Ethics and Organizational Practice

Ethics and Organizational Practice

Questioning the Moral Foundations of Management

Edited by

Sara Louise Muhr

Post Doctoral Researcher, Department of Business Administration, Lund University, Sweden

Bent M. Sørensen

Associate Professor, Department of Management, Politics and Philosophy, Copenhagen Business School, Denmark

Steen Vallentin

Associate Professor, Department of Management, Politics and Philosophy, Copenhagen Business School, Denmark

Edward Elgar
Cheltenham, UK • Northampton, MA, USA

Published by
Edward Elgar Publishing Limited
The Lypiatts
15 Lansdown Road
Cheltenham
Glos GL50 2JA
UK

Edward Elgar Publishing, Inc.
William Pratt House
9 Dewey Court
Northampton
Massachusetts 01060
USA

A catalogue record for this book
is available from the British Library

Library of Congress Control Number: 2009940640

Mixed Sources
Product group from well-managed
forests and other controlled sources
www.fsc.org Cert no. SA-COC-1565
© 1996 Forest Stewardship Council

ISBN 978 1 84844 168 2

Printed and bound by MPG Books Group, UK

Contents

Contributors

Mats Alvesson is Professor of Business Administration at the University of Lund, Sweden, and at the University of Queensland Business School, Brisbane, Australia. He is an Honorary Professor at the University of St Andrews, Scotland and Visiting Professor at Exeter University, England. His research interests include critical theory, gender, power, management of professional service (knowledge-intensive) organizations, leadership, identity, organizational image, organizational culture and symbolism, qualitative methods and philosophy of science. His recent books include *Oxford Handbook of Critical Management Studies* (Oxford University Press, edited with Todd Bridgman and Hugh Willmott), *Understanding Gender and Organizations* (Sage, 2009, 2nd edition with Yvonne Billing), *Reflexive Methodology* (Sage, 2009, 2nd edition, with Kaj Skoldberg), *Changing Organizational Culture* (Routledge, 2008, with Stefan Sveningsson), *Knowledge Work and Knowledge-Intensive Firms* (Oxford University Press, 2004), *Postmodernism and Social Research* (Open University Press, 2002).

George Cairns is Professor of Management at Royal Melbourne Institute of Technology, Melbourne, Australia. His research interests are focused on understanding the impacts of international business on marginalized communities and individuals. Cairns has published in *Human Relations*, *Management Learning* and *Building Research and Information*.

Emma Louise Jeanes is Senior Lecturer at the University of Exeter, England, having previously worked at Cardiff University, Wales, and been a visiting academic at Queensland Univerity of Technology, Brisbane, Australia. Emma has published in journals such as *Journal of Management Inquiry*; *Gender, Work and Organization*; *Creativity and Innovation Management*; and *Public Administration*, as well as being the series editor for the Gender and Organizational Theory book series, Ashgate Publishing, and is currently co-editing *Handbook of Gender, Work and Organization* for Wiley-Blackwell with David Knights and Patricia Yancey-Martin.

Rasmus Johnsen is a post doctoral researcher at the Department for Management, Politics and Philosophy at Copenhagen Business School,

Denmark. In his research, which has focused on pathologies like stress and depression in association with the organization of work in late modernity, he has dealt with subjects related to the broad and colourful history of melancholy in Western culture in order to adress and develop a philosophical, critical and ethical perspective on contemporary modes of management and self-management. He is currently engaged in a larger research project funded by the Velux Foundation, focusing on the management of self-management and pathology.

Dan Kärreman is Professor in Management and Organization Studies at Copenhagen Business School, Denmark. His research interests include critical management studies, knowledge work, identity in organizations, leadership, organizational control, innovation and research methodology. His work has been published in *Academy of Management Review, Human Relations, Journal of Management Studies, Organization, Organization Science*, and *Organization Studies*, among others. He is currently writing a book on theory development with Mats Alvesson.

Jeanette Lemmergaard is Associate Professor in Human Resource Management and Internal Communication at the University of Southern Denmark Campus in Odense, Denmark. She received her PhD in business economics from the University of Southern Denmark in 2003. She has published in journals such as *Journal of Business Ethics, The Service Industries Journal, Employee Relations* and *International Journal of Knowledge and Learning*. Her current research includes strategic human resource management, strategic corporate social responsibility, diversity management, and dysfunctional leadership.

Thomas Taro Lennerfors is a researcher at the Gothenburg University School of Business, Economics and Law, Sweden. His doctoral thesis explored the vicissitudes of corruption, while his current research is focused on understanding owners of large crude carriers. In September 2009 he began post-doctoral studies at the Meiji University School of Commerce, Tokyo, Japan.

Samuel Mansell works as Lecturer in Management at the Essex Business School, England. He has been based at the University of Essex since October 2000. He began by studying accounting and finance with the aim of a lucrative career in investment banking. However, the chance discovery of philosophy led him in search of a more contemplative vocation, so he began a PhD in 2004 supervised by Steffen Böhm, and is presently awaiting his defence. His research interests lie mainly in the field of business ethics: his thesis is entitled 'A critique of stakeholder theory' and he recently published in the *Journal of Business Ethics* on Levinas and corporate governance.

Sara Louise Muhr is a post-doctoral researcher at Lund University, Sweden, where her research focuses on critical perspectives on managerial identity and business ethics, especially in relation to issues around the difficulties of coping with differences and expectations in modern flexible ways of working. Following this broader aim she has worked with various empirical settings such as management consultancy, hospitals and prisons, where she has encountered topics such as work–life subjectivity, gender issues, and leadership. She has published, among others, in *Service Industries Journal, Journal of Organizational Change Management, Management Decision*, and *Journal of Business Ethics.*

Alf Rehn is currently monkeying around at Åbo Akademi University in Turku, Finland, as the Chair of Management and Organization in the Faculty of Economics and Social Sciences, where he tries to establish dominance by loud vocalizations and baring of teeth. He seldom succeeds. Dejected, he then publishes books, essays and journal articles on moralization, culture, ideology, and other ephemeral subjects, while listening to Ethel Merman and Patsy Cline.

Cécile Rozuel is an ethics lecturer at Auckland University of Technology, New Zealand. She recently completed her PhD at the University of Surrey, England, which highlighted the significance of the spiritual and archetypal self in moral behavior. She holds a masters degree in management and an MA in international business analysis. She has published several articles on corporate social responsibility, and her current research interests include integrating Jungian psychology into ethics and management research and praxis, examining the moral dimension of obedience and authority, and exploring the spiritual dimension of sustainability.

Martyna Śliwa is Senior Lecturer in International Management at Newcastle University, England. Her research interests include postsocialist transition, migration and transnationalism, critical approaches to international business, philosophy of management and organization, and representations of organization in literary fiction.

Bent M. Sørensen is Associate Professor at the Department of Management, Politics and Philosophy at Copenhagen Business School, Denmark. He has published in journals such as *Creativity and Innovation Management,*

Scandinavian Journal of Management and ephemera, and edited with Martin Fuglsang, a book titled *Deleuze and the Social*. He is currently interested in self-management and employee subjectivity, especially in relation to organizational aesthetics, that is, how organizational artifacts make available to the employee various self-images to pursue. Alongside this, subjects such as the theological nature of capitalism and Tango Argentino seem to attract him.

Steen Vallentin is Associate Professor at the Department of Management, Politics and Philosophy at Copenhagen Business School, Denmark, where he is also affiliated with the CBS Center for Corporate Social Responsibility (cbsCSR). He has recently been a visiting professor at ESADE Business School in Barcelona. He has published in journals such as *Business and Society and Organization*, and is currently working on a book on CSR, and along with Niels Thygese and Sverre Raffnsøe, the second edition of a book on trust and management.

1. Introduction – after the party. Crisis as foundation

Sara Louise Muhr, Bent M. Sørensen and Steen Vallentin

Allan Greenspan: I made a mistake in presuming that the self-interest of organizations, specifically banks and others, were such as they were best capable of protecting their own shareholders and their equity in the firms.

Henry Waxman: In other words, you found that your view of the world, your ideology, was not right, it was not working.

Allan Greenspan: Absolutely, precisely. . . .

(*International Herald Tribune*, 24 October 2008)

The existentialist philosopher Søren Kierkegaard was familiar with the situation in which Allan Greenspan, former chairman of the US Federal Reserve and a fervent proponent of deregulation and neoliberal economics, found himself when facing the US Government Oversight Committee of the House of Representatives, and its chairman, the Democrat Henry Waxman on 23 October 2008. In 1843, Kierkegaard wrote a book about such a critical event, *Fear and Trembling* (1983), in which he observed that what we today as distinctively *modern* humans should be investigating is *the crisis*. This category is, briefly put, the theme of this book. In the dire turbulence of a financial crisis that has developed into a crisis of world views and, indeed, a moral crisis as well, we want to investigate the 'moral foundations' for managing the complexity of today's business world. Before we provide an overview of the contributions, we want to delve into the notion of crisis itself and what today's crisis may reveal about the dominant version of contemporary capitalism. We will also survey the 'moral' answers to economic dilemmas, which in the last half century have emerged under the aegis of corporate social responsibility. Lately, these efforts has been given a distinctly *philosophical* turn, in the form of post-structuralist thoughts regarding our responsibility towards 'the Other'. Such perspectives are surfacing now, and it is our conviction that they will become more pertinent as the precariousness of our current system becomes more and more visible, and, perhaps, more and more unbearable to the majority of the world's population. For this majority, the crisis is quite real and life threatening.

In the midst of crisis, we turn to *Webster's Dictionary* to learn that a crisis marks 'a stage in a sequence of events at which the trend of all future events, especially for better or worse, is determined'. The word's etymology links it to the Greek *krisis*, meaning 'discrimination' as well as 'decision': Kierkegaard himself linked the moment of decision directly to madness.

Of course, when the economy heats up heading for its next collapse, no voices of crisis are allowed to be heard: the hegemony of neoliberal economics has silenced voices that would not believe in ends and limits of growth. During this period, the market blessed us with growth in welfare and spending abilities at a speed practically unequalled in the history of man. Even the experience of the dot.com bubble, which burst in 2000, did not lead to many second thoughts regarding the deregulating frenzy of the preceding two decades. Rather, through low interest rates and what has been termed 'innovative financial products', the real estate bubble took over the role of supplying the middle class with free capital, which was then converted into consumption. So it is Allan Greenspan who is on trial, and he is surely responsible for the housing bubble through his belief in a low interest rate policy and the viability of sub-prime lending. But Kierkegaard would place every one of us in that chair, and hold us responsible for our participation: it takes a crowd to make a market inflate. The ethical question that guides *Fear and Trembling* remains one of responsibility; Kierkegaard uses the case of Abraham, who faced the possible sacrifice of Isaac, but equally and more relevant for us, he was facing the situation in which our 'view of the world, [our] ideology, was not right, it was not working'. This crisis is the moment of the ethical. It is, equally, the moment, as we shall see, of the political; there is an ethics, if sometimes only a distorted and twisted one, lurking in every political economy, and the crisis brings it forth.

The neoliberal worldview remains, in our view, such a wrenched ethics, or perhaps simply a lack of an ethics. A great number of the world's university economists are considered adherents of the neoliberal Chicago school of economics, a train of thought, which has been celebrating an unequalled success over the last 30 years. To such an extent, we will argue, that it makes sense to talk about its fundamental principles as dogmas, even religious ones. This is seemingly what chairman Waxman was on to when he confronted Greenspan with the latter's withering world view: 'it was not working', he asked. Greenspan replied: 'Absolutely, precisely', and continued: 'You know, that's precisely the reason I was shocked, because I have been going for 40 years or more with very considerable evidence that it was working exceptionally well' (Knowlton and Grynbaum 2008). Forty years may be a long time, but it is no eternity. Neoliberalism, in spite of its dogmatic claims, now finds itself in an hour of reckoning as its temporal and empirical limitations are being brutally exposed. Its tenets no longer appear, if they ever did, as though they are inscribed on stone tablets brought down from the mountain.

The religious nature of neoliberal economics and the piety we have paid to finance capitalism for three decades goes even beyond Walter Benjamin's analysis of capitalism as a religion (Benjamin 1996). The most important concept in neoliberalism is Adam Smith's invisible hand (very sparsely mentioned in *Wealth of Nations* (1937) as well as in what he considered his major work, namely that on ethics, *The Theory of Moral Sentiments* (1801)). As Mark C. Taylor (2004) observes, Smith's concept of ethics was really of theological origin. Smith extends John Calvin's concept of God's invisible providence to encompass the market. In his theology, Calvin contended that whether a believer was to be saved or not was a given that could not be changed, but success in this world would be an indication of success in the coming world: thus, the (north-) western entrepreneur was born (Sørensen 2008). But even if salvation is predestined, it is unknown. God's providence is invisible, yet omnipresent and faultless. With Smith, the market comes to be understood in the same terms: the market is the place where the vices of every one of us is melted into a common good, just as this would happen earlier under the auspices of the Almighty (Taylor 2004). Today, the 'self-interest' that Smith more soberly saw as the engine of the market, has, under neoliberalism, been transformed into pure greed. So, the vice of greed, which even Wall Street apologetics have been condemning lately, becomes basically the very engine of neoliberalism, which sees in a completely 'free market' a real utopian destiny (Gray 2003). Milton Friedman, the father of the Chicago School, would go far in praising this religious utopia; his spiritual forefather, the neo-classical archangel Friedrich A. von Hayek (1998, p. 26) directly pointed to the socialists' 'courage to be Utopian' as their main advantage compared to the 'true liberal'. In hindsight, 60 years later it is clear that the true liberals had learned their lesson. Yet, the religion they had conjured up delivered no redemption, only guilt. The housing bubble may have been a bubble, but the foreclosure and unemployment rates point to a real and material world-wide crisis.

While Naomi Klein's *The Shock Doctrine* (2007) can be read as Friedman's spiritual obituary, we see Kierkegaard's question as all the more pertinent: what remains as our ethical demand, even under overwhelming disaster, even under the shock of modernity, even when a father has raised his knife over his only son's body? This book does not pretend to answer this question, but inserts itself, nevertheless, into such a fundamental, ethical crisis. Even if no answers are given, we may, hope-fully, still be able to scrutinize how ethical theories and moral principles are applied, practised and prioritized in today's society and its organiza-tions. While there is always an existential dimension to ethics, our focus remains the more mundane, but no less interesting world of business and management.

As said, a crisis marks a turning point, and it will be interesting to see, whether the current financial crisis will lead us into an era of more wide-spread moral concern about management. To what extent will the moral concerns that have been raised in regard to financial institutions trickle down into the real economy, so to speak, and affect the way that we think about business and management in general?

Certainly, deregulatory modes of finance capitalism with their built-in belief in the self-sustaining force of self-interest have, for the time being, lost most of their appeal, even in quarters far removed from the opinions of Naomi Klein. Dobson has suggested that while ethics has permeated the disciplines of accounting, marketing and management, 'finance survives as the last bastion of a value-free business discipline' (1997, p. xvii). Now, with the benefit of hindsight, it would seem to most that even finance needs to be infused with values beyond the purely economic and technical.

It may be that the last bastion of freedom from values in business is shaking in its foundations, but it is not yet clear whether or to what extent this will lead to an increased pondering of ethics and morality within busi-ness and management in general. Thus, it may be argued that the problem lies with finance and finance capitalism as such, and that the need for intervention and reconsideration of fundamentals extends no further than that. Also, many would argue, the solution is not for managers to (re) consider ethics, the solution does not hinge on corporate management at all, but rather on state intervention. The ineptitudes of the invisible hand of the market that have come to the fore, calls less for the hand of manage-ment and more for the hand of government to take charge. In the current situation we should rely on law rather than morality. Of course, the hand of government is already doing its work with unprecedented rescue and stimulus packages being pushed through in order to avoid a complete collapse of the economy.

Hence, the crisis is resulting in a rejuvenation of Keynesian economics. But apart from this change of direction of the political economy, we are also keen to look for possibilities of change and turning points in terms of business economics and management. To turn the crisis into a problem of political economy only or primarily is to locate the solution to the problem (moral or otherwise) of irresponsibility in business outside business. It is to accept that the solution rests with the state and is about regulation.

Our point of departure is that we need to be open to the possibility that corporate management and corporate self-regulation can also be part of the solution, and that we need to reflect on this prospect – whether the financial crisis signifies a new dawn for morality in business or not.

Of course, this is nothing new. The private sector has for decades been called upon to help solve or alleviate social and environmental problems, and many companies have heeded the call. It is said that there is today not a single company in the Fortune 500 that does not have some kind of policy regarding responsibility. Companies are engaging in a variety of activities that have hitherto been associated with the state/government or civil society, such as philanthropy and community investment, environmental management, workers' rights and welfare, human rights, animal rights, corruption, corporate governance, and legal compliance. Companies are increasingly presenting themselves as good corporate citizens and making contributions to sustainable development in the broadest sense. Corporate managers are showing a willingness to let their actions and decisions be guided by the demands and expectations of a broad variety of stakeholders rather than the narrow financial interests of owners/shareholders alone.

In the wake of the financial crisis, even former General Electric Chairman Jack Welch, who is often considered to be the 'father' of the shareholder value movement, has renounced his former beliefs. In a *Financial Times* interview conducted in March 2009, Welch said: 'On the face of it, shareholder value is the dumbest idea in the world'. He continued: 'Shareholder value is a result, not a strategy. . . . Your main constituencies are your employees, your customers and your products'. Welch even went as far as to suggest that '[t]he idea that shareholder value is a strategy is insane. It is the product of your combined efforts – from the management to the employees' (Guerrera 2009). Obviously, Welch conveniently wants to disassociate himself from the kind of management that hinges on quarterly profits and share price gains as opposed to long-term development and strong stakeholder relationships. His admission is too late, though. At this point, it is obvious to most that there is a need for a more social and sustainable conception of the firm.

The most commonly used concept in this regard is CSR – corporate social responsibility. Indeed, many would argue that CSR – rather than business ethics – is the most promising way to approach and counter moral deficits in business. CSR would seem more attuned to the reality of responsibility and its societal circumstances than business ethics, which, instead of looking for observable events and relationships in the social world, is 'centered on moral evaluation, judgment, and prescription of human action' (Swanson 1999, p. 507). However, the current crisis is as good an occasion as any to (re)consider what is the most appropriate vocabulary for addressing moral concerns. At first sight the CSR literature certainly seems to provide moral assurance. Howard R. Bowen is often credited with being the inventor of the modern concept of social responsibility (Carroll 1999). In his book *Social Responsibilities of the Businessman* (Bowen 1953, p. 6), he defined social responsibility as 'the obligations of businessmen to pursue those policies, to make those decisions, or to follow those lines of action which are desirable in terms of the objectives and values of our society'. In line with this statement, much of the CSR literature has a strong moral imperative (Scherer and Palazzo 2007). It provides an affirmation of the social and embedded nature of business and the obligations implied by its intimate relationship with society.

Normative contributions to CSR build on a moral concern with business and economic life that has a long history; it goes back at least to the days of burgeoning industrialism in the West. For instance, the French sociologist Emile Durkheim, in the 1890s, described the business professions as being devoid of a professional ethics and regarded economic activity as operating outside the sphere of morals and being almost entirely removed from the moderating effect of obligations. He spoke of the amoral character of economic life as amounting to a public danger because it can be a source of demoralization for those individuals who spend their working lives in the industrial and commercial sphere. Durkheim (1992, p. 12) asked the quite existential question: 'If we live amorally for a good part of the day, how can we keep the springs of morality from going slack in us? ... If we follow no rule except that of clear self-interest, in the occupations that take up nearly the whole of our time, how should we acquire a taste for any disinterestedness, or selflessness or sacrifice?' Ideally, then, CSR can be considered as a modern-day effort to moderate economic rationality and remoralize business by making it accountable to societal demands and expectations regarding responsibility.

However, this is not the whole story about CSR. CSR is most often defined as being voluntary (Carroll 1999), and this feature encapsulates both the hopes and the fears that are associated with the concept. The hope is that with CSR we get more than the bare minimum of responsibility from business – more than we bargained for, so to speak, and that business can indeed be a progressive force for good. The hopeful thus argue that business has an all-important part to play in finding solutions to the social and environmental problems of the day and creating a more sustainable economy. The fear comes from a general suspicion of everything 'corporate' (and its ability to self-regulate in a sustainable manner), and from a particular concern that CSR, when all is said and done, is all about money and mostly for show. Without rules and democratic checks and balances in place, there is no reason to believe that CSR is about long-term investments and commitments, and not just about fleeting political correctness and short-term gains. CSR, the fearful argue, means more power and influence to corporate managers, and, at least potentially, a hollowing out of other (regulatory) modes of governance. In the words of Robert Reich, CSR reflects 'a kind of faux democracy [that] has invaded capitalism' (2007, p. 207). Indeed, he argues, '[t]he soothing promise of responsibility can deflect public attention from the need for stricter laws and regulations or convince the public that there's no real problem to begin with' (ibid., p. 170). Of course, the same kind of argument has been promoted by Friedman (1962 and [1970] 2001) and Hayek (1960) for decades (see also Crook 2005). The diagnoses of CSR are thus similar on the political left and right. It is the suggested solutions that differ – government regulation and free market economy, respectively.

Either way, the fear has precedence. As Frederick (2006, p. 7) points out, CSR has curious origins. Although popular belief is that business opposes CSR, the core idea of social responsibility first took roots in the minds of big business executives. Historically, 'CSR was not born in opposition to the business order but was encapsulated within the capitalist system and became an integral part of the free-enterprise market economy – and was subordinated to that system's central values'. He continues: 'CSR, whatever form it takes, *serves* corporate interests and goals – and has been intended to do so since its inception around the turn of the 20th century'.

Modern developments in CSR are taking it back to its corporate roots, so to speak, and (re)aligning it with the profit motive. Hence, in later years there has been a strong focus on the notion of *strategic CSR*, which is about realizing that CSR can be much more than an externally imposed cost or constraint: 'It can be a source of opportunity, innovation, and competitive advantage' (Porter and Kramer 2006, p. 82). According to Porter and Kramer, value creation should be *the* guiding principle behind CSR: 'The essential test that should guide CSR is not whether a cause is worthy but whether it presents an opportunity to create shared value – that is, a meaningful benefit for society that is also valuable to the business' (ibid., p. 84).

The significance of the turn towards an economic understanding of CSR is not limited to the world of business and academia. It is also making inroads in politics and in governmental approaches to CSR. Although CSR is defined from the corporate point of view, it is an issue that government seems more and more concerned with and eager to address and which is increasingly becoming the object of governmental activity at the level of EU policy and at national, regional and local policy levels. One of the reasons for this activity is the emergence of this new, convenient and seductive 'truth' about CSR, namely that it is good for business and good for the economy. We are thus witnessing the emergence of competitiveness as the new orthodoxy of government in regard to CSR.

In the eyes of European governments, CSR used to be about social issues, social cohesion and inclusive labor markets. The aim was to make business carry its part of the social burden and give something back to society. The language was one of social obligations. Now, CSR is increasingly seen as a strategic advantage and therefore as a lever for, again, value creation, economic growth and competitiveness. The language is one of economic policy, and the message from government is that business should engage in CSR to do well rather than good. This view of CSR conveniently reconciles possible tensions between the interests of society and the interests of business. It dispels fears of government standing in the way of free markets and hindering the free flow of trade and competition when concerning itself with and acting upon corporate responsibilities. Before, government intervention in CSR would be associated with undue and potentially harmful interference imposing restraints and additional costs on business. Now, government works instead to help companies identify/create and act upon strategic opportunities in their environment. Curiously, government promotes CSR by pushing the profit motive, not by restraining it (Vallentin and Murillo 2009). Indeed, we are witnessing an economization of the political that transforms the instruments of public authority, 'replacing laws with guidelines, relying on self- and reflexive regulation and treating normative prescriptions in general as commodities that are to be produced, distributed and consumed by a host of agencies, enterprises and non-profit organizations' (Shamir 2008, p. 2).

Porter and Kramer (2006) argue that CSR tends to pit business against society and to focus on tensions and frictions rather than interdependencies and points of intersection between one and the other. In their view, CSR is a wonderland of strategic opportunities and win–win situations waiting to happen – and mostly absent of points of contention and moral conflict. Their approach is indicative of an emerging neo-liberal imagination in CSR, which dissolves the epistemological distinction between economy and society by grounding social relations in the economic rationality of markets. The result is an economization of morality in the sense that moral duties and considerations lose their character as liabilities and re-emerge as business opportunities (Shamir 2008). We thus see 'a shift from deontological ethics to teleological (consequentialist) ethics that subordinate socio-moral sensibilities to the calculus of possible outcomes, to the test of cost–benefit analyses and to the criteria of reputational-risk management' (ibid., p. 14).

Although such an economizing approach may be considered as absolutely crucial for a widespread mainstreaming of CSR to take place, it also gives reason for concern. Mainstreaming may come at too high a cost.

What happens to CSR in the process? Are we witnessing a kind of economic colonization, appropriation or takeover of CSR at the public policy level? And, if so, what social issues and concerns may be pushed to the side in the process (Vallentin and Murillo 2009)? Scherer et al. (2006) have argued that as long as the norm of profit maximization remains the final point of reference and strategic concerns and 'good ethics is good business' rule the day, it is false labeling to claim to be dealing with 'corporate social responsibility'.

Where does that leave us, then? Well, CSR emerges as a concept that is invested with many different meanings and values, and which has an air of moral ambiguity about it. Although the ongoing mainstreaming of the concept can be considered as progress in the sense that it is all about spreading the message and making it more approachable and digestible for business leaders, it also, to a certain extent, implies an abandonment of ethics and moral concerns. Such concerns are not altogether disregarded, but they become secondary; at best, they become a means to an economic end. This development is hardly surprising in that it merely confirms an often observed ability of capitalism to adjust itself to new challenges, to translate and absorb disturbances and frame them in its own image. From an ethical point of view, however, this is hardly reassuring. It suggests that we need to keep a critical, albeit not skeptical, distance to developments in CSR, and that there is a continued need for ethical reflection and the work of business ethics – in spite of the success of CSR in capturing the responsibility agenda. We need to go back to ethics.

But what kind of ethics do we need? Common definitions of ethics are concerned with attempts to build systematic sets of normative prescriptions about human behavior and codes to govern everyday morals and morality. Philosophers and others 'use the tools of reason to generate rules which should guide our judgment in particular and general circumstances' (Parker 1998, p. 1). However, as Parker also points out, 'the project of ethics . . . seems to have spent an awful lot of time going nowhere' (ibid.). The idea of foundational ethical codes is no longer taken seriously by very many, which suggests that ethical reflection has to proceed without hope of reaching anything resembling an ultimate point of moral justification. Modern normative approaches to business ethics are perfectly able to function without recourse to any (supposedly) final assurances of right and wrong. Their ultimate goal is not to dissolve moral doubts and insecurities, ambiguities and dilemmas but rather to bring them out in the open. They do not promote ethics in terms of rules and rationality but rather seek to undermine and question such being.

The promise of a just world thus seems hollow and recent literature has attempted to disturb and question this promise. Critchley (2007, p. 92) for example asks 'what might justice be in a violently unjust world', and makes us reflect over the fact that there is no perfect solution and there is no promise of a just world. What we can do is to constantly question and be critical towards general practice and thus make sure that we never stop trying. This book is a contribution to the critical perspective on business ethics, and thus tries to question the autonomy and self-evidence of the 'good' in business ethics.

The word 'ethics' is therefore not as simple as some business ethicists often seem to suggest. Some might argue that a critical approach ends in a relativist 'anything goes' position, but as this book shows, a critical conception means that we take into account the difficulties that ethical decisions necessarily entail, the undecidability experienced when having to make an ethical decision (see for example Derrida 1992, 1995) and the infinity of responsibility, that is the impossibility of ever being responsible enough (Levinas 1969, 1981).

This view of responsibility obviously places a critical burden on CSR, especially considering the strategic turn developments within this field have recently taken. CSR risks becoming something that is done for economic reasons, a means to another end, and companies engaged in CSR can be accused of only caring for the other because the other serves a business purpose, not for a more profound ethical reason (see for example Jones et al. 2005, p. 122). As Derrida argues, ethics needs to hold a level of secrecy (Derrida 1995) to avoid falling into the circular movement of economics, which is devoid of ethics (Derrida 1992). For an act to be ethical one cannot expect a given return on an ethical act. In fact the ethical act must remain a secret or even better completely unknown or unnoticed. What Derrida means with this is that as soon as ethics becomes a calculation of benefits, it is not about being good to others, but about securing personal gains. In that way, it is not said that CSR is a bad thing, it can very well be good, but codes and rules are just never enough, responsibility also needs to have a certain personal aspect (Muhr 2008). On the same note, Levinas argues that responsibility is not a duty or a matter of complying with a rule, but rather an ability to respond to and not ignore the other's call. Responsibility is in this way never final, it is always infinite in the sense that one can never be responsible enough, there is always more to do, other others to respond to. Responsibility is therefore shown in a response, which is always given in the light of undecidability and unknowingness. There are always limits to full responsibility (Loacker and Muhr 2009). One can never be fully responsible, but as long as we constantly try, we are, according to Butler, not being irresponsible. And if we are after all, 'we will surely be forgiven' (Butler 2005, p. 136).

Even this short introduction holds many different viewpoints and refers to many different ethical issues. That is exactly the point. The point of this book is not to define a 'new business ethics', but rather to discuss its limits (see also Jones 2003). With this book we therefore want to question the assumption that we can meaningfully talk about a 'right' decision or what it means to be 'good'. We therefore want to expose business ethics to its crises rather than formulate its solutions. We are in a time of crisis and as such a time shows there are no definite answers to what it means to be responsible. Rather a time of crisis invites questioning and challenging common sense. This book is a collection of texts that critically investigates what ethics means. The ten chapters that follow thereby critically question the general assumption that there can be *a* business ethics.

In Chapter 2, Martyna Śliwa and George Cairns discuss values and ethics in the context of international business (IB). They critique mainstream sources of business education for a too restricted and narrow view on ethics and values. Instead, they set out to reconstitute it based on a different set of ethical principles and values. The authors propose an ethical paradigm for building IB theory and practice drawing upon a contemporary interpretation of Aristotle's concept of *phronēsis*, or 'prudence', found in his *Nicomachean Ethics*.

The value perspective is continued in Chapter 3 where Jeanette Lemmergaard explores ways of enacting Scandinavian value-based management, that is, managing through communicating social values and ethical stances. Through a case-study she illustrates the dilemmas and paradoxes of how value-based management is conducted in a Danish knowledge-intensive organization. She concludes her chapter with a discussion of why value-based management is more than just defining and formulating appealing phrasings. More important – and more difficult – it is the ongoing process and commitment at all organizational levels.

In Chapter 4, Dan Kärreman and Mats Alvesson take a particular interest in the concealment of the moral dimension. With this in mind they develop the concept of ethical closure, which they define as the ways ethical considerations are arrested, blocked, and short-circuited. The chapter then focuses on identifying specific categories of ethical closure (sealing, bracketing, double dehumanization, and moral commodification) in a Swedish media organization. The authors argue that the combined effect of the categories of ethical closure makes it difficult for newsmakers to engage in ethical reflection in matters that concern their work. Since processes of closure counteract ethical reflection through indirect displacement, rather than direct oppression, they also become difficult to resist. By arguing this, the authors criticize the code-based view on ethics and they instead discuss the possibility that ethical codes of conduct may fuel rather than solve certain ethical problems.

In Chapter 5, Steen Vallentin explores the role of public opinion in defining corporate responsibilities, and thereby makes a case for a political understanding of CSR. Public opinion is a highly influential political force that has many points of intersection with business, but recognition of its significance does not necessarily imply recognition of its democratic value. Public opinion is certainly a democratic ideal, but it is a contested ideal: hero to some, villain to others. Thus, the chapter emphasizes the contested and ambiguous nature of public opinion and its different articulations – and the need for a political understanding of CSR to embody a critical mode of *reflection*. This embodiment seeks to elucidate the conflicts and problems that come to the fore in political struggles over the meaning and value of CSR. More specifically, the chapter is concerned with the ways in which public opinion is framed and given political meaning by the opposing camps in the on-going battle of ideas over CSR.

In Chapter 6, Samuel Mansell explores the possibilities and limits of moral argument in informing the development of corporate legislation. Through a thorough philosophical consideration, of what is implied in the concept of a moral argument, the author presents us with an in-depth analysis of among others, the work of John Stuart Mill. Based on this, he outlines a dialectical framework in which a moral basis for regulation can be conceived. The author thus shows that 'objectivity' need not be considered as the dogmatic imposition of an ideology, which closes down all space for discussion. Indeed, the very notion of contesting an idea by providing better reasoning and evidence in support of an alternative is according to the author inconsistent with the denial that one may be 'correct' or incorrect' in the assertion one makes.

In Chapter 7, Cécile Rozuel engages in the field of moral psychology. Opposite the former chapter she thus takes a much more individualistic approach and links morality to the realization of being a self. Rouzel emphasizes Carl G. Jung's psychology and argues that it has a distinctive ethical dimension, which articulates around the concept of conscience and the archetype of the self. Knowing oneself and becoming an individual are purported to be moral tasks. From this point of view, she perceives the human being as a complex, but whole being, with physical, rational, emotional and spiritual dimensions. Through two case-studies, she explores sense-making of moral experiences in what she, following Jung defines as 'the persona' and its correlate 'self-image'.

In Chapter 8, Emma Louise Jeanes and Sara Louise Muhr argue for an ethics based on the theoretical perspective Samuel Mansell in Chapter 6 was critical towards. In taking this stand, they are critical of the prospect of ethical guidance as they argue that guidance and control also takes away individual responsibility for behaving ethically. Instead, these authors argue for a Levinasian ethics of the Other, which places ethics at the heart of social relations. Levinasian ethics is an ethics without a system of judgment, but an ethics by which one experiences a calling into question in the face of others. Through a case-study of a human rights project in South Africa, the authors further explore the limits to guidance and argue that rules are never enough to ensure moral behavior. Instead, the universality of justice comes from the singularity of the respect for another human being as Other.

In Chapter 9, Alf Rehn investigates what a moral foundation of management might look like. To do this, he invites the reader to revisit the very roots of human economies. By bringing in notions from economic anthropology and primatology the author shows that notions such as empathic response and honor are concepts that have been either ignored or discounted as archaic or too trivial. The author reclaims the importance of empathic response and honor and uses them to query the very notion of a business ethics and to suggest an actual moral foundation of management. In doing so, he argues that the power/knowledge regime of management studies suffers from an ethical problem of limiting the discourse to things that can be managed within an agreed-upon ideology of what constitutes management. By bringing in themes that break with the tradition in organization studies, the author then raises the issue of epistemological comfort as a necessary part of ethics. The author calls on us to ask ourselves whether the limitations we are imposing on our field of study needs to be studied as a form of ethics, and whether these limitations in fact make us less ethically aware.

In Chapter 10, Rasmus Johnsen engages in the debate concerning clinical psychopathy among employees and managers. He enters this debate with a critique of the distinction between 'psychopath' and 'normal' and argues that in the first place being able to speak about organizational psychopaths reflects the problematic issues in understanding socially unacceptable behavior as mental illness. The author then warns against the dangerous implications in using pathology instrumentally in power struggles on the labor market. In doing this, he argues that the organizational psychopath represents a boundary phenomenon of monstrous hybridization. He then analyses the organizational psychopath as a modern version of the werewolf and argues that it becomes a matter of how the 'human' has come to be understood through the human–animal divide. Like the werewolf, the organizational psychopath represents the lack of spontaneous judgments and moral acts of authentic human behavior and can therefore not be seen as a proper human resource.

In the last chapter, Chapter 11, Thomas Taro Lennerfors critically investigates the principal–agent notion of corruption, and argues that current research might do more to limit our understanding of corruption than to guide it forward. Taking a psychoanalytic perspective, the author argues that one cannot understand corruption if one ignores desire. To engage further with a psychoanalytical understanding of corruption the author emphasizes the necessity of understanding the so-called 'two bodies doctrine'. The two bodies doctrine basically means that by splitting one's self, one can free the authentic self of the burden of corrupt behavior. In a Zizekian reading of this, the author shows that when a person occupies an office, a symbolic place of power, his or her body gets supplemented with an inseparable, sublime substance. The author concludes the chapter by arguing that corruption is not only the actions of an agent. Instead, the main crime is the place, a place that is vested ideologically with desire.

REFERENCES

Benjamin, W. (1996), *Selected Writings*, Cambridge, MA: Belknap Press of Harvard University Press.

Bowen, H.R. (1953), *Social Responsibilities of the Businessman*, New York: Harper & Row.

Butler, J. (2005), *Giving an Account of Oneself*, New York: Fordham University Press.

Carroll, A.B. (1999), 'Corporate social responsibility – evolution of a definitional construct', *Business and Society*, **38** (3), 268–95.

Crane, A. and D. Matten (2007), *Business Ethics – Managing Corporate Citizenship and Sustainability in the Age of Globalization*, 2nd edn, Oxford: Oxford University Press.

Critchley, S. (2007), *Infinitely Demanding: Ethics of Commitment, Politics of Resistance*, London: Verso.

Crook, C. (2005), 'The good company – a sceptical look at corporate social responsibility', *The Economist*, 20 January.

Derrida, J. (1992), *Given Time*, Chicago, IL: University of Chicago Press.

Derrida, J. (1995), *The Gift of Death*, Chicago, IL: University of Chicago Press.

Dobson, J. (1997), *Finance Ethics – The Rationality of Virtue*, Lanham, MD: Rowman & Littlefield Publishers.

Durkheim, E. (1992), *Professional Ethics and Civic Morals*, London: Routledge.

Frederick, W.C. (2006), *Corporation, Be Good! The Story of Corporate Social Responsibility*, Indianapolis, IN: Dog Ear Publishing.

Friedman, M. (1962), *Capitalism and Freedom*, Chicago, IL: University of Chicago Press.

Friedman, M. ([1970] 2001), 'The social responsibility of business is to increase its profits', in W.M. Hoffman, R.E. Frederick and M.S. Schwartz (eds) (2001), *Business Ethics – Readings and Cases in Corporate Morality*, Columbus, OH: McGraw-Hill, pp. 156–60.

Gray, J. (2003), *Al Qaeda and What it Means to be Modern*, New York: New Press.

Guerrera, F. (2009), 'Welch condemns share price focus', *Financial Times*, 12 March.

Hayek, F.A. (1960), 'The corporation in a democratic society: in whose interest ought it and will it be run?', in I. Ansoff (ed.) (1969), *Business Strategy*, Harmondsworth: Penguin Books, pp. 225–39.

Jones, C. (2003), 'As if business ethics were possible, "within such limits. . ."', *Organization*, **10**, 223–48.

Jones, C., M. Parker and R. ten Bos (2005), *For Business Ethics: A Critical Text*, London: Routledge.

Kierkegaard, S. (1983), *Fear and Trembling. Repetition*, Princeton, NJ: Princeton University Press.

Klein, N. (2007), *The Shock Doctrine. The Rise of Disaster Capitalism*, London: Allen Lane.

Knowlton, B. and M.M. GrynBaum (2008), 'Greenspan makes rare admission of fallibility', *International Herald Tribune*, 24 October.

Levinas, E. (1969), *Totality and Infinity – An Essay on Exteriority*, Pittsburgh, PA: Duquesne University Press.

Levinas, E. (1981), *Otherwise Than Being or Beyond Essence*, Pittsburgh, PA: Duquesne University Press.

Loacker, B. and S.L. Muhr (2009), 'How can I become a responsible subject? Towards a practice-based ethics of responsiveness', *Journal of Business Ethics*, **90** (2): 265–77.

Margolis, J.D. and J.P. Walsh (2003), 'Misery loves companies – rethinking social initiatives by business', *Administrative Science Quarterly*, **48** (2), 268–305.

Muhr, S.L. (2008), 'Reflections on responsibility and justice – coaching human rights in South Africa', *Journal of Management Decision*, **46** (8), 1175–86.

Orlitzky, M., F.L. Schmidt and S.L. Rynes (2003), 'Corporate social and financial performance: a meta-analysis', *Organization Studies*, **24** (3), 403–41.

Parker, M. (1998), 'Introduction: ethics, the very idea?', in M. Parker (ed.), *Ethics and Organizations*, London: Sage.

Porter, M.E. and M.R. Kramer (2006), 'Strategy and society – The link between competitive advantage and corporate social responsibility', *Harvard Business Review*, **84** (12), 78–92.

Reich, R.B. (2007), *Supercapitalism*, New York: Alfred A. Knopf.

Scherer, A.G. and G. Palazzo (2007), 'Towards a political conception of corporate responsibility: business and society seen from a Habermasian perspective', *Academy of Management Review*, **32** (4), 1096–120.

Scherer, A.G., G. Palazzo and D. Baumann (2006), 'Global rules and private actors: toward a new role of the transnational corporation in global governance', *Business Ethics Quarterly*, **16** (4), 505–32.

Shamir, R. (2008), 'The age of responsibilization: on marked-embedded morality', *Economy and Society*, **37** (1), 1–19.

Smith, A. (1969), *The Theory of Moral Sentiments*, New Rochelle, NY: Arlington House.

Smith, A. (1937), *An Inquiry into the Nature and Causes of the Wealth of Nations*, New York: Random House.

Sørensen, B.M. (2008), 'Behold, I am making all things new': the entrepreneur as savior in the age of creativity', *Scandinavian Journal of Management*, **24** (2), 85–93.

Swanson, D.L. (1999), 'Toward an integrative theory of business and society: a research strategy for corporate social performance', *Academy of Management Review*, **24** (3), 506–21.

Taylor, M.C. (2004), *Confidence Games: Money and Markets in a World Without Redemption*, Chicago, IL: University of Chicago Press.

Vallentin, S. and D. Murillo (2009), 'CSR as governmentality', Copenhagen Business School Center for Corporate Social Responsibility working paper no, 04-2009, pp. 1–38.

Vogel, D. (2005), *The Market for Virtue – The Potential and Limits of Corporate Social Responsibility*, Harrisonburg, VA: Brookings Institution Press.

2. Developing a new ethics of international business: possibilities and role of educators

Martyna Śliwa and George Cairns

1. INTRODUCTION

This chapter engages with the subject of values and ethics within the field of international business (IB), in particular, in relation to the current paradigm of IB knowledge as represented through mainstream[1] sources produced for the purposes of educating students towards developing skills and competences as future actors involved in IB activities. Our aim is, first, to critically interrogate the ethical assumptions behind contemporary IB knowledge, and second, to explore the possibilities for reconstituting it based on a different set of ethical principles and values. Our overview of the values and ethics underpinning IB theories and managerial practice promoted in the mainstream texts leads us to conclude that they do not provide a basis for the establishment of responsible and sustainable systems, norms, incentives and behaviors. We therefore try to answer the question, to what extent and in what way can we, as IB academics and educators, contribute to the development of IB knowledge, which would challenge the current rhetoric of neo-liberal market economics and profit maximization. In doing so, we propose an ethical paradigm for building IB theory and practice drawing upon a contemporary interpretation of Aristotle's concept of *phronēsis*, or 'prudence', found in his *Nicomachean Ethics.*

We locate our discussion within the tradition of a critical pedagogy that is committed to 'personal and societal transformation towards more just, free and equitable conditions through an integrative combination of critical analysis and collective action' (Fenwick 2005, p. 31). Writings of a critical nature, in particular in relation to management education, have been developed in response to a shift towards the application of market logic to the way in which academic institutions are managed and to the kind of content they convey to those they educate (cf. Welsh and Dehler 2007). Authors within the field of critical management education

(CME) have voiced concerns about the emergence and subsequent dominance of the current paradigm of 'education for the organization's sake' (Antonacopoulou 2002, p. 193) and have pointed to the conditions of 'the intellectual tyranny of the economic mindset' (Hendry 2006, p. 268) in present-day universities. There have also been attempts to set out principles for critical pedagogic engagement, including:

- a commitment to questioning the assumptions and taken-for-granteds embodied in both theory and professional practice . . .
- an insistence on foregrounding the processes of power and ideology . . .
- a perspective that is social rather than individual . . .
- the realization of a more just society based on fairness, democracy and 'empowerment' of identifying and contesting sources of inequity and the suppression of the voices of minorities.

(Perriton and Reynolds 2004, p. 65)

Despite the fact that the project of critical pedagogy in management education has evoked considerable research interest, practical resources for those wishing to teach management-related subjects critically remain scarce. In addition, whilst they can be relatively easily identified for the purposes of teaching general management and organization theory, educators are left with little choice when teaching more specialist subjects, such as operations management, finance, accounting, strategy or international business. In our own recent research we have engaged with the topic of teaching IB critically through an application of a critical analytical framework for interrogating the content of mainstream IB textbooks (Śliwa and Cairns 2009) as well as proposing a stakeholder-focused approach based upon the application of scenario method (Cairns et al. 2008; cf. van der Heijden et al. 2002). In the discussion presented in this chapter we argue that it is important for researchers and educators in the area of IB to contribute to the project of CME through writing educational materials; such as textbooks, case studies and articles; that address the subject of IB knowledge from what we refer to as a 'phronetic perspective'.

To this end, the remaining parts of this chapter are structured as follows. First, we briefly discuss the intellectual roots of IB knowledge in the historical, economic and social context of its emergence. We then move on to consider more recent theoretical developments in the field, specifically their link with the emergence of the multinational enterprise (MNE) as the key player in IB in the second half of the 20th century. We show how the goals of the MNE are presented as the priority within contemporary IB practice, as disseminated through the major body of IB research and in mainstream textbooks. In particular, using a range of firm-based theories of IB as examples, we show how, within the rhetoric of profit maximization and shareholder value, they subjugate the interests of other groups of stakeholders. We argue that, since these theories underlie management knowledge constructed within the discipline of IB, the ethical assumptions, which are implicit in IB textbooks, are grounded in a narrow paradigm, privileging the shareholders and managers of the MNE. We offer illustrative examples of this in relation to organizational practices within the domains of operations, HRM and accounting at a global level. Subsequently, we offer suggestions regarding the development of a phronetic approach to IB knowledge; one that would move away from the ethics of profit maximization and shareholder return; that would take into account the interests of a variety of parties involved in and affected by IB; and that would present IB-related theories and practices in such a way that critical reflection would be promoted.

2. ETHICS AND THEORIES OF INTERNATIONAL BUSINESS

In the space of this chapter, we cannot address the full range of theories of IB in detail, but we draw upon selective examples from a range of sources in order to highlight several key issues:

- International business has developed from an historical basis of exploitation of political, economic and military strength differentials;
- Contemporary IB theories are grounded in the continuance of these differentials as a source of competitive advantage for the 'good' of the firm;
- Reliance upon such theories renders IB inherently 'unethical' in relation to the good of society at large at a global level.

In relation to its historical antecedents, Czinkota et al. (2005) describe how IB has been used as a tool of governmental policy throughout history; whether as an enabler of development, or as an instrument of coercion and control. Early theories underpinning IB; for example mercantilism, theory of absolute advantage and theory of comparative advantage; were built around the concept of the nation state as the main actor in trade exchanges, and upon an assumed imbalance of power relationships between nations with regard to the distribution of physical and financial resources. In these theories, the underlying notion of 'good' was that of benefit to the individual nation state, and of social and moral improvements for groups relative to their own previous situation. However, they did not see as problematic any notion of inequality of wealth distribution across groups and between nations.

Whilst IB has a long history, recent developments in the fields of indus-trialization and globalization, advances in transportation, and the growth of multinational enterprises (MNEs) have led to an increase in its eco-nomic, social and political significance. During the second half of the 20th century, the central focus of IB moved from products to services and from country-based to firm-based theories. The period was exemplified by the establishment of economic dominance by multinational companies, which in literature was reflected by a preoccupation with consideration of indus-tries and markets. Accordingly, the definition of 'good' as centered on the nation state has been replaced by one that places the firm as the main actor in IB transactions. Contemporary theories, such as Linder's (1961) country similarity theory and Vernon's (1966) product life cycle theory, seek to enable the firm to achieve the highest possible returns for its finan-cial shareholders. Similarly, global strategic rivalry theory (e.g. Krugman 1981; Lancaster 1980) outlines a variety of ways in which MNEs can seek to gain advantage over their competitors. In these theories, the ethical imperative is that of profit maximization for the global players and their shareholders, whereby any negative impact on societies is not addressed. This does not mean that negative social outcomes are not acknowledged. In his theory of national competitive advantage, Porter (1990) recognizes the existence of inequalities between and within nations and sees them, not as a negative aspect of IB to be overcome, but as a potential source of com-petitive advantage and a necessary condition for industry globalization. Following a similar logic, Dunning's (1993) 'eclectic theory' outlines how successful foreign direct investment (FDI) by the firm is based upon the combination of three conditions: ownership advantage, location advan-tage, and internalization advantage. The second of these points to the need for the continued existence of economic inequalities between home and host countries, such that those who are used as labor by global companies will, by definition, attract a low level of earnings. This translates into them having a relatively low level of purchasing power and, as a result, they lack the ability to buy those products and services that they might wish to. In this way, the condition of poverty for sections of society is built into con-temporary IB theories as a necessary enabler of industry globalization and reduction in the costs of doing business.

Perhaps, for a critically minded reader, it is unsurprising that the IB-related theories presented in mainstream textbooks carry an implicit assumption about IB activities being essentially desirable and socially valuable. It might also be seen as obvious that, similar to other texts grounded in the managerial discourse, they present 'an understanding of organizations as rational entities and of management as politically and morally uncontentious' (Grey 2003, p. 349). However, we would argue that, since few of those who construct IB theories, write textbooks for students and teach IB currently locate themselves within the tradition of critical management studies (CMS) and CME, there is scope for pointing to what some might see as obvious: that neither at its roots nor in more recent conceptualizations, is a broad deontological ethics embedded in notions of IB. Any ethical values that can be implied are those of a narrow and exclusive perspective, evoking action, the morality of which is concerned with the benefits for the few, rather than addressing the exploitation of the many.

3.　THE MORALITY OF IB PRACTICE

In the previous section, we have argued that the ethics underpinning the conceptual roots of IB – both classical and more recent ones – promote action, which benefits a few powerful actors, rather than society as a whole. At present, the main entities addressed within mainstream IB literature are MNEs, and conceptual and empirical research within the discipline privileges the interests of their top managers and financial stakeholders. As such, the knowledge constructed and conveyed through textbooks, directed at students of IB and managers of companies involved in IB practices, reflects the morality of managerialism and neo-liberalism inherent in contemporary IB theories. Recommendations for conducting business at an international level in accordance with this moral paradigm address all functional areas of management discussed within IB textbooks, including: production, marketing, research and development (R&D), human resource management (HRM), accounting and financial management. We recognize that it is possible to argue that, as far as business ethics is concerned, self-interested behavior of companies leads to the best possible outcome for society as a whole, or that, as claimed by Milton Friedman (1962) in his book *Capitalism and Freedom*, the maximization of shareholder value is the best way for corporations to serve societal interests. Indeed, the assumption that maximizing total firm value will result in maximizing social welfare underpins conventional firm theory (Jensen 1988) and the view of 'enlightened self-interest' as a socially desirable approach to business ethics lies behind the philosophy of corporate social responsibility. However, we concur with Banerjee (2007, pp. 1–2) that enlightened self-interest 'can only go so far in producing positive social outcomes' because 'the imperatives of profit accumulation and shareholder value maximization do not always create win–win situations but often result in dispossession, [whereas] the current political economy results in an economic capture of the social that marginalizes millions of people in the world'. Therefore, we feel the need to critically appraise the ends to which the IB practices commonly discussed in textbooks lead. Within the limited space of this chapter, we look at illustrative examples from the canon typically adopted in business school education. The areas we focus upon are: production, HRM and accounting.

One of the examples offered in the recently published text on international business by Cavusgil et al. (2008) is that of the extent of internationalization of manufacturing and assembly operations by the computer firm Dell. The authors present this case in the context of contemporary trends in international production and logistics operations; such as outsourcing, global sourcing and offshoring; whereby 'the search for the best sources of products and services' is seen as 'an ongoing task for managers' (2008, p. 484). Cavusgil et al. illustrate how just one product – the Dell Inspiron Notebook Computer – is assembled from parts originating from numerous locations across the world, including Malaysia, Mexico, China, Taiwan, South Korea, Singapore, Thailand, the Philippines, Japan, Costa Rica and Germany. The commentary provided by the authors does not address questions such as the environmental cost of transportation involved in building computers within the framework of global sourcing or the power relationships within the global supply chains. Rather, it conveys to the reader the message that what matters is whether global configuration of activities contributes to the company's success, since it is unproblematically assumed that contemporarily 'firms shop around the world for inputs or finished products to meet efficiency and strategic objectives and remain competitive' (2008, p. 484).

Another example, with reference to managing human resources internationally, is provided in Czinkota et al.'s (2004) text on the *Fundamentals of International Business*. In discussing issues pertaining to 'managing a global workforce', the authors focus on HR practices involved in employing managers for overseas assignments. The candidates, it is argued, should be characterized by certain sets of competences, combined with high levels of adaptability, and should have specific personal traits which are seen as potentially contributing to their success as expatriate managers. These selection criteria, such as adaptability, however, are not constrained to the candidates themselves, but extend to cover their families, whereby family members become subject to 'in-depth interviews. . . from various perspectives' (2004, p. 352). This type of screening is conceived as necessary from the point of view of the company's financial priorities, and aims at reducing the losses related to 'the cost of transferring a manager abroad and the high attrition rates' (2004, p. 352).

As far as employment within IB of people other than expatriate managers is concerned, Czinkota et al. (2004 p. 357) mention three perspectives on 'labor strategy', namely '(1) the participation of labor in the affairs of the firm, especially as it affects performance and well-being; (2) the role and impact of unions in the relationship; and (3) specific human resource policies, in terms of recruitment, training and compensation'. The subject of non-managers employed globally by MNEs is approached exclusively from the point of view of fulfilling the company's objectives of turnover and profit generation. The voices of those employed by the MNEs across the world, or the subcontractors located at different locations within the global value chains dominated by the major players are, however, absent from the discourse.

In a similar vein, the emphasis on profit maximization can be found in discussions of accounting-related issues, as presented in texts on international business. For example, Shenkar and Luo (2008) introduce the readers – prospective managers of companies operating internationally – to transfer pricing strategies which are used by MNEs in order to 'earn economic benefits such as tax avoidance by manipulating the price of intra-MNE transactions' (Shenkar and Luo 2008, p. 425). The authors offer illustrations of how, through over- or under-pricing products or intra-company transactions, the MNE is able to reduce the amount of taxes paid in each of the countries in which it operates. The ability to do this is presented as beneficial for MNEs, based upon the unproblematically accepted assumption that 'when tax rates are different in two countries, MNEs favor low transfer prices for goods and services bought by, and high transfer prices for goods and services sold by, an affiliate in a low-tax jurisdiction' (2008, pp. 426–7). Other benefits for MNEs mentioned in the context of transfer pricing refer to avoiding exchange controls, and hence overcoming governmental restrictions on imports of goods or withdrawal of funds from a given country, and to increasing profits from joint ventures in order to enable 'the party to gain unilateral profit from controlling the joint venture's import and export activities' (2008, p. 426). Whilst the explanation of transfer pricing strategies is followed by a discussion of regulations and penalties developed in response to MNEs' transfer pricing practices, this is framed within the context of conformance with the legal requirements of a given country, rather than the moral dimension of tax avoidance and its implications for a range of stakeholders. Likewise, the emphasis on the benefit for the MNE, rather than a concern for the well-being of other parties involved in and affected by their activities, is present in the section on the use of tax havens, where, without contesting the ethical aspect of their existence, it is taken for granted that they are there since 'high tax rates in many countries have forced MNEs to seek refuge in tax havens' (2008, p. 429).

From the above examples, taken from contemporary international business textbooks, we posit that the morality underpinning the IB knowledge conveyed to the students of the subject is one of exploitation of opportunity and financial gain to serve the benefits of MNEs and their shareholders.

4.   SEEKING A NEW ETHICS OF IB – DRAWING UPON *PHRONĒSIS*

Based upon our readings of these various examples of presentation of key issues in IB in the canon of textbooks, we posit that they privilege the hegemonic economic model of IB practice, not only subordinating other considerations but, by and large, silencing other voices and excluding them from the discourse. They show how global production and markets lead firms to see the search for ever-lower costs of production as a prime driver. When the work process can be physically detached from the market, jobs will be moved across the world in search of the most efficient operational base, as forms of decision-making on global workplace location develop that are based upon recognition and maintenance of economic differentials. In the IB literature, these differentials – as well as critical consideration of key issues of cause and effect, inclusion and exclusion, winners and losers – are not seen as problems to be addressed through changing the contemporarily predominant models of IB practice.

In presenting the 'Ethical dilemmas of critical management education', Fenwick (2005, p. 36) raises the question of '(h)ow can critical management educators ethically justify engaging learners in an orientation that may be impossible to enact in existing structures of practice?' We would argue that, as educators, we have an influence upon those who in the future will manage and work for organizations involved in international activities and therefore we have a contribution to make in terms of changing existing structures of IB practice through encouraging our students to critically examine their underlying ethics and values, as well as their consequences for a range of parties, and through presenting our students with examples of IB practices which are not usually discussed in mainstream textbooks. Like Banerjee (2007), Jones et al. (2005); as well as such diverse supporters and critics of globalization as ex-WTO advisor Philippe Legrain (2002), former World Bank economist Joseph Stiglitz (2002), and critical journalists Paul Kingsnorth (2003) and Naomi Klein (2000, 2008); we posit that a new ethics of IB requires, at a minimum, some reconstitution of the existing frameworks and institutions. We believe that, as researchers and educators, we should not assume that the trajectory of

IB ethics is determined only by commercial organizations, supra-national organizations and possibly social movements, and that our role is limited to educating managers as 'morally neutral technicians' (Hendry 2006, p. 269). Rather, we suggest adopting a more active role for ourselves – in this particular case, we draw upon the Aristotelian concept of *phronēsis*, in order to offer one option for developing a new approach to IB ethics, based upon a re-humanizing of organization, such that the proper purpose of business is seen as serving the ends of a broad range of parties rather than of itself. Aristotle considers *phronēsis* to be the most important of the 'intellectual virtues'; the ability of 'man to be able to deliberate about what is good and advantageous for himself', and to be 'capable of action with regard to things that are good or bad for man' (Aristotle [350 BC] 2004, p. 150). The concept of *phronēsis* is subject to discussion and development in contemporary social science (for example, Birmingham 2004; Cairns and Śliwa 2008; Clegg 2006; Clegg and Ross-Smith 2003), most notably by Danish academic Bent Flyvbjerg (2001, 2003).

Flyvbjerg (1998, 2001) challenges the notion that contemporary democracy is transparent, inclusive and conducive to the realization of a 'common good', and that decisions made by politicians and business interests are rational. He posits that politicians and managers approach complex problems such that 'power *defines* what counts as rationality and knowledge and thereby what counts as reality' (Flyvbjerg 1998, p. 227, emphasis in original). Here, the exercise of power determines not only what problems are brought forward for consideration, but also how they are conceived and presented. Flyvbjerg argues that the 'democratic' process is most likely one of exclusion and the pursuit of self-interest by powerful individuals and bodies. He proposes (Flyvbjerg 2001, p. 60) a new focus on complex social issues, through application of a phronetic approach in which the following value-rational questions are addressed at the outset:

- Where are we going?
- Is this development desirable?
- What, if anything, should we do about it?
- Who gains and who loses, and by which mechanisms of power?

Flyvbjerg considers that a truly democratic process of governance requires transparency and accountability, and development of dialogical communication that incorporates all stakeholder perspectives and draws upon all relevant and effective media. This dialogue must also acknowledge the mediating processes of power and rationality.

Drawing upon Flyvbjerg's conceptual framework, Jentoft (2006, p. 1) proposes that thinking on problems involving complex societal issues requires early and open consideration of the implications and impact of political and policy decisions in the broader realm of community and society. He states that 'the concerns, principles and goals of the management process are matters of preference and choice, and hence political struggle' and that 'the name of the game is changing, as "management" is increasingly being replaced by the broader concept of "governance"'. It is in seeking ways of enacting a new form of management that involves consideration of a broad range of social values and ethical stances that Jentoft calls for a phronetic approach.

In Jentoft's text, we find a resonance with the Aristotelian concern for what is 'good or bad for man'. In relation to complex and possibly ambiguous problems; that involve deliberation on social, economic, ecological and other implications of their resolution; Jentoft sees the answer to what is 'good' as a matter for negotiation within the framework of a truly democratic society. Jentoft's governance perspective 'emphasises the interaction between the state, the market and civil society, recognising the strengths and weaknesses of each and the need to draw on their respective capacities' (2006, p. 9), 'inviting a more reflexive, deliberative and value-rational methodology than the instrumental, means-end oriented management concept' (2006, p. 1). Jentoft recognizes that problems are not always what they appear to be, often stemming from outside the context that they are made visible within, and he urges the approach of 'scouting outwards', in terms of geographical, disciplinary and chronological contexts. In relation to the third context, and to Flyvbjerg's (2001) fourth question, above, he asks, 'Are future generations sacrificed for the benefit of the present one?' (Jentoft 2006, p. 2). Jentoft's text is based upon analysis of the relationships between the range of affected actors, policy makers and society at a regional level, in relation to fisheries policy. However, we consider that the questions he raises and the approaches he advocates might be applied in a broader geographical context in relation to issues of IB, moving it beyond the 'instrumental, means-end oriented management' we find promoted in many of the texts.

As can be seen from the above discussion, the phronetic approach to IB knowledge that we propose pays considerable attention to the notion of stakeholders and their interests. In this context, it is necessary to explain how our interpretation of phronetic engagement differs from what can be found in stakeholder theory. Contemporary IB literature does include some references to the concept of 'stakeholder'. However, where stakeholders are mentioned, they are defined narrowly, in relation to groups and individuals that are linked 'via some role-related activity, to the corporation' (Freeman 1994, p. 411); have an impact upon decisions made (cf. Janoff and Weisbord 2005), or have a financial interest in their outcome (cf. van der Heijden et al., 2002). Our starting point is to adopt a broader view of stakeholders, as '(a)ny identifiable group or individual who can affect the achievement of an organization's objectives or who is affected by the achievement of an organization's objectives' (Freeman and Reed 1983, p. 91). This definition considers stakeholders 'as individuals, human beings . . . moral beings' (Freeman 1994, p. 411), and thus conceives of the stakeholder–firm relationship as a 'moral relationship' (Mitchell et al. 1997). Here, the 'ultimate test of corporate performance' (Donaldson and Preston 1995, p. 80) lies, not in meeting conventional financial criteria, but in satisfying multiple stakeholder interests – which, of course, implies the need for redefining of the purpose of a firm (cf. Banerjee 2007). As such, an approach to IB knowledge grounded in *phronēsis* corresponds with a normative approach to stakeholder theory rather than the prevailing instrumental approach which 'accommodates the fundamental economic assumptions of the theory of the firm while ignoring many social and eco- nomic conflicts between corporations and some stakeholders' (Banerjee 2007, p. 28). We concur with Banerjee (2007) that, for a stakeholder theory to promote social good it must be applied, not on instrumental but on normative terms, and it must involve a conceptual move away from the primacy of shareholder interests and profit maximization as the essential purposes of the firm. We posit that approaching IB knowledge from a phronetic perspective – bearing in mind that to Aristotle, *phronēsis* was associated with broad considerations of 'what is good and bad for man' – creates space for changing the currently dominant paradigm of IB towards one in which the 'social' rather than the 'corporate' is given primary import- ance. In seeking to challenge the presently taken for granted neo-liberal economic foundations of the discipline of IB, this perspective is commen- surate with a critical normative application of stakeholder theory.

5. A PHRONETIC ANALYSIS OF IB PRACTICES

In order to engage with the question of what IB knowledge and practice grounded in a phronetic approach would look like – and in the context of Flyvbjerg's and others' work on *phronēsis* – we now point to some of the limitations of the current prevalent model of IB knowledge and practice, by considering the examples we presented earlier through the lens of the four value-rational questions posed by Flyvbjerg (2001).

In relation to the first question – 'where are we going?' – we see the initial task of IB researchers and educators in problematizing its very subject. As we have outlined in this chapter, mainstream IB textbooks are written from the point of view of firms involved in international business activities and promote the kinds of conduct conditioned by the interests of MNEs' shareholders and managers. We call for development of IB knowledge and practice that are underpinned by notions of what is good for a broad range of involved and affected parties, both currently and in the future. At present, as the textbook examples lead us to contend, the implications of the rhetoric of geographic expansion and maximization of financial return of MNEs are far from positive, when viewed from the perspective of all human beings. In terms of how operations of MNEs are organized, we are moving towards an ever more globalized system of sourcing and distribution, which brings about resource exploitation and depletion, and increased levels of pollution resulting from global operations and logistics. The desire to always find the cheapest provider also leads to exacerbation of global poverty and inequalities, the consequence of which is the deepening of socio-economic fragmentation. This – as our reading of examples from international HRM suggests – is coupled with the development of a specific model of worker subjectivity, one within which the lives of workers and their families are subordinated to the objectives of the firm. Moreover, the currently predominant paradigm of IB knowledge is primarily concerned with the work of managers employed by MNEs and does not consider it as ethically necessary to dedicate more attention to the interests of people other than managers who also work for MNEs. In addition, following from our engagement with mainstream textbook discussions of accounting practices of MNEs; such as the use of transfer pricing and tax havens; we see contemporary IB knowledge as promoting a model of political economy in which; through an unproblematic prioritization of MNEs' objectives of maximizing their profits and minimizing the amount of corporate taxes paid; there is little space left for emphasizing the responsibility of companies for enabling governments to fulfill their role in providing public goods, such as health care, education and social benefits, for all citizens.

The realization of where – according to the trajectory outlined by mainstream IB texts – we, as broadly defined stakeholder groups, are going leads us to consideration of the second of Flyvbjerg's (2001) questions in his framework for a phronetic approach to democratic governance, i.e. 'Is this development desirable?' Following from what we have highlighted above, our answer is 'no'. The environmental degradation, which often results from global business operations, is not good for either contemporary society, or for future generations. The scale of global poverty and the deepening socio-economic inequalities across the world may put the powerful few in a privileged position, but certainly are not good for the masses, for example, those who carry out sweatshop labor in export processing zones (EPZs). Reducing human beings to committed workers for whom the objectives of the firm are more important than their and their families' well-being, is – at least from the perspective of those on the receiving end of such instrumental HRM policies – not a desirable development, either. The image of a world in which companies are free to choose not only where they source, produce and sell, but also how much – if any – tax they are going to pay in the countries in which they conduct their business cannot be viewed as desirable for the majority of members of society, since it is in their interest to benefit from the governmental provision financed by corporate taxes. Such an image seriously reduces the possibility of conceptualizing commercial organizations in IB as entities whose existence contributes to developing and supporting civil societies, in which all citizens are given the chance to build sustainable livelihoods for themselves and their families.

As academics involved in IB education, in response to Flyvbjerg's (2001) third question – 'What, if anything, should we do about it?' – we call for development of IB knowledge in accordance with a phronetic approach. More specifically, we suggest that there is a need to challenge the hegemony of neo-liberal discourse, which currently pervades IB texts, and to address the subject of IB from the perspective of much more broadly defined stakeholders, both at present and in the future. This would involve examining the ethical assumptions of contemporary IB knowledge and their resultant morality, and exposing the ways and extent to which it privileges the interests of corporations at the expense of other parties involved in and affected by IB practices. Following from here, a phronetic IB knowledge would need to be rooted in a different set of ethical assumptions, whereby the interests of the broadly defined society, rather than the firm, would be central – with the aim of contributing to building a truly democratic society.

As far as Flyvbjerg's (2001) fourth question is concerned – 'who gains and who loses, and by which mechanisms of power?' – a phronetic approach to IB would imply the need for changing the extant power structure promoted by contemporary IB practices. At present, the most obvious 'winners' are the shareholders and top managers of MNEs, whose power is increased through their alliance with supranational institutions. This, in turn, legitimizes their hegemony within the neo-liberal view of social priorities. Other parties, as we have outlined above, are in different ways disadvantaged by activities of MNEs, the morality of which is underpinned by the narrow, instrumental, firm-focused view of ethics conveyed in mainstream IB texts. Moving away from the current paradigm of knowledge and opening up space for discussing alternative models of economy and society would, perhaps, help make IB work for the benefit of society, rather than solely for MNEs and their top management and shareholders.

We do not see our call for reconstituting IB knowledge in our academic practice as promoting some form of 'superior moralizing' (Samra-
Fredericks 2003) when engaging with students of IB. As discussed earlier
in this chapter, the current paradigm of IB is by no means value-free and
we consider it our task to reframe it in accordance with a different set of
values. This is not because we believe that we have the right to take a lofty
ethical position of speaking from the perspective of the whole of humanity, but because we recognize that at present, globally, 'there are many
disempowered and marginalized groups who are adversely affected by
corporate activity yet unable to participate in any "stakeholder dialogue"'
(Banerjee 2007, p. 33). Since the present model of IB knowledge reinforces
this situation of unequal power relationships between companies engaged
in IB activity and other groups, we have the opportunity to contribute to
a shift in the 'discursive power' (McAfee 1999) reproduced in mainstream
IB publications through the development of research articles, case studies,
textbooks and other materials grounded in a phronetic perspective and
commensurate with the principles of CME. In this way, in the sphere of
IB, we respond to Banerjee's (2007, p. 127) call for 'examin(ing) the relationships between major actors and institutions as well as the structural
and discursive mechanisms of power that underlie these relationships'.

Aristotelian *phronēsis* has a strong emphasis on practice and we would
like to stress the need for us, as academics and educators, to be involved
in the practices associated with the production of what is considered as
'truth' within the discipline of IB, since 'we are subjected to the production
of truth through power and we cannot exercise power except through the
production of truth' (Foucault 1980, p. 3). In our call to reconstitute IB
knowledge around a different set of values and ethics, we stress, in particular, the need to expose the values behind and the consequences of the theories and practices prevailing in the field of IB at present, in order to reveal
how the predominant model of IB is created and sustained (Cox 1981);
to move away from the primacy of profit maximization and shareholder
return, and to redefine the purpose of organizations involved in IB as centered around the 'social' rather than the 'corporate'; to critically analyse
the political economy of IB and to problematize the power relations within
it by addressing the perspectives of those groups which are currently
marginalized within the mainstream discourse, for example indigenous
communities in the poorer regions of the world, and those activities which
are rarely written about, but currently constitute profitable IB activities,
for example the arms trade; and to dedicate space to alternative forms of
IB, based on more equal relationships between involved parties and being
environmentally sustainable. By realizing that we, as academics, have
the power to construct 'statements which provide a language for talking

about – way of representing knowledge about' (Foucault 1972, p. 143) IB, and by taking an active role in changing the hegemonic discourses through our practices as authors and educators, we have a contribution to make in terms of influencing 'what is and what is not, what can be done and what cannot and what should be and what should not' (Clegg 1989, p. 142) in contemporary IB. A phronetic approach to IB knowledge, commensurate with a critical normative stakeholder perspective, can therefore have an impact not only upon what happens in the classroom but also upon the organizational, institutional and social practices linked to the 'regime of truth' (Foucault 1980) of the discipline of IB.

6.   FINAL REMARKS

In this chapter, we have provided a brief overview of the theoretical basis of IB and have pointed out how notions of profit maximization, share-holder return and corporate self-interest underpin much of the present-day mainstream IB literature. We have also discussed a number of examples from extant IB textbooks in order to reveal how the way in which IB knowledge is presented and the practices it promotes lead to privileging certain groups – mainly top managers of MNEs and their shareholders – at the expense of other categories of stakeholders. We have argued for the need to construct an alternative approach to IB knowledge, commensurate with a critical normative stakeholder perspective. Our suggestion is that a change in the currently dominant IB discourse can be brought about through developing IB knowledge inspired by contemporary interpreta-tion of Aristotle's concept of *phronēsis*. We see the task of developing such knowledge as resting on us – academics and educators in the field of IB. Through phronetically informed textbooks, book chapters, case studies and articles published for the purposes of critical IB education, we can put this approach into practice and contribute to redefining the boundaries, purposes, content, power structures and broader impacts of the discipline of IB. We have the chance to encourage our students to critically reflect upon IB practices and, in their thinking, to address not only the 'what' and 'how', but also the 'why' and 'to what effect' of these practices. By prob-lematizing the power relationships present in the dominant IB discourse we have the opportunity to open up a dialogue about alternative power-sharing arrangements (Payne 2005) between involved and affected parties.

We consider the major relevance of the phronetic approach to IB inquiry to be that it is an interpretive approach, which places a broad range of actors at the centre stage, engaging with their values and beliefs, and with their interpretations and understandings of their 'reality'. Whilst the phronetic approach enables us to challenge hegemonic theories of IB that focus on the firm and its interests, it is not grounded in some moral relativism, which accepts all views as equal. Being normative in its orientation, it involves making informed judgments which will favor and privilege some options over others, and reflection upon the consequences of different courses of action. Like mainstream IB thinking, the phronetic approach is grounded in practice – but we would stress that, whilst the central concern of the phronetic approach is that of context and of engagement with the values, beliefs, and assumptions of the actors in this context, the concern for practice does not place *phronēsis* in the realm of the a-theoretical, setting up an 'unhelpful false dichotomy' (Feyerabend 1999) between theory and practice. Like Ruderman (1997), we see *phronēsis* as being informed by '*theoria* (that) can foster flexibility, by helping prudence to gain critical distance on popular but misguided views and to resist the often rigid moralism of the community or regime' (1997, p. 411). We concur that Aristotle 'does not allow his practical or moral concern for justice to silence the theoretical investigation of what justice is (and cannot be)' (1997, p. 411).

Adopting a phronetic approach to the generation of IB knowledge requires us to engage with a much broader range of stakeholders in their own context of thinking and acting over time, to be able to gain an understanding of events in terms of their origins, emergence, outcomes and implications. We propose that Aristotle's concept of *phronēsis*; and its contemporary development in the works of Flyvbjerg (2001, 2003) and others, offers theoretical possibilities for a more humanistic IB project that either brings about fundamental change to the practices and institutions of IB or, at the very least, leads to a radical restructuring of the existing institutions.

NOTE

1. Here, we clarify that we identify 'mainstream' textbooks on IB as those that (a) are published by international publishing houses, (b) are in their nth edition, (c) are claimed within the texts as being 'leading' or 'best selling', and (d) are supported by electronic and web-based teaching resources.

REFERENCES

Antonacopoulou, E. (2002) 'Corporate universities: the domestication of management education', in C. Wankel and R. DeFillippi (eds), *Rethinking Management Education for the 21st Century*, Greenwich, CT: Information Age Publishing, pp. 185–207.

Aristotle ([350 BC] 2004), *The Nicomachean Ethics*, translated by J.A.K. Thomson (1953) and Rev. H. Tredennick (1976), London: Penguin Books.

Banerjee, B. (2007), *Corporate and Social Responsibility*, Cheltenham, UK and Northampton, MA, USA: Edward Elgar.

Birmingham, C. (2004), 'Phronesis: a model for pedagogical reflection', *Journal of Teacher Education*, **55** (4), 313–24.

Cairns, G. and M. Śliwa (2008), 'The implications of Aristotle's *phronēsis* for organizational inquiry', in D. Narry and H. Hansen (eds), *The Sage Handbook of New Approaches in Management and Organization*, London: Sage, pp. 318–28.

Cairns, G., M. Śliwa and G. Wright (2008), 'Developing the stakeholder perspective in international business education through application of scenario thinking', paper presented at the Academy of International Business – Australia and New Zealand Chapter Symposium on Research and Teaching in International Business, University of Sydney, 10 December.

Cavusgil, S.T., G. Knight and J.A. Reisenberger (2008), *International Business. Strategy, Management and New Realities*, Upper Saddle River, NJ: Pearson Education.

Clegg, S.R. (1989), *Frameworks of Power*, London: Sage.

Clegg, S.R. (2006), 'The bounds of rationality: power/history/imagination', *Critical Perspectives on Accounting*, **17** (7), 847–63.

Clegg, S.R. and A. Ross-Smith (2003), 'Revising the boundaries: management education and learning in a postpositivist world', *Academy of Management Learning and Education*, **2** (1), 85–98.

Cox, R.W. (1981), 'Social forces, states and world orders: beyond international relations theory', *Millennium: Journal of International Relations*, **10** (2), 126–55.

Czinkota, M.R., I.A. Ronkainen and M.H. Moffett (2004), *Fundamentals of International Business*, Mason, OH: South-Western.

Czinkota, M.R., I.A. Ronkainen and M.H. Moffett (2005), *International Business*, 7th edn, Mason, OH: South-Western.

Donaldson, T. and L.E. Preston (1995), 'The stakeholder theory of the corporation: concepts, evidence and implications', *Academy of Management Review*, **20** (1), 65–91.

Dunning, J. (1993), *The Globalization of Business*, London: Routledge.

Fenwick, T. (2005), 'Ethical dilemmas of critical management education', *Management Learning*, **36** (1), 31–48.

Feyerabend, P. (1999), *Conquest of Abundance: A Tale of Abstraction Versus the Richness of Being*, Chicago, IL: University of Chicago Press.

Flyvbjerg, B. (1998), *Rationality and Power – Democracy in Practice*, Chicago, IL: University of Chicago Press.

Flyvbjerg. B. (2001), *Making Social Science Matter: Why Social Inquiry Fails and How It Can Succeed Again*, Cambridge: Cambridge University Press.

Flyvbjerg, B. (2003), 'Making organization research matter: power values and phronesis', in B. Czarniawska and G. Sevón (eds), *The Northern Lights: Organization Theory in Scandinavia*, Copenhagen: Liber Abstrakt – Copenhagen Business School Press, pp. 357–82.

Foucault, M. (1972), *The Archeology of Knowledge and the Discourse on Language*, New York: Pantheon Books.

Foucault, M. (1980), *Power/Knowledge: Selected Interviews and Other Writings, 1972–1977*, New York: Pantheon Books.

Freeman, R.E. (1994), 'The politics of stakeholder theory: some future directions', *Business Ethics Quarterly*, **4** (4), 409–21.

Freeman, R.E. and D.L. Reed (1983), 'Stockholders and stakeholders: a new perspective on corporate governance', *California Management Review*, **XXV** (3), 91.

Friedman, M. (1962), *Capitalism and Freedom*, Chicago, IL: University of Chicago Press.

Grey, C. (2003), 'Debating forbidden knowledge', *Management Learning*, **34** (3), 349–51.

Hendry, J. (2006), 'Educating managers for post-bureaucracy', *Management Learning*, **37** (3), 267–81.

Janoff, S. and M. Weisbord (2005), 'Future search as "real-time" action research', *Futures*, **38** (6), 716–22.

Jensen, M. (1988), 'Takeovers: their causes and consequences', *Journal of Economic Perspectives*, **2** (1), 21–44.

Jentoft, S. (2006), 'Beyond fisheries management: the phronetic dimension', *Marine Policy*, **30** (6), 671–80.

Jones, C., M. Parker and R. ten Bos (2005), *For Business Ethics*, London: Routledge.

Kingsnorth, P. (2003), *One No, Many Yeses*, London: Simon and Schuster.

Klein, N. (2000), *No Space/No Choice/No Jobs – No Logo*, London: Flamingo.

Klein, N. (2008), *The Shock Doctrine*, London: Penguin Books.

Krugman, P. (1981), 'Intraindustry specialization and the gains from trade', *Journal of Political Economy*, **89** (5), 959–73.

Lancaster, K. (1980), 'Intra-industry trade under perfect monopolistic competition', *Journal of International Economics*, **10** (2), 151–75.

Legrain, P. (2002), *Open World:/The Truth About Globalisation*, London: Abacus.

Linder, S.B. (1961), *An Essay on Trade and Transformation*, New York: John Wiley.

McAfee, K. (1999), 'Selling nature to save it? Biodiversity and green developmentalism', *Environment and Planning D*, **17** (2), 133–54.

Mitchell, R., B. Agle and D. Wood (1997), 'Toward a theory of stakeholder identification and salience: defining the principle of who and what really counts', *Academy of Management Review*, **22** (4), 853–86.

Payne, A. (2005), *The Global Politics of Unequal Development*, New York: Palgrave Macmillan.

Perriton, L. and M. Reynolds (2004) 'Critical management education: from pedagogy of possibility to pedagogy of refusal?', *Management Learning*, **35** (1), 61–77.

Porter, M. (1990), *The Competitive Advantage of Nations*, New York: Free Press.

Ruderman, R.S. (1997), 'Aristotle and the recovery of political judgment', *American Political Science Review*, **91** (2), 409–20.

Samra-Fredericks, D.A. (2003), 'A proposal for developing a critical pedagogy of management from researching organizational members' everyday practices', *Management Learning*, **34** (3): 291–312.

Shenkar, O. and Y. Luo (2008), *International Business*, Thousand Oaks, CA: Sage.

Śliwa, M. and G. Cairns (2009), 'Towards a critical pedagogy of international business: the application of *phronēsis*', *Management Learning*, **40** (3), 227–40.

Stiglitz, J. (2002), *Globalization and its Discontents*, London: Allen Lane/Penguin.

Van der Heijden, K., R. Bradfield, G. Burt, G. Cairns and G. Wright (2002), *The Sixth Sense: Accelerating Organizational Learning with Scenarios*, Chichester: John Wiley.

Vernon, R. (1966), 'International investment and international trade in the product life cycle', *Quarterly Journal of Economics*, **80** (2), 190–207.

Welsh, M.E. and G.E. Dehler (2007), 'Whither the MBA? Or the withering of MBAs?', *Management Learning*, **38** (4), 407–25.

3. More than words – an analysis of Scandinavian value-based management

Jeanette Lemmergaard

1. INTRODUCTION

The call for a more humanistic approach to ethics, which was emphasized in the previous chapter, will be responded to in this chapter. As such, the aim of this chapter is to explore ways of enacting Scandinavian value-based management, that is, managing through communicating social values and ethical stances.

In his classic book *The Functions of the Executive*, first published in 1938, Chester I. Barnard postulates that the managing director performs three functions in an organization. First, he provides and maintains a system of communication. Second, he promotes essential and cooperative efforts from individuals, and finally, he formulates and defines purpose and objectives. This chapter argues that Barnard's view on management and the function of the manager is not different from the view on management underlying the Scandinavian version of value-based management. Despite the fact that value-based management emphasizes moral value in contrast to economic value as a managerial guiding star, at least in the Scandinavian version of value-based management, the underlying managerial mechanisms represent a rather conventional view on management. The rhetoric is different, but the underlying assumptions are the same. To explore deeper into the nature of organizational values and the concept of value-based management, this chapter first discusses the concept of Scandinavian value-based management and then analyses this empirically through a case study analysis.

First, this chapter explores the concept of Scandinavian value-based management and discusses the dilemmas inherent in it. Then data are introduced from an empirical study in the form of an illustrative case study of how value-based management is conducted in a Danish knowledge-intensive organization. The case example is based on numerous in-depth interviews with the managing director of the organization, an electronic survey measuring the managers' and the full-time employees' perception of the organizational values, and a two-day participant observation study taking place during the organization's value-based management kickoff seminar. The chapter is questioning the diffusion of the concept and argues that whether articulated or not, the Scandinavian version of the concept resembles the concept of Scandinavian management and is therefore very much a conventional and running concept similar to the line of thinking that Barnard represents. The chapter concludes with a discussion of the implications of this study for the future of value-based management practice.

2. BEHIND THE CONCEPT OF VALUE-BASED MANAGEMENT

In terms of concept development and theoretical reflection, value-based management is a confusing concept. Various theoretical traditions use the term value-based management for different purposes, and a comprehensive literature review (Lemmergaard 2004a) shows that there is no clear-cut approach to the concept. Lack of consistency in the academic literature on what can be characterized as value-based management has lead to numerous implementation approaches. Similarly, analyses of the practitioners' application of value-based management principles demonstrate disagreements about the implementation of the concept. Not only does this lack of consistency among academics and practitioners with regard to understanding the concept aggravate confusion, but the confusion and inconsistency is also one of the reasons why many implementations of the concept has been unsuccessful. Many organizational leaders have simply come to the conclusion that the concept has fallen short of its expected benefits, and this has led to the concept being discontinued at least as a consciously implemented management tool. And from being an innovative concept promoted at the forefront of management progress in the 1990s, the concept has rapidly diffused. Generally, the concept has been conceptualized in so many different ways that it could be argued that the concept is so broad and diverse that it is useless. Simultaneously (or even perhaps consequentially), value-based management is rather wrongfully being considered a management fad among both academics and practitioners.

3.   DEFINING SCANDINAVIAN VALUE-BASED MANAGEMENT

Value-based management in the Scandinavian tradition is a business philosophy and a management system for competing effectively based upon the inherent value, dignity, and empowerment of organizational members. The concept is described as a tool for multidimensional management and control leaning against humanist values that can create a strong dynamic and competitive organization. Value-based management in this tradition is a matter of views, values, and convictions, frequently emphasizing ethics. Following this tradition, everyday behavior in the organization is regulated through strong and visible values and convictions, sometimes even replacing formal rules and regulations. Morality and individual responsibility are considered a supplement to and a possible replacement for rational, rule-based management. As such, value-based management can be compared to the special Scandinavian management culture, where employees as well as management have a high degree of autonomy with respect to work procedures, goals, and priorities, and where flexibility and tolerance towards unstructured matters are managerial keywords. The amount of individual freedom is high (self-governed groups, management, and union committees, etc.), and the flexibility and tolerance towards unstructured matters are essential.

In practice, value-based management covers everything from abstract value concepts to views on what is right and wrong. The concept is built on the assumption that a number of one-off values that each represent something special to the organizational members forms a united whole. The set of values are interrelated, containing elements of both compatibility and conflict. The values are fundamental and a leading force in determining behavior, and they create the groundwork of the organization. As such, the values create the foundation for conducting value-based management. In other words, the one-off values create the pool of core values that creates the foundation for value-based management, which is postulated to give an organization a competitive advantage. It is, however, not a matter of five positive sentences printed on glitter paper, but a matter of underlying attitudes and emotions expressed for example through the day-to-day management style and the organizational processes and practices. It is a management system which offers a logical framework for designing an organization's structures and processes in a way that an ownership culture is installed which enables the organization to carry on its purpose and objectives most effectively. Organizational values are socially shared cognitive representations of institutional goals and demands (Rokeach 1973), that provide the decision rules for interpreting the complex and numerous signals within the organizational environment and influence the organizational structure (Kabanoff et al. 1995), culture (Pettigrew 1979), identity (Ashforth and Mael 1989), climate, and strategy (Lemmergaard 2004b).

However, in order to build a strong credible management team a well-articulated company mission and a consistently practiced set of core values must be established. The mission statement is intended to articulate (or even create) a community of interest and a common culture, as it delivers a clear sense of direction and purpose. A well-articulated mission statement that is reflected in the day-to-day managerial practices and in the organizational processes is a good way to give value and meaning to the organizational members. However, the organizational members must accept the purpose of the mission, since otherwise it will not produce cooperative activity. Also, communication is necessary to translate mission into action. Here communication should be understood as language – verbal and written – but also as, what Barnard (1938) calls observational feeling, which is the ability to be able to understand, without words, not merely the situation but also the intention. Links between mission, values, and practices result from experience and training as well as continuity in association and lead to organizational members developing common perceptions and reactions to particular situations. In line with the Scandinavian management philosophy, values are made visible through dialogue and are not a top-down governed monologue (Thyssen 2002). It is, however, the management team that must convince the organizational members of the value of a shared vision or shared goals. They must sell vision and not impose it. Whereas the top management team determines the values, the organizational identity and climate often emerge from shared experiences.

It could be argued, that value-based management in a Scandinavian perspective has been dominated by a pre-event way of thinking and by viewing value from a moral sense. In this way, value-based management is less about pragmatic behavior and behavior regulation, and more about deeply rooted, partly emotional, and in particular attitudinal assumptions (Thyssen 2002). This way of thinking builds upon management as a cognitive and empathic process, where the point of departure is the purpose and objectives of the organization often expressed through the mission statement. It is through the purpose and the objectives of the organization that ideas, value, and actions directly emanate (Thyssen 2002; Grenness 2003). But as mentioned above, the purpose does not produce cooperative activity unless the organizational members accept it. However, implicit in this argument lies the assumption that organizational members will carry out even disagreeable jobs if they can accept them as relevant to the aims of the organization.

In sum, the concept of value-based management involves more than a model and some special priority areas with specified measures. The traditional Scandinavian version of value-based management emphasizes the importance of organizations consequently and consistently redis-covering their values in thoughts, words, and actions. Organizational members and organizational managers in particular should practice what they preach regardless of any pressure. This, however, should be done with attendance to the fact that commitment will rise and fall. The com-mitment of any organizational member will fluctuate depending on the satisfactions or dissatisfactions obtained. Thus, the total willingness of all organizational members to cooperate is unstable. Therefore, value-based management is a continuous process that requires an ongoing formulation and reformulation of purpose and objectives in order to secure the essen-tial services from the organizational members. It is the fundamental values that serve as guidelines, which are followed, when it comes to making compromises and defining priorities. And regardless of whether the basic values are economically or morally founded, they must be reflected in the business strategy and vice versa, also from a competitive and economic point of view. The same applies for all the messages – verbal and non-verbal – that the organization sends out. Values must be communicated to become significant, and hereby communication becomes essential in linking the common purpose with those willing to cooperate in achieving it.

4.   DIFFERENT VALUE-BASED MANAGEMENT SYSTEMS

Examples of more prominent Scandinavian value-based management tools are ethical accounting, value-based management through ethical codes, and/or ethical narratives. Scandinavian academics have especially positioned themselves in this area through the development of ethical accounting. Ethical accounting is using philosophical considerations as its starting point (Pruzan and Thyssen 1990; Morsing 1991; Hjelmer 1997) and is built on the assumption that individuals act in a social context where the common identity of the affiliation determines the behavior (Meyer and Arentsen 1997). The tool has its roots in the ethics of discourse (Habermas 1981), where consensus among all stakeholders, reached through the rational dialogue, determines what is considered acceptable behavior. Openness and mutual recognition characterize the consensus-seeking dia-logue. It is through dialogue you can find the values, that you wish to be recognized upon, to commit yourself to, and to which you wish to commit a third party (Morsing 1991: Hjelmer 1997; Meyer and Arentsen 1997). The consensus way of thinking, however, must not be considered narrow-minded, as conflicts and contradictory opinions are the very substance of a creative environment (Thyssen 2002).

Working with the ethical accounting tool, however, is not unproblematic as the tool presumes that values are hierarchical in nature. This underlying assumption implies a priority-based ordering where the hierarchy is more important than the contents. In that way, the hierarchy of the values determines behavior, however, in a context determined by, for example, culture and social institutions (Pruzan 1994). Combined with the use of metrics to measure the ethical and moral stance of the organization, ethical accounting is potentially leading the organization towards a dark spiral of moral decline as metrics can have unintended and unanticipated consequences. Ethical accounting tools rely on assembling data, which enables the company to determine value performance against some predetermined effectiveness criteria. The accounts help the organization to determine which elements of the value framework are in place and which are not. However, the problem is that 'you get what you measure', and since organizational members – managers and as well as employees – are smart and creative in their efforts to succeed, the metrics become the total focus of the organization. As individuals within the organization start planning how to 'fix' those stats or 'bend' the figures to suit their strengths, the best intentions of identifying goals and setting targets does not necessarily lead to the desired results.

Another instrument, which takes its point of departure in the moral value definition, is the formulation of ethical codes and basic values (Somers 2001). Besides the challenge of formulating the exact words or phrases, the real challenge is to make the basic values applicable when making the actual decision. One the one hand, the basic values must be clearly laid out, easy to remember, and not too detailed. On the other hand, the values must, however, not be self-evident positive words, upon which anybody can agree, because everything, and as a consequence nothing, is included in the chosen wording (Schwarts 2002; Gibbs 2003). Highly detailed ethical codes of conduct will, however, assume a rule-based nature. Such rule-based management provides security on the one hand, but on the other hand, it removes responsibility (Gibbs 2003), and whether it is a matter of value-based management in the moral sense of the word can be doubted. Often when presenting ethical codes and fundamental values, organizations experience resistance from the organizational members and the intention of articulating and perhaps even creating a community of interest fails. One reason why organizational members often become cynical about the organizational values is that they do not recognize the organization that they work for in the values. At best, such value formulations are a waste of paper and at worst, they strengthen distrust in management. However, if tied to for example appraisal, promotion, and payment systems the value statements will be accepted even by the less committed members of the organization.

A third example of a value-based management tool within the Scandinavian tradition is a deliberate work with the narratives from everyday organizational life, for example through stories that give reasons for the values and show in which direction the organization is moving (Nymark 2000). The contents and format of the values are challenged, for example through what is remembered and retold. The challenge is to make the values reflect the desired ideal picture through consciously and actively influencing the social constructive reality. Thus, value-based management is a matter of organizational culture, identity, and image (Jensen 1999; Schultz et al. 2000). Whether formulated as a narrative or as value statements as discussed above, it is important that the organizational members recognize the organization that they work for in the writings. Otherwise the writings will only represent the language of a fake community, similar to what Gouldner (1952) once called 'pseudo-*Gemeinschaft*'.

5.   DIFFERENT APPROACHES – SAME FOCI

Comparing the different approaches to the concept of value-based management a striking resembles to the concept of Scandinavian management becomes clear. It could even be argued that the concepts are representing the same managerial conviction under different labels. The Scandinavian Management concept has been around since the 1980s (Sjøborg 1985). The Scandinavian Model is based on cooperation between employers, employees, and politicians (Grenness 2003). Scandinavian Management is, generally speaking, action-oriented and based on values such as openness, equality, participation, and power-sharing. These values tend to foster flat organizational hierarchies that are consensus-orientated, where ideas are reciprocally exchanged, and where decision-making is democratic (Grenness 2003). Besides appreciating employee initiative and participation, the Scandinavian Management tradition also tends to have a long-term perspective on employment relationships.

At times the most effective manner in which to define an orientation or idea is to demonstrate what it is not. Comparing the Scandinavian management philosophy to management in general shows some fundamental differences. All in all, whereas the international management literature and in particular, American management literature, takes its point of departure in a traditional strategic and economic way of thinking, the Scandinavian management literature departs in the adaptation of the basic moral and humanist values. Table 3.1 shows several key distinctions

Table 3.1   Different approaches to managerial thinking

	Classical thinking in the strategic and economic tradition	Scandinavian thinking in the behavioral tradition
Definition of value	Economic value	Moral value
Focus	Value creation Value measurement	Value understanding Value consensus
Reasoning and point of departure of tools development	Negative reasoning Flat and decentralized management structures combined with a high level of process orientation have created a need for self-governing, flexible, and responsible employees Rules and procedures are replaced by independency and influence There are demands on the inner value of the organization, not least in relations to recruitment and retention of employees	Positive reasoning The employees are no longer an anonymous, standardized labor input, but engaged and responsible enthusiasts with a high level of personal commitment The work is identity-creating, and personal development is required as well as a professional career and interesting work Creation of a common vision and common basic values, which promote dynamic organizational structures
Objectives	Focus on measurements of results Ensure that financial objectives are rooted in operational plans for action Focus on defining key areas and on constant follow-up Communication tools for allocation of risk and capital	Determining, communicating, and anchoring of the values of the organization Coordinate individual and organization goals Indirect management
Behavior control	Direct compliance	Indirect commitment
Conflict solving	Disagreements are used in a constructive way	Consensus-seeking

Table 3.1 (*continued*)

	Classical thinking in the strategic and economic tradition	Scandinavian thinking in the behavioral tradition
Theoretical models and examples of tools	Strategic models. Porter's value chain, Prahalad's core competence model, and Balanced Scorecard Federal Sentencing Guidelines Economic models, e.g., Economic Value Added (EVA™), CFROI/CVA and Discounted Cash Flow (DCF)	The ethical accounts Code and other formulated behavior-regulating statements Storytelling Understanding and building culture

Source: Lemmergaard (2004a).

between traditional management thinking and Scandinavian management thinking.

The basic difference between the two traditions is the definition of value. The non-Scandinavian point of departure within strategy and economy is both culturally and institutionally determined and contrasts sharply with the dominating Scandinavian approach to the value concept, which takes its point of departure in a humanist definition of value. Whether the definition of value is based on an economic or a moral tradition is significant for the choice of management tools. International academics, particularly within the more traditional approach to management, distinguish between value defined from a moral and an economic tradition. The Scandinavian tradition, on the contrary, builds on a moral understanding, where moral and ethical values are adjusted among multiple stakeholders. This difference in basic assumptions leads to very different applications of management principles and to working with organizational values.

However, the underlying values of the Scandinavian management tradition do raise dilemmas and underpin the faddish characteristics of especially the Scandinavian version of value-based management. The dilemmas inherent in the Scandinavian version of value-based management are analysed using data from an empirical analysis of a Danish knowledge-intensive organization managed by principles of value-based management. By looking into the climate of an organization, we move closer to the root of explaining the values.

6. THE CASE STUDY

The following analysis of the case-organization is based upon three levels of analysis. First, numerous in-depth interviews with the managing director of the organization were conducted. The managing director was encouraged to tell her story of leadership in a subjective, reflexive manner with a strong emphasis on description. Second, an electronic quantitative survey was conducted measuring the value-orientation of the full-time employees and the management team. A questionnaire replicating Koys and DeCotiis' Psychological Climate Construct was distributed electronically to all full-time employees ($n = 44$) of the case organization in March 2007 – 43 usable questionnaires were returned, resulting in a 98.0 percent response rate. Finally, a two-day participant observation study took place during the organization's value-based management kickoff seminar. During the seminar informal interviews were held, direct observations were conducted, and different documents were analysed.

The findings of this exploratory study are revealing, though simply indicative as they arise from a small convenience sample of a single Danish organization. As such, the findings reflect their own observations rather than empirically established facts.

6.1 Working from the principles of value-based management

The case-organization is one of the leading language translation companies in Scandinavia. The company has a 28-year track record in providing document translation services in all major world languages. The company specializes in providing translation services in a range of fields including technical, medical, legal, financial, and marketing translations. The case-organization includes besides approximately 40 full-time employees, a considerable number of freelance workers. Approximately 400 freelance workers work on a regular basis for the case-organization.

The managing director of the case-organization was appointed in 2003. She has been with the company since 1983 first as translator and from 2000 as a middle manager. She perceives leadership as a visionary act similar to theories of Kousnes and Posner (1987) and Sashkin (1988). Visionary leadership involves cooperation, networking, teamwork, and creativity. It requires a leader with an exceptional gift for non-rational communication and inspiration, where inspiration (Alvesson and Svenningsson 2003) is seen as obtaining outstanding accomplishments (House and Aditya 1997). Ideally, visionary leaders are charismatic (House 1977), and seen as people 'who rises above and beyond the specification of formal structure to provide members of the organization with a sense that they are

organized' (Smircich and Morgan 1982, p. 260). These theoretical characteristics fit with the impressions obtained from observations from the
two-day seminar, and from the formal and informal interviews with both
the manager and other organizational members. The managing director
of the case-organization appears energetic and her emotional expressive-
ness and warmth is notable. However, she also displays a self-promoting
personality by allowing others to know how important she is.

> I see myself as the guiding star. . . . I set the direction in a frame where rules are
> replaced by norms and values. It is the values that bind us [i.e., the employees
> of case-organization] together. We are one big happy family. You see that
> for example when you visit our Copenhagen office. [name of an employee] is
> wearing slippers, we have candlelight and flowers at our desks, and you always
> find freshly made coffee and cakes in the kitchen.

The managing director is very eager to create a solidarity concerning the
basic values of the organization, so that the organization always bases its
activities on these basic values. She sees the employees of her company as
the most valuable asset. She sees the values as mediators influencing the
organizational context and structure on members' attitudes and behavior.
The values define the stimuli that confront the individual, place constraints
on the freedom of choice within the organizational context, and determine
reward/punish behavior.

> The most valuable asset of this company – maybe of any company – is the
> people. Therefore I'm willing to go to great lengths to make sure it is fun to go
> to work. With enough resources and time our product can be easily replicated.
> However, it is extremely difficult to replicate good working values. It is hard
> work and takes a bit of luck to gather a workforce of highly motivated loyal
> employees who are having fun. We believe in honesty and trust, and we know
> where to draw the line. Of course new colleagues need to learn this – and it takes
> time. Sometimes you need to weed out some of your values. Of course you need
> to take care not to get rid of values that some employees care about.

This is line with the Scandinavian management principles, which is primarily a matter of creating consistency between the desired behavior and
the actual behavior through correlation and harmony among words,
thoughts, and actions. In this way, the value frame of the organization is
personalized (Kirkeby 1998), which contrasts the economic approach to
value. However, as emphasized by the managing director:

> The most important thing is not the words, but the ongoing process and the
> organizational commitment. My leadership paradigm is built on employee
> autonomy and responsibility. These two words describe the main values that
> I provided for my colleagues. It is up to them to create the possibilities within

this framework. If they fail, I have failed in articulating the core values, and I might risk losing credibility.

It is the purpose of the value-based management principles displayed in the case-organization that the values are meant to be the overriding frame of reference for both managers and employees. By extensive dialogue, it is the objective that all participate and generate a kind of ownership of the common values. Generally the one-off values are applied both internally and externally, and the values are meant to be both inspirational and motivating. Since the values are embodied into all employees it is, at least in theory, expected that the values substitute rules, manuals, and descriptions of work procedures. Also, it is expected that the leadership style can be characterized by a high degree of trust, autonomy, and individual responsibility.

6.2 Measuring values

In the Scandinavian tradition, value-based management is primarily a matter of creating consistency between desired and actual behavior through correlation and harmony among words, thoughts, and actions. However, words as such are not important. Most important is the ongoing process and commitment at all organizational levels. Value-based management, in this context, is therefore more about behaviors than about management, not least because of the indirect management style, which is attached to the practical tools in connection with the moral way of thinking when it comes to value understanding.

To make value-based management principles work, an empathic management team is required, which is in close contact with its employees. Moreover, a sensible communication strategy is required, which makes the relationships transparent. One way to detect whether the manager is in contact with the employees is to identify similarities and differences between collective organizational values and individual managerial values. In this study, Koys and DeCotiis' (1991) 'Psychological Climate Construct' was chosen as an instrument to measure the organizational value orientation. From empirical findings, Koys and DeCotiis (1991) concluded that an organization's value and management orientation can be characterized along two descriptive dimensions: (1) values and (2) organizational structure, reward, and control mechanisms. Koys and DeCotiis (1991) define psychological climate as 'an experimental-based multidimensional, and enduring perceptional phenomenon, which is widely shared by the members of a given organizational unit' (1991, p. 266). It is an individual's description of his/her organizational experiences that are relatively stable over time, and widely shared by the members of the relevant organizational unit.

Koys and DeCotiis (1991) arrived at their definition and dimensions of climate through an extensive literature review of many of the more influential studies in this field. They found more than 80 differently labeled dimensions of climate in the literature, which they clustered into 45 original dimensions through an elimination of all objective measures (for example, absenteeism, turnover, tardiness, labor disputes, and accidents) and evaluative measures (for example, general satisfaction, and satisfaction with supervisor and co-workers) plus all properties related to organizational structure (for example, centralization, organizational size, task structure, and administrative procedures). Koys and DeCotiis' (1991) study indicated that the lack of consensus in the literature is more apparent than real as the results of their analysis demonstrated reasonably adequate reliability and internal consistency on the proposed measures.

The 45 dimensions were empirically categorized into eight summary concepts each with five items, which they subdivided into two dimensions; (1) values and (2) organizational structure, reward, and control mechanisms. The first dimension constituted the values of an organization, and was described in terms of cohesion, trust, support, and fairness. Cohesion was related to the perception of togetherness or sharing among employees. Trust was related to the perception of freedom to communicate with peers, also about sensitive or personal issues. Support was related to the superior–subordinate relationship and included the willingness to let organizational members learn from their mistakes, without fear of reprisal. Finally, fairness was related to the perception that organizational practices were equitable and predictable.

The second dimension of the psychological climate of an organization constituted the organizational structure, reward, and control mechanisms, and was described in terms of autonomy, pressure, recognition, and innovation. Autonomy related to the perception that organizational members experience self-determination with respect to work procedures, goals, and priorities. Pressure related to the perception of time demands with respect to task completion and performance standards. Recognition related to the perception that organizational members' contributions were acknowledged, and, finally, innovation related to the perception that change and creativity were encouraged.

All in all, the definitions are somewhat overlapping which, according to Koys and DeCotiis (1991), is due to the fact that any given organizational experience can be described in more than one way. As exemplified by Koys and DeCottis 'an organization characterized by participative decision making . . . may be described as being both cohesive (that is, people work together as a team) and providing recognition (that is, employees' skills and opinions are recognized)' (1991, p. 269). The dimensions of the psychological climate are not meant to determine any evaluative measures, in contrast to, for example, the level of job satisfaction, but represented perceptions of the context in general in which an individual is supposed to behave and respond.

It could be argued that the climate instrument does not direct attention or guide research in any useful way. However, the multidimensional nature of climate can also be seen as both an asset and a liability when researching the intersection of organizational and individual behavior. Although, climate is complex, it is not limitless. At some point the dimensions of climate interconnect, and create a finite system. Therefore, this piece of research is build on the assumption that Koys and DeCotiis' psychological climate model (1991) represents a useful model that does not oversimplify the values of an organization, but mirrors them.

The results of the presented study show no differences between the climate dimensions of pressure, recognition, and fairness when comparing the score of the managing director and mean scores of the employees. For the climate dimensions of trust, autonomy, cohesion, support, and innovation the employees of the case organization have a significant lower score than the managing director. A possible explanation for this finding could be that the managing director is more attentive to the values of the organization than the organizational members in general. From findings from the participant observation and from in-depth interviews with the managing director of the case organization, it is clear that she has a strong awareness of the organizational values, and that she believes to be practicing value-based management. The managing director is a firm believer in 'walking the talk' management principles. But she also attempts to bring organizational members' values in line with her own values through her socialized charismatic leadership style. On the basis of the statements and comments from the managing director, it could even be argued that she is almost attempting to untangle the organizational members from previous attachments and tie them strongly to the organization as a safeguard in an increasingly fragmented world. This attempt – in the name of value-based management – is, however, not a new phenomenon but is in many ways equal to for example Fayol's recognition that *esprit de corps* matters.

Despite the intention of the managing director of the case-organization to use her power for the good of others through attention to values and employees' well-being, it was rather clear that the members of the organization were only partially accepting the values. An explanation for this partial acceptance could be that the organizational members perceive that it would increase their possibilities of status and reward as well as their warm feeling if they were doing what was valued. In general, the employees did recognize that the managing director was trying to create a comfortable, pleasant, and intellectually stimulating work environment. However, they were also on several occasions pointing towards the fact that they could not recognize the organization that they worked for in that description. It could therefore be argued, that the organizational members simply displayed dedication to the organization in the pursuit of supposedly collective purpose, and exercised self-surveillance in order to erase signs of disloyalty for the purpose of reaching, for example, personal career goals.

7.   MORE THAN WORDS

The Scandinavian consensus-seeking approach to value-based management builds upon the plurality of values and upon how values develop, are adapted, and modified in the interaction among individuals. The Scandinavian version of value-based management, thus, is more about behavior represented by reaction, attitudes, and views based on emotional convictions rather than it is about management. Value-based management is linked to behavior because of the indirect management style, which is attached to the practical tools in connection with the moral way of thinking when it comes to value understanding. Value-based management is not achieved through five positive sentences (Jensen 1998; Maclagan 1998). If the basic values of various organizations are compared, it is only rarely impressive. Quite often a professional writer or a public relations officer could have done better (Beyer 2000). According to the Scandinavian tradition, however, it is not a matter of words, but of the underlying attitudes and emotions, where the creation process, the consensus-building, and the commitment of the basic values are important (Thyssen 2002). The management style, a day-to-day personal behavior according to common values and a framework of the employees' personal values are important, not those five positive sentences as such (Beyer 2000). But often the five positive sentences are followed out of a sense of necessity and survival than a response to real value-based management just as demonstrated in the case-organization above. Employees in general want to succeed, but success must not be at the expense of the heart and soul of the organizational members. Therefore, the real managerial challenge is the ethical responsibility that managers have when influencing their employees.

Working with value-based management from a Scandinavian perspective, organizations often, if not always, depart in the personal values of the managers when defining and clarifying the organizational values. In other words, management is in this approach not different from leadership in a human relation perspective where leadership is seen as a mechanism for influencing the behavior of individuals, or as expressed by Barnard (1938) 'the inculcation of belief in the real existence of a common purpose is an essential executive function'. Of course the exhaustive consensus-seeking dialogue and exchange of subjective perceptions of the values that is often part of the Scandinavian management philosophy provides the opportunity to select those specific values that all organizational members perceive as significant and worth preserving. But, the values are identified based on the question: What do we wish to be known for? And here the responsibility for abstract, long-term decisions on purpose lies with the managers. Hence, there is a need to influence those individuals at lower organizational levels with general purposes and major decisions if the organization is to be a cohesive organic whole. Claiming that value-based management in practice can rest upon a common vision and common basic values, which promote dynamic organizational structures is at the best naïve and self-delusional; at worst it is a calculative and manipulative way of seducing internal as well as external stakeholders. Management or leadership is the process of influencing self, others, and organizations, through growth and change, towards achieving results and fulfilling a vision or a purpose.

The Scandinavian consensus-seeking approach to value-based management is in many ways similar to the rational thought of the ancient Greek philosophers, who claimed that since we are all humans, we all want the same things. However, world history reveals a long and troubled conflict about core values. Values not only have conflicted, they have also called for battle, and history is a story of individuals who seem happier to be defined by their differences than to be joined by what they share. So, how can managers believe that in a fast changing business world a foundation of all shared values can be established? Maybe this is also why, in light of efforts to ensure value-based conduct, value lapses continue to cause significant damage and losses in the business world. Moreover, value-based management and value-based reasoning is a continuous process achieved by sustaining morale, and by maintaining schemes of incentives, deterrents, supervision, and control. The continuity of the process is needed as organizational members are continuously leaving and entering the organization. Moreover, organizational members also change due to education and training or simply due to changes in the life cycle.

8. MEN ARE NEITHER GOOD NOR BAD

Barnard (1938) argues that the art of management is to eschew conflict in formal order-giving by issuing only those formal orders which are acceptable, and disagreements must be dealt with by informal means. By expanding the means of communication, and thus reducing the need for formal decisions, the principles of Scandinavian value-based management rests on similar assumptions. The core values are expressed in the interpersonal relationships and are meant to guide and being expressed in the doings required at work on a daily basis, for example in strategies of exemplification and promotion secure and maintain desired images of the organization and its management. Hereby, the values form the view of situations of all organizational members and influence what is done and what is thought. The values are fundamental beliefs that rule in the organization and influence behavior. As such, the values, for example, express which business arrangements an organization wishes to take part in and which it does not want to attend. In much the same way, the values presumably also express what the organization will hold on to even in times of recession or crisis.

However, when working on value-based principles managers are potentially facing the conflict between being loyal to themselves as opposed to being a symbol of the core values of the organization, while at the same time being reflecting critically to the core values of the organization (Thyssen 2002). For conducting true value-based management, managers must be able to 'walk the talk'. Anyone aspiring to demonstrate good management in the current scenario of constant change must therefore above all be able to conduct self-management. Without the ability to self-manage, the manager will be viewed upon as being false, lacking credibility, and lacking real appeal. In other words, committed and competent managers, capable of influencing others and organizations, must be able to demonstrate results in managing the challenge of change themselves, of delivering results themselves, and of moving themselves towards some higher level of purpose.

Another dilemma attached to the conduct of value-based management is the issue of being able to present a simplified set of basic values, while at the same time maintaining the complexity in the various interpretations of the values. Managers might simply find it impossible to maintain their trustworthiness when a simplified set of basic values is presented in a few sentences. The findings from the case-study presented here, though simply indicative as they rise from a small convenience sample, are revealing. The managing director is very much aware of the fact that she is operating within a specific cultural context. Key values that are representing her management style are co-operating, consensus-seeking, participation, and power-sharing. However, she falls into the trap of trying to build consensus by reducing the core values of the organization to a limited number of positive sentences that can be presented on glitter paper. By initiating a consensus-building process among all employees, the managing director of the case organization undermines the already existing common ownership of the corporate core values. Hereby, the failure to increase consensus in the case-organization strengthens the argument, that conducting value-based management in the Scandinavian tradition is more about leadership and value-based behavior than about value-based management.

A third dilemma related to value-based management is attached to the paradox that exists between the reinforcing hierarchical management and the apparent responsiveness towards what is common and value-based. In the case-organization, the solution to this paradox is anticipated by the organizational members having committed themselves to the organization in a way where they have almost taken the vows of organization life. A majority of the organizational members not only work for the organization, but belongs to it as well. Such approaches aiming at the hearts of the organizational members have unsurprisingly been criticized, for example by Whyte's (1961) formulation of the 'organization man'. Supporters of the commitment-led organizations, however, argue that organizations recruit those who will fit in and those who will get along well with the other organizational members. Hereby, the incoming organizational members will not have any disturbingly exceptional characteristics, but will for the most part echo the manager's voice, and not challenge it.

9.   CONCLUDING REMARKS

This chapter has questioned the diffusion of the concept of value-based management and has argued that whether articulated or not, one version of the concept resemblances the concept of Scandinavian management and is therefore very much a running management concept. The approaches to value-based management cover a wide field of techniques with more traditional and instrumental views of management to techniques that build upon communication and voluntariness (Brytting and Trollested 2000). The initiatives also cover a wide field of broad, non-committal statements of interest to binding statements. But overall, the concept is about values, which is also the reason why working with value-based management varies from organization to organization. Depending on the basic definition of value, it is decided which model to use in the organization in question.

Implementing value-based management principles, practitioners tend to focus on value measurements and ethical guidelines in line with the techniques that are used within the economic value way of thinking. Value-based management in a Scandinavian context, based on a humanist understanding, thus presents a unilateral perspective of the concept.

Regardless of the approach, in practice, value-based management is a matter of combining principles and techniques from strategic planning, management, organizational behavior, and business administrative disciplines. In the right combination between economic and humanistic values a useful synergy can be found, and only through an understanding of this is it possible for the organizations to succeed in implementing well-functioning value-based management practices.

Supporters insist that value-based management practices produce positive ripple effects and argue that value-based management is the essence of management. Opponents, however, argue that value-based management practices are merely euphemisms for a management style basically driven by extensive profit excess. This chapter argues that value-based management is a running concept and value-based management is for everyone. Even the choice of not having a value-orientation signals a choice of values, which is why value-based management is here to stay. The nature of value-based management, however, tends toward a higher level of formalization, but the field will continue to be characterized by various academic and practical approaches. It is a way of thinking that has hardly found its final shape and name. Among practitioners, the trend of discussion already seems to be toward the importance of being able to distinguish between technical and practical possibilities and between the legal framework and responsibility. It should, though, be mentioned that no matter how it is approached, value-based management is not a key to solving the ethical dilemmas of an organization or to handling actual staff policy problems (Beyer 2000).

If management is prepared to present a version of value-based management that, for example, accepts responsibilities then they are, indirectly at least, also forced to accept the reciprocity implied. Truly accepting responsibility sharing involves making organizational members feel powerful and being able to accomplish tasks on their own. It refers to passing decision-making authority and responsibility from mangers to organizational members. In other words, the reciprocity requires some kind of universalism that positions managers and subordinates in similar ways. It must be taken into account though that managers have the special responsibility of maintaining the organizational communication, securing the essential services from the organizational members, and formulating the overall purpose. In this way, value-based management is not different to other management philosophies, and as argued above, the concept resemblances the concept of Scandinavian management that in particular stresses the participation of organizational members in day-to-day decision-making processes. Consequently, value-based management is a rather conventional and running concept. And when organizations fail in implementing value-based management principles it often rests on their failure to communicate their mission, purpose, and values as well as they might. There is no one best value-based management tool, but there are many good value-based management tools. And independent of the chosen tool, success comes with sincere communication.

REFERENCES

Alvesson, M. and S. Svenningsson (2003), 'Managers doing leadership: the extra-ordinarization of the mundane', *Human Relations*, **55** (12), 1435–59.

Ashforth, B.E. and F. Mael (1989), 'Social identity theory and the organization', *Academy of Management Review*, **14** (1), 20–39.

Barnard, C.I. (1938), *The Functions of the Executive*, Cambridge, MA: Harvard University Press.

Beyer, P. (2000), *Vaerdibaseret Ledelse: Den Aeldste vin på den Nyeste Flaske*, Copenhagen: Thomson.

Brytting, T. and C. Trollestad (2000), 'Managerial thinking on value-based management', *International Journal of Value-Based Management*, **13** (1), 55–77.

Gibbs, E. (2003), 'Developing an effective code of conduct', *Financial Executive*, **19** (4), 40–41.

Gouldner, A. (1952), 'The problem of succession in bureaucracy', in R.K. Merton, A.P. Gray, B. Hockey and H.C. Selvin (eds), *Reader in Bureaucracy*, New York: Free Press.

Grenness, T. (2003), 'Scandinavian managers on Scandinavian management', *International Journal of Value-Based Management*, **16** (1), 9–12.

Habermas, J. (1981), *Theorie des Kommunikativen Handelns*, Frankfurt am Main: Suhrkamp.

Hjelmer, U. (1997), *Etisk Regnskab: Vaerdistyring og Resultatmaaling*, Copenhagen: Frydenlund grafisk.

House, R.J. (1977), 'A 1976 theory of charismatic leadership', in J.G. Hunt and L.L. Larson (eds), *Leadership: The Cutting Edge*, Carbondale, IL: Southern Illinois University Press, pp. 189–207.

House, R. and R. Aditya (1997), The social scientific study of leadership: quo vadis?', *Journal of Management*, **23** (3), 409–73.

Jensen, F.D. (1998), *Vaerdibaseret Ledelse – Styring mellem Regler og Visioner*, Copenhagen: Jurist- og Oekonomforbundets Forlag.

Jensen, P.B. (1999), 'A value- and integrity-based strategy to consolidate organization, marketing, and communication – the case of Jyske Bank', Department of Organization and Management, Faculty of Business Administration, the Aarhus School of Business, Denmark, working paper 99-8.

Kabanoff, B., R. Waldersee and M. Cohen (1995), 'Espoused values and organizational change themes', *Academy of Management Journal*, **38** (4), 1075–104.

Kirkeby, O.F. (1998), *Ledelsesfilosofi. Et Radikalt Normativt Perspektiv*, Copenhagen: Samfundslitteratur.

Kousnes, J.M. and B.Z. Posner (1987), *The Leadership Challenge: How to Get Extraordinary Things Done in Organizations*, San Francisco, CA: Jossey-Bass.

Koys, D.J. and T.A. DeCotiis (1991), 'Inductive measures of psychological climate', *Human Relations*, **44** (3), 265–85.

Lemmergaard, J. (2004a), 'Betydningen af det manglende "s": value(s)-based management er ikke værdibaseret ledelse', *Ledelse & Erhvervsøkonomi*, **68** (3), 183–92.

Lemmergaard, J. (2004b), *Tolerance for Ambiguity. The Intersection Between Ethical Climate, Psychological Climate, and Ethnic Diversity*, Odense, Denmark: University of Southern Denmark Press.

Maclagan, P.W. (1998), *Management and Morality*, London: Sage Publications.

Meyer, T. and T. Arentsen (1997), 'Dialogos – Den etiske laereproces. Vaerdibaseret organisering – at styre, regulere og kontrollere i samspil', in V.C. Petersen and M.S. Lassen (eds), *Vaerdibaseret Ledelse – et Alternative til Styring, Regulering og Kontrol?*, Copenhagen: Dansk Industri.

Morsing, M. (1991), *Den Etiske Praksis: en Introduktion til det Etiske Regnskab*, Copenhagen: Handelshoejskolens Forlag.

Nymark, S.R. (2000), *Organizational Storytelling: Creating Enduring Values in a High-Tech Company*, Hinnerup, Denmark: Ankerhus.

Pettigrew, A. (1979), 'On studying organizational cultures', *Administrative Science Quarterly*, **24** (4), 570–81.

Pruzan, P. (1994), 'Etik, vaerdibaseret ledelse og det etiske regnskab', in S. Hildebrandt and E. Johnsen (eds), *Ledelse Nu – 10 Danske Professorers Bud på Aktuel Ledelse*, Copenhagen: Boersen Boeger, pp. 97–154.

Pruzan, P. and O. Thyssen (1990), 'Conflict and consensus: ethics as a shared value horizon for strategic planning', *Human Systems Management*, **9** (3), 135–51.

Rokeach, M. (1973), *The Nature of Human Values*, New York: Free Press.

Sashkin, M. (1988), 'The visionary leader', in J.A. Conger and R.N. Kanungo (eds), *Charismatic Leadership: The Elusive Factor in Organizational Effectiveness*, San Francisco, CA: Jossey-Bass.

Schultz, M., M.J. Hatch, and M.H. Larsen (2000), *The Expressive Organization. Linking Identity, Reputation, and the Corporate Brand*, New York: Oxford University Press.

Schwartz, M.S. (2002), 'A code of ethics for corporate code of ethics', *Journal of Business Ethics*, **41** (1–2), 27–43.

Sjøborg, E.R. (1985), *Riding the Tide: Skandinavisk Management mot År 2000*, Oslo: Bedriftsøkonomens Forlag.

Smircich, L. and G. Morgan (1982), 'Leadership: the management of meaning', *Journal of Applied Behavioral Science*, **18** (3), 257–73.

Somers, M.J. (2001), 'Ethical codes of conduct and organizational context: a study of the relationship between codes of conduct, employee behavior and organizational values', *Journal of Business Ethics*, **30** (2), 185–95.

Thyssen, O. (2002), *Vaerdiledelse: Om Organisationer og Etik*, Copenhagen: Gyldendal.

Whyte, W.H. (1961), *The Organization Man*, Harmondsworth: Penguin.

4. Understanding ethical closure in organizational settings – the case of media organizations

Dan Kärreman and Mats Alvesson

1. INTRODUCTION

Organizations have traditionally been understood as instrumental and social spaces, where products and relationships are conceived and manufactured. Increasingly, organizations are also understood as moral spaces, where humans continually form and exercise ethical judgment (Jackall 1988; Bauman 1989, 1994; Kjönstad and Willmott 1995; Mangham 1995; Parker 1998a; Jones and Wicks 1999; Tucker et al. 1999; Weaver et al., 1999; Bird 2002). A growing body of scholarly work points out the various ways organizational activity includes ethical issues and dilemmas. Some perspectives picture ethical imperatives mainly as a restriction on organizational activity, comparable with market forces, competition, government regulation, and customer preferences (Morgan 1998; Sorrell 1998). There is some truth in this, but from reasons spelled out below, we are drawing upon a more expansive understanding of the relationship between ethics and organizational activity. In particular, we are going to pay specific attention to the inversed relationship: how organization processes affects the articulation of ethics and judgment.

Our point of view has some resonance with what Kjönstad and Willmott (1995) call 'empowering ethics', which underlines the learning and developmental aspects in ethics, and what Butterfield et al. (2000) refer to as 'moral awareness', the recognition that an issue is important to consider in terms of moral standards. We assume that ethical dilemmas are potentially everywhere and can't really be captured and solved through a set of moral rules regulating appropriate behavior. Thus, in this chapter we will understand ethics as a sensitivity or a mode of understanding that is cultivated – or inhibited – locally and from within, rather than a restrictive – or enabling – force applied from outside.

Consequently, as indicated above, we understand ethics as something shaped by organizational activity, rather than the other way around. People learn codes of conduct, and their local meaning and application, *within* organizations (Watson 1998). Different forms of organization give different room for ethical considerations, and consequently shape ethics differently. We take a specific interest in ethical considerations in one type of (semi-) professional organizations – media organizations. To be more precise, in this chapter we pay particular attention to ethical closure – the ways ethical considerations are arrested, blocked, and short-circuited.·

The choice of media organizations is not arbitrary. Media is a powerful institution in modern Western society and plays an active role in shaping and propagating values, meanings and norms. It is thus an important and interesting phenomenon in itself. The existence of an explicit ethical code for the industry as a whole, in the Swedish context, that is supposed to regulate media workers' moral conduct also has particular relevance for the purposes of the study.

The chapter aims to (1) identify specific categories of ethical closure in an organizational setting, (2) illuminate the relationship between key aspects of the organizing of media work in a Swedish context and the space for ethical reflection and (3) discuss the possibility that ethical codes of conduct may fuel rather than solve certain ethical problems. The first aim is clearly the most significant. The third aim is partly an elaboration of a sub-theme addressed through the first aim, but as it raises some broader implications and goes to the heart of much business ethics thinking we draw particular attention to it.

The idea that organizational processes influence and shape ethical judgment is hardly original. Several influential studies have observed, and analysed, the formative relationship between ethical judgment and various organizational processes. Typically, these studies advance from a general point of view and paint with broad sweeps, pointing, for example, at organizational processes – in particular the rise of managerialism – as informative clues on the current state of Western civilization (MacIntyre 1984; Bauman 1994) or at the bureaucratic phenomenon as a necessary, but not sufficient, ingredient in the sociology of the Holocaust (Bauman 1989; Vetlesen 1994).

There is, however, a small, but growing body of studies addressing the impact of organizational processes on ethical judgment, rather than as illustrations of a larger picture (for example, Paine 1994; Watson 1994, 1998). Perhaps the most well-known work in the genre is Jackall's (1988) study on what he calls the moral mazes of managerial work. In his book, Jackall sets out to capture the ethics-in-use of managers in large bureaucracies, rather than their espoused values. As he observes: 'the notions of morality and ethics have a decidedly prescriptive, indeed moralistic flavor. They are often rooted in religious doctrines or vague cultural remnants of religious beliefs, like the admonition of the Golden Rule' (Jackall 1988, p. 4).

However, Jackall treats managers' occupational ethics as sociological entities: as empirical realities possible to uncover. Jackall shows that American managerial occupational ethics is primarily shaped by the oppositional forces of, on one hand, the need to conform to internal pressures towards instrumental achievement and to adapt to a predictable social order, and, on the other hand, external pressures to 'look good' in the face of the public. In particular, he points at and explores the enigmatic and highly ambiguous moral terrain managers face, and their habitual and routine ways of coping with it. Jackall demonstrates that organizational contexts have decisive impact on the ethical sensibilities developed, allowed and expressed in particular occupations. We believe that the basic thrust of his argument is not only valid for managers, as demonstrated by Jackall's study, but also for other occupational groups. In this chapter we will use Jackall's insights on the organizational framing of ethical judgment as a starting point for our analysis.

2. THE IDEA OF ETHICAL CLOSURE

In its most elementary form, ethics boils down to the distinction between what is good and what is evil (bad, harmful) (MacIntyre 1967; Parker 1998b; Brytting 1997; Bird 2002). There is a tendency in organizational ethics research to focus on codes of conduct (see, for example, Tucker et al. 1999, for a review). Such codes of conduct typically consist of lists of actions that are either considered to be good or bad (or right or wrong). The codes are believed to exercise influence on actions and decision making in organizations. However, as briefly mentioned earlier in this chapter, we think that this way of addressing ethics tends to treat it as yet another restrictive force on organizational behavior. When for example Weaver et al. (1999) argue that 'formal ethics programs' can be viewed as managerial control systems, they are taking the business ethics approach to its logical conclusion, where 'formal ethics programs' are a way of managing the workforce – no more, no less.

This perspective is of course not 'wrong'. It may have some practical advantages as it may discourage some, easily specified, immoral behavior. It is, however, narrow and thin, in Geertz's (1973) sense. Thus, it misses unique qualities inherent in ethics and morality. As Bird (2002, p. 28) points out, moral actions are necessarily voluntary. Without choice, the moral dimension simply ceases to exist. Moral actions are reasoned actions. To unreflectively adhere to ethical codes of conduct is not the same thing as performing moral actions. In this sense, ethics constitute a particular mode of understanding that guides human conduct and practice, rather than 'merely' operating as a restrictive force. From this perspective, ethics includes a particular vocabulary, with particular meaning and significance for action. We find it useful to analyse ethics and morality as language-games that humans command, or have the capacity to command, given sufficient exposure and training – rather as humans master a language.

Moral development is thus, much like the development of any vocabulary, a social practice (cf. Bird 2002). As Vetlesen puts it:

> [I]ndividuals are not free to pick just any moral objects they would like. Perception does not start from scratch; it is guided, channeled, given a specific horizon, direction, and target by society. Society, not the single individual, selects the appropriate objects of moral concern and the like; other objects it rules out, conceals from view, demanding from the individual to do so as well. (Vetlesen 1994, p. 194)

As mentioned above, we take a particular interest in the concealment of the moral dimension. From our point of view such concealment is created through the denial of framing issues in ethical terms – what we from now label 'ethical closure'. With ethical closure we mean systematic denials of the application of moral vocabulary and, thus, informed ethical judgment. Since there is some ambiguity around the term 'closure' – which sometimes might indicate closing off or sealing something, or indicate the fulfilment of something – we want to emphasize that the term as we use it gestures towards closing off an argument rather than resolving it.

Ethical closure has similarities to what Bird (2002) labels moral blindness. According to Bird, moral blindness occurs whenever people fail to recognize relevant ethical considerations. However, moral blindness includes all sorts of failures to recognize the ethical dimension. Ethical closure, in this sense, is a more specific concept: it focuses on systematic effects emerging from identifiable social processes, thus excluding random effects and human shortcomings.

The concept of ethical closure has a close affinity to the concept of discursive closure, as developed by Deetz (1992). Ethical closure attempts to illuminate a kind of communication breakdown within a particular field of inquiry and reflection, while the concept of discursive closure points to the generalized form for such communication breakdowns. Discursive closure plays, according to Deetz, a pivotal role in creating systematically distorted communication (Habermas 1984; Forester 1989; Deetz 1992; Alvesson 1996). Put shortly, discursive closures 'exist whenever potential conflict is suppressed' (Deetz 1992, p. 187). Discursive practices, Deetz observes, may on one hand lead to the potential suspension of preformed convictions and relatively unconstrained production of understanding, or, on the other hand, the suspension of dissent, difference, and discussion.

> Discursive practices . . . can either lead to . . . [the] open formation [of the self] by further exploration of the subject matter or divert, distort, or block the open development of understanding. When discussion is thwarted, a particular view of reality is maintained at the expense of equally plausible ones, usually to someone's advantage. (Deetz 1992, p. 189)

It is the latter type of discursive practices that propels discursive closure. Since the practices themselves consist of tactical moves, rather than substantive claims, they often appear inoffensive and unobtrusive. This is further underscored by the fact that such discursive practices are often seemingly evoked for the common good, 'to keep the order', 'to avoid rocking the boat', and, ironically, 'to let everybody have a say'.

There are numerous processes that potentially create discursive closure. Deetz discusses and elaborates seven important ones: disqualification, naturalization, neutralization, topical avoidance, subjectification of experience, meaning denial and plausible deniability, legitimation, and pacification. Obviously all processes of discursive closure may be involved in creating ethical closure. However, in this chapter we will pay specific attention to two of these processes: *naturalization* and *subjectification of experience*. Our reason is primarily empirical: these two processes are particularly involved in creating the kinds of ethical closure we observed among newsmakers.

Naturalization occurs when a particular view of a subject matter is put forward, and accepted, as the way things are. In relation to social reality, naturalization often appears as a result of reification – the treatment of social relationships and subjective constructions as natural, fixed and external objects. Processes of naturalization deny alternative formulations of experience. Such discursive moves are often used to stop or block discussion at the moment where it becomes interesting. For example, a naturalizing move is typically made by declaring 'this is the way it is' in a way that makes it difficult or impossible to ask the more interesting question: 'Yes, but how did that happen?' Naturalizing moves make such a question seemingly irrelevant, since it is claimed that this is a natural state of affairs, implicating that alternative formulations are against the natural order.

Subjectification of experience – the idea that experience and meaning are strictly personal and private – stems from an anthropological oddity of modern Western society: the subjectification of experience as embodied and expressed in the institution of the individual (Meyer 1986). It is also foundational for a particular perspective on ethics and morality: the emotivist position. According to Macintyre (1984), emotivism has been equally successful as its companion individualism, to the extent that it 'has become embodied in our culture' (1984, p. 22). Emotivism states that moral judgments have no rational justification. They are rather expressions of attitude, preference, or feeling (Mangham 1995). Moral judgments are first and foremost means for influencing other people's attitude or conduct. They do not make any meaningful truth-claims, in the sense that one moral position can be truer or falser than another. Moral positions, from the emotivist perspective, are in that sense equal to tastes and opinions. They are debatable, of course, but such debates are not possible to resolve rationally.

Here is not the place to point out all the pitfalls and shortcomings in the emotivist position. We will restrict ourselves to discuss two weak spots in the emotivist argument. First, it draws heavily on the separation between values and facts. Most emotivists claim that rational discourse is indeed possible, as long as it concerns facts. As proponents of critical theory, amongst others, long have pointed out (cf. Horkheimer and Adorno [1947] 1979; Habermas 1987), it is simply impossible to maintain a sharp distinction between facts and values, since facts necessarily are selected and constructed from a value point of view. Other values would produce other facts.

Second, the emotivist position assumes that experience and meaning is private and personal: locked into the emotional and cognitive apparatus of the individual. However, the various linguistic turns in social science (Deetz 1992; Alvesson and Kärreman 2000) have increasingly undermined such assumptions. Today, many social scientists and philosophers would claim the opposite: that meaning and experiential structures precede the individual in space and time, that the individual is thrown – as phenomenologists would express it – into an already formed, interpreted and experienced world. From a cultural point of view one could say that socially shared meanings and values provide much more significant reference points for people's ethical reasoning than idiosyncratic tastes. Butterfield et al. (2000) found that when an individual perceives a social consensus around an issue being ethically problematic, his or her moral awareness will be triggered, indicating the social rather than individualistic nature of ethical thinking.

The subjectification of experience provides discursive closure by pushing issues from the public realm to the private realm. As the case of emotivism illustrates, this move may even articulate the whole issue of ethics as a strictly private matter. As such, it ceases to exist as a matter of public discussion. Ethical convictions and judgments are turned into personal attitudes and opinions, true only to myself and my current personality or 'character' (MacIntyre 1984).

Both naturalization and subjectification deny the socially constructed character of reality. Instead of recognizing that social phenomena are constituted through social action and collective definitions of what is true and good, reality is uncritically reproduced as either too objective or subjective to warrant scrutiny.

3. ETHICAL CLOSURES IN SWEDISH MEDIA ORGANIZATIONS

The empirical material stems partly from an ethnographic case study of a Swedish evening newspaper (at the time of the study, Sweden had three evening newspapers) and partly from in-depth interviews with 12 journalists. The case study is based on participative observation over nine months, two or three days a week, 15 more or less formal interviews, and numerous informal conversations. The second set of data is comprised of interviews with editors and reporters from a wide array of positions (including editors-in-chief, editors, senior columnists and reporters) and media outlets (morning papers, evening papers, and national and local radio). Since the ethnographic material allowed for depth, informant selection for the second set of interviews was aimed to generate breadth.

The ethnographic material has provided the richest and the most profound insights in to how Swedish journalists form and articulate ethical judgment. It has been particularly revealing to observe how Swedish journalists juggle with the practical, professional and ethical aspects of reporting while doing work. Although the ethnographic material has provided depth and richness, it may also restrict the validity of our results, since the ethnographic material draws exclusively from one media organization. It can be argued that evening newspapers are neither representative, nor particularly illuminating for how mainstream news organizations operate.

However, Swedish journalists are remarkably homogenous, both as a social group and in terms of espoused values (Nohrstedt and Ekström 1994). This is partly due to the fact that most, if not all, journalists are shaped in a similar mould. The early career steps almost invariably include internships and short-time temporary work, often in different parts of Sweden, at a variety of media organizations. Internships and temporary positions at evening newspapers are, in this context, commonly perceived as important qualifications because evening newspapers are perceived to be highly competitive and performance-oriented workplaces. In this sense, evening newspapers provide benchmarks for aspiring journalists.

Fieldwork has been conducted through an open and emergent approach, asking questions about how the interviewees view moral issues in their work organizations. We have primarily used qualitative methods. We have adopted a perspective with an emphasis on interpretation, looking for deeper meanings behind more obvious aspects of the empirical material. Thus, we have opted for a critical-hermeneutic perspective that primarily constructs analysis and interpretation in terms of reading and understanding.

3.1 The meaning of ethics among Swedish journalists

Ethics has a particular meaning for Swedish journalists, shared in the sense that almost every Swedish journalist is aware of a set of principles and relate to these in one way or another. One of our informants summarized these as follows:

> Ethical dilemmas in journalism are most often constituted by the, on the one hand, legitimate interest to expose as much material of common interest as possible, and, on the other hand, the fact that people may be hurt by such exposure. It is important to remember, though, that the journalistic ethics does not aim at eliminating damages due to publication. If it would, there would not be much to print, at least not with any substance. (Former morning newspaper and evening newspaper editor-in-chief)

This dilemma is often framed – reduced – into the question whether one should provide material that identifies the people in a story, or not. Judging from our material, as well as other studies (Nohrstedt and Ekström 1994; Ekström and Nohrstedt 1996), this is *the* ethical question for journalists. However, as some informants made clear, journalistic ethics covers more than name publishing:

> There exists a well-documented and elaborated ethical responsibility, codified in the rules of the game. They are the ethical foundation for the trade. . . . They are developed in a collaboration with several stakeholders; the union, the owner's organization and the publisher's club [a professional organization]. It is part of the freedom of press-articles in the constitution, that the press is self-regulated, rather than government-regulated. And it regulates issues of name publishing. It regulates the separation between editorial content and advertising. And it concerns the journalist's integrity, how involved one can be – which means that one cannot. (Morning paper senior columnist)

Name publishing, editorial purity, integrity – put bluntly, it is around these issues Swedish newsmakers are expected to develop a professional conscience, guided by agreed-upon 'rules of the game'. These are the issues that are generally perceived as relevant for the occupation, ethically speaking.

Journalists do not generally claim that these issues exhaust the realm of ethics. However, it is quite clear that other issues, that at least the outsider would expect to have ethical relevance for journalists, have a difficult time qualifying as issues that are relevant for the profession. Such issues include respect for private life rather than intruding and exploiting it; telling the truth (as far as possible) rather than producing half-truths, misleading information, or even lies; illuminate important phenomena (thus serving society and democracy or informing the public of global problems) rather than focusing on nonsense (such as celebrity gossip).

Journalists do not deny that these issues are ethical issues. But they are not considered to be particularly relevant for the profession – at least not on the workplace level – in the sense that they are issues that are regularly intraprofessionally considered from an ethical point of view. They are, in that sense, 'dead' as ethical issues.

This narrow understanding of ethics is constructed and maintained through particular processes of ethical closure. Judging from our empirical material, it is possible to identify four specific processes of ethical closure that operate in the Swedish newsmaking context. We label them *ethical sealing*, *ethical bracketing*, *double dehumanization*, and *commodification*. Below we elaborate the content and characteristics of each process.

3.2 Turning judgment into 'rules of the game' – the codification and reification of ethical conduct

Ethical sealing occurs when a particular set of moral judgments and issues is selected and maintained as *the* set, singling out a limited number of demarcated themes as objects of ethical consideration in for example an official set of ethical rules for a corporation or a profession. This move shrinks the scope for ethical judgment and creates ethical closure by (a) making a narrow, but seemingly crucial, space for it, and (b) turning it into a following of guidelines and rules. Ethical sealing draws mainly on naturalization, which may seem as a bit odd, since it ought to be difficult to argue that ethical judgments are 'natural', and not human achievements. The process of ethical sealing relies on reifying practices in this regard. This is beautifully illustrated in the newsmaker context by the way ethical judgments are converted into rules of the game. As such, they are looked upon as bureaucratic protocol to be followed or bent, rather than a particular perspective on the human existence.

> The journalistic ethics in use in Sweden is, more or less, a following of rules. So it is not, apart from a historical point of view, based on moral judgment.

Everything is put together in a pamphlet: this is what you are allowed to do. The limits and boundaries are expressed there, everything is regulated in there. Everything, from Freedom of Press-bills to the ethical, moral rules of the game, as they are called, and which really is nothing but recommendations. (Evening newspaper editor-in-chief)

The codified, and almost formal, nature of 'the rules of the game' makes them impersonal and lends them a pretense of objective existence. They are there and are to be followed as something natural and self-evident. The reference to extrapersonal institutions (unions, employer organizations, professional organizations, and legislative bodies) as key guardians of the book of rules further detaches them from their origins as outflows of concrete human judgment, thus making them appear more 'objective' and less part of subjective human experience. Morality is here based on the seemingly superior rationality of certain institutions. As a consequence, moral judgment becomes an exercise in converting rules into practice; into yet another area regulated by bureaucratic protocol. Ethical sealing is in this sense another example of the substitution of technical for a moral responsibility in bureaucratic settings, as described by Bauman (1989, p 98ff).

Ironically, what is set to safeguard ethical conduct in vital ways rather undermines it (cf. ten Bos 1997). However, as ten Bos points out, rules are also resources for ethical reflection and may not necessarily stifle all forms of ethical reflection. In this sense, ethical sealing thus simultaneously enhances and eclipses domains of ethical judgment. Sealing is thus not purely about ethical closure. It facilitates the accomplishment of certain 'minimal' standards within at least a narrow terrain. In the end, the process of ethical sealing creates *moral reservations*, where engagement in ethical reflection is both legitimate and encouraged, but also narrowly prescribed and regulated. Particular sets of issues and judgments are singled out as valid, whereas others are pushed to a fringe existence. In the end, ethical sealing results in the conversion of informed conduct, guided by practical reason, into restricted behavior, determined by technically motivated application of a body of rules. Ethics in practice then shows resemblance with bureaucracy.

3.3 Lost in the divide – the privatization of moral judgment

Ethical bracketing is another important process that provides ethical closure in the Swedish newsmaker context. Ethical bracketing allows newsmakers to manage the breach between 'official morality' as expressed through ethical sealing, and other ethical convictions that may be held by individuals. As discussed above, ethical sealing primarily operates on a topical level. That is, it provides ethical closure through systematically enhancing a certain set of moral judgments and issues, and eclipsing others.

Ethical bracketing, on the other hand, operates on the personal level. Such a process is necessary since newsmakers are likely to hold ethical convictions and exercise moral judgments that transcend the boundaries of the 'official morality'. However, 'excessive' moral convictions and judgments may create problems in the work process, since they may call for action that is incompatible with action deemed necessary to make the story stick (Jackall 1988). Of course, if such a dilemma arises within the boundaries of what is ethically sealed, there are certain guidelines and rules for how to proceed. However, if they arise outside the limits of the moral reservations provided through ethical sealing, individuals are expected to suspend, or more accurately, temporarily bracket their normal ethical standards and moral judgments.

> New employees, particularly temps and interns, often jolt when they understand that they are supposed to knock on the door of, let's say, the dead boy's home and ask his parents for a photo to publish in the paper, for example. But you are expected to be a Viking and accept that that's the way it is to work at a paper. (Evening newspaper copy-editor)

The individual newsmaker has little possibility to voice morally motivated objections, in a situation as the one pictured in the quotation. To be more precise, he or she can voice as much moral indignation as he or she likes, but it will not be recognized as a voice speaking with moral authority. Rather, it will be recognized as 'out of bounds'. Its reception may range from the sympathetic: as understandable but irrelevant personal pain; over the ignorant: as meaningless noise; to ridicule: as wimpy whining, but it will regardlessly be viewed as besides the point.

The process of subjectification of experience, as described above, mainly propels ethical bracketing. It allows journalists to maintain their own ethical standards and judgments, as long as they don't interfere with newsmaking procedures. Since moral convictions are systematically viewed as private and individual concerns, apart from the set of convictions that exist in the moral reservation created by ethical sealing, they are also viewed as something that each individual must manage.

> Let's take an example, the boy who got lost in the woods in Smalltown. In the end, we ask ourselves, will we approach the parents or not? And we usually do. But you can never force a reporter to do it. I can't say: '– Do it.' '– No, it's so uncomfortable', they might say. And that's OK. So you have to . . . at the same, you know that in nine cases out of ten, they [the parents etc.] will talk

> with you. I mean, if they don't want to, you have to be very careful, because
> you can't force them. . . . You can never force a reporter to make those calls.
> But, on the other hand, you will always suggest them to make them. (Evening
> newspaper editor)

It is OK but somewhat suspicious, as indicated above, to withdraw from
a task on moral grounds, as an individual. However, because of the subjectification of experience, this will be viewed as an individual choice,
due to personal idiosyncrasies, rather than a morally motivated decision.
Typically, newsmakers respond by bracketing personal moral convictions
and judgment capacity, since newsmaker practices often create situations
that demand action that is difficult to make compatible with conventional
moral standards. There are only a limited number of occasions in which
one can decline a task before becoming labeled as unfit for the job, and
there simply are no arenas where reservations would be recognized as
voicing valid moral concerns.

3.4   The instrumentalized newsmaker

The combined effects of sealing and bracketing put a third kind of ethical
closure, *double dehumanization*, a concept borrowed from Vetlesen (1994),
into play. Sealing creates an environment where professional ethical judgment is reserved for a narrow set of topics, and where personal ethical
judgment has no possibility to speak with moral authority in the work
context, since that particular position is occupied by the sealed sets of
judgments. Bracketing provides a mechanism that makes it possible for
individuals to maintain privately held moral convictions and work in a
context where actions incompatible with their personal moral convictions
routinely and systematically occur.

Usually, this makes it easier for newsmakers to instrumentalize themselves in their professional role: they view themselves as instruments of
the trade. The idea of being instruments substitute the notion of being a
human agent, guided by conscience and practical reason (an end), with
the notion of being a functional utility (a mean) regulated by external
constraints. Journalists are 'the messengers, not the message', and they are
'only printing stuff people want to read'. They are no longer humans: they
are conduits of information and mere expressions of supply and demand.
Ethical closure is motivated not by references to a restricted set of official
ethical rules or to a purely personal (subjective) view on morals. It is the
logic of instrumentalization, the emphasis on a technical response to the
imperatives of media and market forces that produces closure. Neither a
predefined closed arena of morality, nor a personalization of opinion, is

needed for instrumentalization to take place. The domination of instrumental reason may stand on its own feet, but is sometimes facilitated by ethical sealing and bracketing. Sealing fits into an instrumental rationality in the sense that ethics is compartmentalized and taken care of in a well packaged and compartmentalized way, leaving major parts of operations free from disturbing considerations.

The process of double dehumanization dehumanizes and instrumentalizes relentlessly. Since newsmakers usually interact with other people; witnesses, victims, villains, heroes, sources, confidants, and so on, these people are also instrumentalized and dehumanized in the process – hence double dehumanization (cf. Kärreman and Alvesson 2001). They are, of course, instrumental in the sense that they are necessary for producing stories. But they are also converted into instruments, rather than human beings, by instrumentalized newsworkers that attempt to stage the story – the message – in the most effective way.

As noted earlier, such staging may include the use of moral perspectives. But the moral point of view is not used here as a way of guiding human conduct. It is used as an effect, as a way of adding drama and sensation. The following extract, taken from a routine meeting between day- and nightshift personnel at an evening newspaper, provides an illustration:

> *Day editor*: This piece, I don't know whether it should be in the national edition, but it goes straight to the gut. There have been several severe accidents at a crossroad outside the hospital in Arvika. Two accidents with fatal outcomes have occurred in only a couple of weeks. In one case, well, the father is still in intensive care with life-threatening damages. The little daughter was buried yesterday. The mother . . . they were on their way to pick her up, so she witnessed the crash. Anyway, we have got her down to the crossroad for a picture, and there will be a petition tomorrow in favor of a rebuilt crossroad. It goes straight to the gut, really.
>
> *Night editor*: Portrait of the daughter and the spouse?
>
> *Day editor*: Yes, I hope so.

The extract is unusual in its compact demonstration of the double dehumanization of newsmakers and the use of human tragedy, with moral indignation as the main dramaturgical ingredient, as a story-enhancing effect. Typically, double dehumanization is less obvious, although still possible to identify in most instances of newsmaker procedure. The voice of moral indignation, so useful for evening newspaper newsmakers in particular, but also a story-line standard for newsmakers in general, is what makes the story newsworthy. However, such moral indignation has almost nothing to do with morality and ethics proper. It is merely a pose, used to maximize a particular effect.

3.5   Trading in morality: the commodification of ethics

We have, to some extent, already touched upon the fourth kind of ethical closure we have identified among Swedish newsmakers, particularly in the paragraph above. We have labeled it moral commodification since as a process, it transforms ethics and morality from a particular mode of re- flection into a valuable commodity in the marketplace. Newsmakers trade in offering products that appeal to the customer's morality, typically in a spontaneous, self-evident and common-sensical way. The commodifica- tion of ethics occurs because good stories need drama, at least according to newsmakers, and because most media organizations are commercial enterprises. One way of adding drama to a story is to cast it in moral terms. Such moral casting typically introduces narrative elements that make it easier to frame the story in a dramatic fashion. It provides a chance to establish heroes, villains, and victims within a moral story.

Since good stories are equivalent to selling stories, particularly at an evening newspaper (Kärreman and Alvesson 2001), moral drama becomes a selling point. Morality offers a tool of the trade that makes a story more compelling, interesting and/or dramatic. The commercial nature of most media organizations frames and further emphasizes ethics and morality as parts of the product package – as commodities.

Moral commodification provides ethical closure because it disqualifies the notion of ethics and morality as specific modes of understanding, and turns them into something that may or may not add value to the product. Thus, it becomes possible to address moral issues without engaging in ethical reflection at all. Rather, ethics and morality are, as noted above, reduced to drama-enhancing effects.

Commodification of ethics occurs in all types of media. However, in the Swedish context, it seems as if evening newspaper people have a particular self-conscious relationship to moral commodification. These newsmakers quite often refer to market conditions. They compete in a marketplace, they claim, where competition is intense. There is a market for moral storytelling – a market in which Ethics Inc. operates. Ethical judgment gets mixed up in conjectures on the readership's shared moral standards. Second-guessing the ethical judgments of the typical reader becomes as important, or even more important, as making independent ethical judg- ments. Ultimately, what the market is perceived to want replaces inde- pendent ethical judgments.

4. THE ROUTINE PRODUCTION OF ETHICAL CLOSURE: CONTEXTUAL FEATURES AND ORGANIZATIONAL ARRANGEMENTS

It is perhaps tempting to explain ethical closures as effects of a lack of or unsophisticated and poorly implemented codes of conduct. This is true, in a tautological and trivial sense, but it also misses the point with the concept of ethical closure. Such 'explanations' miss how particular contexts produce circumstances that facilitate, foster, and even inevitably lead to ethical closures of different kinds. Ethical closures can be explained and understood from the particular contexts where they are working. In our case, we will put emphasis on the way organizational arrangements facilitate and enable the production of ethical closures. We will point at four organizational structural features that enable the kinds of ethical closures discussed in the chapter: the rhythm of the work flow, division of labor, division of ethical responsibility, and solipsistic social relations.

The practical business of newsmaking is typically divided into recurring sequences of work within short time-spans. The periodic character of most, if not all, news media creates a work situation where output formats regulate, sometimes even dictate, work procedures (Tuchman 1978; Gans 1979). Newspapers, TV, and radio rely on a steady inflow of stories and commentary. Deadlines are omnipresent. Time is scarce. Print space is scarce.

> You are not allowed to write 6000 characters because there is not enough space in the paper. Everybody knows that. And you have to write a certain kind of preamble, because it has to fit into a certain layout. You have to accept those rules. (Editor-in-chief)

Most newsmakers tend to point at this particular aspect of work when explaining ethical shortcomings. However, their main concern is rarely rigid formatting, or lack of print space. According to newsmakers, scarce time and tight deadlines are the main contributors to ethical shortcomings.

> To the extent journalists don't meet their own perceived moral standards, it is because of time pressures. The pressure is so intense and everything has to move so quickly. You don't have time to reflect. (Editor-in-chief)

Although it is questionable if time pressure is the main cause behind ethical closures, it is clear that time pressures create situations where newsmakers may have to choose between reflection and production. Steady production and reflective conduct are both valued at a premium in most news organizations, but since production mostly is seemingly unproblematic from an ethical point of view, production is routinely chosen before reflection. This is, of course, further underscored by ethical sealing and division of ethical responsibility (see below) which – on a surface level – guarantee that minimal ethical reflection occurs somewhere in the editorial production process.

As with most modern organizations, the typical media organization relies heavily on elaborate and sophisticated division of labor. Labor is divided both horizontally and vertically. In the horizontal dimension, labor is usually divided and specialized in two areas: work functions and topical coverage. In the case of work functions, division of labor is typically grounded in various kinds of technical expertise. Newsmaker work is also typically divided based on topical coverage. This means that newspapers, in particular, but also other media, organize the news flow in various topical categories: business, domestic, sports, international, entertainment, culture, and so on. Newsmakers are expected to be able to move between the boundaries of topical division: reporters specialized in domestic affairs should, in principle, be able to work in the sports department. However, newsmakers normally specialize in one or a few topics and stick to it.

Labor is also typically, if not always, divided vertically. Formal vertical division of labor may vary in its scope. A small local newspaper may for example restrict formal vertical division of labor to two levels: a supervisor and supervised journalists. On the other hand, large newspapers may have several levels in their hierarchy of formal authority.

The significance of formal vertical division of labor is generally downplayed by newsmakers. They often claim that hierarchical authority has little influence on everyday operations, and that too visible use of hierarchical authority would be counterproductive.

> There exists a hierarchy here, with an editor-in-chief, two deputy editor-in-chiefs, a managing editor with a sort of general responsibility for the daily work with the news, plus the managing editor for each department. But it is not that disciplinary, it is relatively free . . . it is not that authoritative, so to speak. Your managing editor will not yell at you. There will be discussions and then there will be a consensus on how to carry on with the work. Each department has large degrees of freedom. The business department, for example, decides what they want to do for themselves. There is nobody who will tell them 'Now let's do this, this is what we will do'. There is a general policy that most agree upon. And then we work from there. Sports are minding their business, Politics theirs, and so on. (Morning newspaper senior columnist)

Nevertheless, as labor process theorists, organizational sociologists, and others have demonstrated (Jackall 1988; Bauman 1989, 1994; Knights and Willmott 1990), division of labor is hardly as innocent as most newsmakers tend to believe. Division of labor is often a gain in efficiency for the organization, and perhaps in the possibility of developing expert knowledge for individuals. But it also includes costs. Such costs typically involve fragmentation and the separation of decision and execution. Fragmentation and separation of decision and execution make it difficult for individuals to create a meaningful picture of the activity that is carried out in the organization, and thus to relate their own work to the various outputs produced in the organizations. It also makes it difficult to influence the end product of your work.

> I have control over my stuff until the minute I deliver them to the managing editor. Until I have finished the writing. Then it falls freely. You can ask any reporter how it feels to deliver a story that one thinks is good, and the pictures. . .. You think 'I'm delivering a complete kit here, this is damn good'. And then you see it in the paper the day after and you realize that you delivered it to a donkey. (Evening newspaper senior columnist)

Such frustration is not untypical in media organizations, and perhaps in all modern organizations. Although the informant in the excerpt above suggests incompetence or even sabotage on behalf of the receivers of his 'kit', the problem is rather that they have little knowledge of his particular vision, or little possibility to realize it. Copy-editors, on their side, often complain that they receive confusing and almost incomprehensible material from the field workers (reporters and photographers). Sophisticated division of labor generally tends to make work results and responsibilities diffuse, or 'floating' in Bauman's (1989, 1994) vocabulary, and provide structural conditions for far-reaching separation between organizational members. Needless to say, diffuse responsibilities and structural separation both facilitate and reinforce processes of ethical closure. It facilitates processes of ethical closure through providing structural contingencies that make them difficult to resist. It reinforces them through fragmenting responsibilities to the extent that it makes bracketing – both ethical and other kinds of bracketing – the only possible way to cope.

Actual division of labor is normally decided within an organization. However, government regulation may sometimes force organizations to particular divisions of labor. As is the case in media organizations, such mandatory division of labor, although well intended, may create building blocks for ethical closures. In media organizations, the law divides legal responsibility. Individual journalists are not legally responsible for the accuracy and truthfulness of their stories in Sweden. Instead, the law leaves this responsibility exclusively with one person in the media organization: the 'responsible publisher'. Newsmakers typically have no objections to this system. They tend to accept it, which may be a bit odd since it means, in pragmatic terms, that power over editorial content is, in the end of the day, exclusively concentrated to the responsible publisher.

> What is really special with the position of the responsible publisher is that it is completely uncorroded by the various Swedish experiments in worklife democracy. It is a position that makes one person responsible, and [gives] this person absolute power. It is an anachronistic dictatorship, that oddly enough is accepted by all concerned, by this freedom-loving group. It is a paradox. (Former morning newspaper and evening newspaper editor-in-chief)

It is the responsible publisher who is punished for wrongdoings conducted in the name of the media organization. This means that, from a legal point of view, the individual newsmaker does not operate within his or her own ethical frame of reference but, by proxy, within the ethical frame of reference of the responsible publisher. When individual newsmakers face ethical dilemmas that cannot easily be resolved within institutionalized rules of thumb, they also face choices that simply are not theirs:

> Decisions concerning publication of name do not normally bother me much. If we publish, well, it wouldn't affect me. I mean, in some cases it is so obvious that all you have to do is to make the decision. But if it is a close call, I just let it flow up in the hierarchy [to the responsible publisher], because it would be him ending up in jail. So he better make the decision. (Evening newspaper managing editor)

In this sense, the system with 'responsible publisher' makes individual newsmakers insignificant as moral agents. Legally speaking, they are nothing but remote-controlled extensions of the 'responsible publisher'. This system may have other advantages, but it undoubtedly invites newsmakers to take comfort in bracketing their ethical convictions and moral judgments, and ultimately reduce the inclination to position themselves as ethical subjects.

Newsmakers working in news organizations are rarely in direct contact with their colleagues due to division of labor, as noted above, and to shift work. Tasks, functions and duties are distributed in time and space. Most tasks and functions are performed by at least two persons separated in time and space. Opportunities to direct and interpersonal contacts between individuals performing identical functions and tasks are minimal. Communication and sharing of experience are limited to phone conversations and exchange of documents.

At the same time, newsmakers regularly face unexpected events. They must often make difficult decisions with short notice and in general work under a strict time pressure – the newspaper must be put together every

24th hour. Due to the low degree of social interaction between larger groups of people – most interactions and meetings only involve two or three persons – and infrequent contacts between people doing the same job – due to shift work – chances to develop a shared understanding through everyday interaction are few and far between.

This means that newsmakers typically work in situations where division of labor and responsibility is elaborate, narrow, and specific, but where social relations are loosely and thinly coupled (Weick 1976; Orton and Weick 1990). Individuals work under high degrees of separation, even where the workflow makes them highly interdependent. A typical newspaper story may be co-created by people who actually never see or communicate directly with each other. A reporter who may make some telephone calls and then write the piece may, for example, contribute with the text. Pictures are either bought from picture agencies or taken by a newspaper photographer. Work will be coordinated by a managing editor, which usually means that the editor orders pictures from the department of photography, and has a few words with the reporter. The text and the pictures are eventually delivered to a copy-editor, who will add headlines to the story, and also decide the presentation of the piece, together with his or her managing editor.

This is, of course, typical for professional and semi-professional work. Reporters, photographers, and copy-editors are expected to be able to perform their work on their own, with minimal intervention from superiors and colleagues. After all, they are the experts. However, this also means that there are few places or spaces where organization members regularly meet in a fashion that allows them to engage in conversations that transcend what is minimally necessary for putting the paper together. The lack of opportunities to develop rich social relations with peers and other organizational members facilitate subjectification of experience. It also neutralizes moral reflection by denying proximity. According to Bauman (1989), proximity is essential for 'the moral impulse' (cf. ten Bos 1997):

> That proximity-cum-responsibility context within which personal images are formed surrounds them with a thick moral wall virtually impenetrable to 'merely abstract' arguments. Persuasive or insidious the intellectual stereotype may be, yet its zone of application stops abruptly where the sphere of personal intercourse begins. 'The other' as an *abstract category* simply does not communicate with 'the other' *I know*. (Bauman 1989, pp. 187–8, emphasis in original)

Bauman is referring to 'the other' outside the organization (for an analysis of an ethics for the other, see Jeanes and Muhr this volume). However, there is no reason to think that proximity starts and stops at organizational borders. If I have few opportunities to find out whether my experiences are strictly personal or shared by others – if I am systematically denied proximity – it is likely that I eventually will feel confusion around the character of the experience. The confusion may vary from person to person. Some may confuse potentially shared experiences with personal experiences. Others may confuse personal experience for shared. All may confuse abstract stereotypes for personal knowledge. Either way, the result will be confusion, caused by the solipsistic mistake of placing one's own preformed interpretations at the center.

5.   CONCLUSION

In this chapter, we have taken an interest in the social construction of counterforces to moral awareness and ethical reflection in organizational settings. We have introduced the concept of ethical closure in an attempt to reveal and analyse such counterforces. We have attempted to understand ethics as a particular mode of understanding that is not only exercised but also shaped in organizational settings. Ethical closure occurs, we claim, when people are systematically denied – or 'voluntary' refrain from – engagement in ethical reflection. In this chapter, we have attempted to connect the concept of ethical closure with the related concept of discursive closure, as developed by Deetz (1992). In particular, we have pointed to how ethical closures, in a manner similar to discursive closures, operate through unobtrusively diverting attention from potential ethical reflection, rather than through overt prohibition and restriction.

Drawing from empirical material from media organizations we have identified four processes of ethical closures: sealing, bracketing, double dehumanization, and moral commodification. Processes of *sealing* typically assign the role of ethical judgment to a narrow set of issues – and thereby eclipsing others – where ethical 'reflection' normally is guided, indeed confined, by elaborate systems of rules. *Bracketing* allows newsmakers to disconnect from individual ethical frameworks, and thus make actions they otherwise would find ethically questionable, possible. This is also facilitated by *double dehumanization*, which constructs newsmakers as well as those people addressed as instruments, allowing little space for the wider considerations of goals and values. Finally, *moral commodification* – the reframing of ethics from a particular mode of understanding to a selling effect – allows newsmakers to address and utilize ethical issues without engaging in ethical reflection at all. It means a kind of displacement of ethics into the market.

Although quite distinct as processes, the four kinds of ethical closures discussed here may be empirically interlinked and operate in a mutually reinforcing fashion. For example, sealing, bracketing, and double dehumanization provide space for moral commodification, and moral commodification, when established, further reinforces processes of sealing, bracketing, and double dehumanization. Their combined effect makes it difficult for newsmakers to engage in ethical reflection in matters that concern their work. Since processes of closure counteract ethical reflection through indirect displacement, rather than direct oppression, they also become difficult to resist.

Resistance is further eroded and inhibited by the way organizational/contextual features provide fertile ground for the ethical closures we have identified in media organizations. The rhythm of work, with its tight deadlines and short job-cycles, gives little space for ethical reflections. Division of labor diffuses and fragments responsibility. The division of ethical responsibility, peculiar for the Swedish context, centralizes all legal responsibility to one person in the organization and converts other newsmakers from moral agents to mere agents. The solipsistic social relations provide few, if any, occasions where ethical judgments can be collectively articulated, evaluated, and formed.

The kinds of ethical closure, and the contextual features that facilitate and foster them, identified and discussed in this chapter are to some extent specific for media work, and news work in particular. The process of moral commodification, for example, seems to be particular for media work although there are some other areas of work where moral commodification is likely to be an issue, for example in advertising and lobbying agencies and their client organizations. However, such businesses are in many ways also media organizations, with a sufficiently generous, but not meaningless, definition of the term. Thus, they also fall into the category of media work.

Other processes that we have identified in this chapter are arguably more general, meaning here not only restricted to media organizations. Ethical bracketing is likely to occur in most modern bureaucratic organizations, partly due to the emotivist bias in Western culture (Macintyre 1984) and the following subjectification of experience, and partly due to the nature of bureaucracy (Jackall 1988; Bauman 1989, 1994). Double dehumanization is probably also common in capitalist society. Market economy strongly encourages the treatment of human subjects as means for profit and actors on this market are expected to develop a strong instrumental orientation in this respect.

The final process of ethical closure identified in this chapter, sealing, is likely to be less particular than moral commodification, and less general (frequent) than bracketing and perhaps also double dehumanization. One might suspect that sealing is likely to occur in settings where there is an 'official' moral code established. Consequently, most (semi-) professional organizations, which are prone to develop or incorporate specific codes of conduct, are likely to show more or less evidence of processes of ethical sealing.

The concept of ethical closure has general relevance. Wherever ethical reflection is applicable, ethical closures may be set to operate. Actual processes of ethical closure are likely to differ between occupations and organizational settings, but the outcome would be the same: the blocking and denial of ethical reflection.

It is an important task to identify the various forms and processes of ethical closures at work in different contexts, may they be occupational or organizational. There is a need to further develop and elaborate our theoretical sensitivities in this field of inquiry. We offer this chapter as a modest but hopefully valuable empirically illustrated outline to a general conceptualization of ethical closures in organizational settings.

REFERENCES

Alvesson, M. (1996), *Communication, Power and Organization*, Berlin/New York: de Gruyter.

Alvesson, M. and D. Kärreman (2000), 'Taking the linguistic turn in organizational analysis: challenges, responses, consequences', *Journal of Applied Behavioral Science*, **36** (2), 136–58.

Alvesson, M. and K. Sköldberg (2000), *Reflexive Methodology*, London: Sage.

Bauman, Z. (1989), *Modernity and the Holocaust*, Cambridge: Polity Press.

Bauman, Z. (1994), *Alone Again: Ethics after Certainty*, London: Demos.

Bird, F.B. (2002), *The Muted Conscience: Moral Silence and the Practice of Ethics in Business*, Westport, CT: Quorum Books.

Brytting, T. (1997), *Företagsetik [Corporate Ethics]*, Malmö, Sweden: Liber.

Butterfield, K., L.K. Trevino and G. Weaver (2000), 'Moral awareness in business organizations: influences of issue-related and social context factors', *Human Relations*, **53** (7), 981–1018.

Deetz, S. (1992), *Democracy in an Age of Corporate Colonization: Developments in Communication and the Politics of Everyday Life*, Albany, NY: State University of New York Press.

Ekström, M. and S.A. Nohrstedt (1996), *Journalistikens Etiska Problem [The Ethical Problems of Journalism]*, Stockholm: Rabén Prisma/Svenska Journalistförbundet.

Forester, J. (1989), *Planning in the Face of Power*, Berkeley, CA: University of California Press.

Gans, H. (1979), *Deciding What's News*, New York: Vintage Books.

Geertz, C. (1973), *The Interpretation of Cultures*, New York: Basic Books.

Habermas, J. (1984), *The Theory of Communicative Action.* vol. 1, Boston, MA: Beacon Press.
Habermas, J. (1987), *Toward a Rational Society*, Cambridge: Polity Press.
Horkheimer, M. and T. Adorno ([1947] 1979), *The Dialectics of Enlightenment*, London: Verso.
Jackall, R. (1988), *Moral Mazes. The World of Corporate Managers*, New York: Oxford University Press.
Jones, T. and A. Wicks (1999), 'Convergent stakeholder theory', *Academy of Management Review*, **24** (2), 206–21.
Kärreman, D. and M. Alvesson (2001), 'Making newsmakers. Conversational identities at work', *Organization Studies*, **22** (1), 59–90.
Kjönstad, B. and H. Willmott (1995), 'Business ethics: restrictive or empowering?', *Journal of Business Ethics*, **14** (6) 1–20.
Knights, D. and H. Willmott (eds) (1990), *Labour Process Theory*, London: Macmillan.
Lincoln, Y. and E. Guba (2000), 'Paradigmatic controversies, contradictions, and emerging confluences', in N. Denzin and Y. Lincoln (eds), *Handbook of Qualitative Research*, 2nd edn, Thousand Oaks, CA: Sage, pp. 163–88.
MacIntyre, A. (1967), *A Short History of Ethics*, London: Routledge and Kegan Paul.
MacIntyre, A. (1984), *After Virtue*, Notre Dame, IN: University of Notre Dame Press.
Mangham, I.L. (1995), 'MacIntyre and the manager', *Organization*, **2** (2), 181–204.
Marcuse, H. (1964), *One-Dimensional Man*, Boston, MA: Beacon Press.
Meyer, J.W. (1986), 'Myths of socialization and personality', in T. Heller, Morton Sosna and David E. Wellbery (eds), *Reconstructing Individualism: Autonomy, Individuality and the Self*, Stanford, CA: Stanford University Press pp. 208–21.
Morgan, G. (1986), *Images of Organization.* Beverly Hills, CA: Sage.
Morgan, G. (1998), 'Governance and regulation: an institutionalist approach to ethics and organizations', in M. Parker (ed.), *Ethics and Organizations*, London: Sage, pp. 221–37.
Nohrstedt, S.A. and M. Ekström (1994), *Ideal och Verklighet: Nyhetsjournalistikens Etik i Praktiken [Ideal and Reality: the Ethics of News Journalism in Practice]*, Örebro, Sweden: Högskolan i Örebro.
Orton, J.D. and K. Weick (1990), 'Loosely coupled systems: a reconceptualization', *Academy of Management Review* **15**, (2), 203–23.
Paine, L.S. (1994), 'Managing for organizational integrity', *Harvard Business Review* March–April, 106–17.
Parker, M. (ed.) (1998a), *Ethics and Organizations*, London: Sage.
Parker, M. (1998b), 'Ethics, the very idea?', in M. Parker (ed.), *Ethics and Organizations*, London: Sage, pp. 1–14.
Sorrell, T. (1998), 'Beyond the fringe? The strange state of business ethics', in M. Parker (ed.), *Ethics and Organizations*, London: Sage.
ten Bos, R. (1997), 'Essai: Business ethics and Bauman ethics', *Organization Studies*, **18** (6), 997–1015.
Tuchman, G. (1978), *Making News: A Study in the Construction of Reality*, New York: Free Press.
Tucker, L., V. Stathakopolous and C.H. Patti (1999), 'A multidimensional

assessment of ethical codes: the professional business association perspective', *Journal of Business Ethics*, **19** (3), 287–300.

Vetlesen, A.J. (1994), *Perception, Empathy, and Judgment: An Inquiry into the Preconditions of Moral Performance*, University Park, PA: Pennsylvania State University Press.

Watson, T. (1994), *In Search of Management*, London: Routledge.

Watson, T. (1998), 'Ethical codes and moral communities: the Gunlaw temptation, the Simon solution, and the David dilemma', in M. Parker (ed.), *Ethics and Organizations*, London: Sage, pp. 253–68.

Weaver, G.R., L.K. Trevino and P.L. Cochran (1999), 'Corporate ethics programs as control systems: influences of executive commitment and environmental factors', *Academy of Management Journal*, **42** (1), 41–57.

Weick, K.E. (1976), 'Educational organizations as loosely coupled systems', *Administrative Science Quarterly*, **21** (1), 1–19.

5. The business of business and the politics of opinion

Steen Vallentin

Sentiment is a corrupting and debilitating influence in business. It fosters leniency, inefficiency, sluggishness, extravagance, and hardens the innovationary arteries. . . . The governing rule in industry should be that *something is good only if it pays*. Otherwise it is alien and impermissible. This is the rule of capitalism.

Theodore Levitt, 1958

I call myself a liberal in the true sense of liberal, in the sense in which it means of and pertaining to freedom.

Milton Friedman, 1975

1. INTRODUCTION

Recently, several calls have been made for a politically enlarged conceptualization of corporate social responsibility (CSR) (Margolis and Walsh 2003; Scherer and Palazzo 2007; see also Dubbink 2004; Matten and Crane 2005, Matten and Moon 2008, Vallentin 2009). These calls have been motivated by the dramatic increase of corporate power and influence in the global economy – with the rise of the multinational corporation and corporate entanglement in a variety of activities and issues that have hitherto been associated with the state/government or civil society, namely philanthropy and community investment, environmental management, workers' rights and welfare, human rights, animal rights and corruption. Private companies can not only be considered as citizens in and by themselves (vis-à-vis the notion of *corporate citizenship*), they are also increasingly assuming, sharing or taking over the function of protecting, facilitating and enabling other citizens' rights. Examples of this include business involvement in educational and community development programs, provision of health and educational services for workers in developing countries, and protection of civil rights in countries with oppressive regimes such as Nigeria or Burma (Crane et al. 2004). In certain respects, private companies are assuming a statelike role and becoming more and more governmental (Matten and Crane 2005; Walsh 2005). This is a reflection – both cause and effect – of an on-going *politization* of business: the actions, decisions and responsibilities of private companies are increasingly exposed to public scrutiny and societal demands and expectations that have formerly been associated with government and the functions of public authorities and institutions.

This leads toward a political understanding of CSR. Drawing on Rorty (1991) and Habermas (1996), Scherer and Palazzo (2007) argue for a political conception of CSR that establishes a primacy of democracy to philosophy: 'It does not start with philosophical principles but with a political analysis of the changing interplay of governments, civil society actors, and corporations, and the institutional and cultural consequences of that dynamic' (ibid., p. 1098). However, in giving primacy of democracy to philosophy there is a fundamental choice to be made of whether to emphasize consensual or conflictual aspects of democratic processes. Political approaches to CSR that emphasize the democratic value of consensus often tend to lead to more of the same, that is, alternative forms of normative and idealized reasoning about business and society (even if they are motivated by a perceived need to break away from such reasoning). This chapter is concerned with the role of *public opinion* in defining corporate responsibilities, and I will argue that this conceptual emphasis calls for a conflictual understanding of the politics of CSR. Public opinion is a highly influential political force that has many points of intersection with business, but recognition of its significance does not necessarily imply recognition of its democratic value. Public opinion is certainly a democratic ideal, but it is a contested ideal, hero to some, villain to others, and the differences of opinion – in regard to public opinion and CSR – often seem irreconcilable because they are ideological in nature and therefore immune to change.

Instead of arguing for the superiority of a particular normative conception of public opinion, I will emphasize the contested and ambiguous nature of public opinion and its different articulations. Instead of letting the political emerge as a kind of *salvation*, a supposedly superior solution to the problem of providing a properly embedded and material justification for CSR, I will strongly emphasize the need for a political understanding of CSR to embody a critical mode of *reflection*. A mode of reflection that is not preoccupied with finding new answers to the same old normative questions, but instead seeks to elucidate the conflicts and problems that come to the fore in political struggles over the meaning and value of CSR. More specifically, this chapter is concerned with the ways in which public opinion is framed and given political meaning by the opposing camps in the on-going battle of ideas over CSR. In other words, I will explore the uses of public opinion in CSR discourse.

As argued elsewhere (Vallentin 2009), this kind of approach does not imply a devaluation of normative approaches to CSR as such. It merely points to the need for a plethora of complementary research strategies to be operative in the field of business and society. There is (also) a need for research to maintain a critical, albeit not sceptical, distance from developments in this field, and for political enlargements that are less concerned with the democratic safeguarding of corporate activities and more concerned with the social and strategic reality of how CSR is actually being debated and acted upon.

The chapter will proceed first by juxtaposing the consensual view of politics as salvation and the more critical mode of politics as reflection. Section 2 discusses the important contributions of Scherer and Palazzo (2007) and Preston and Post (1975). In section 3 I present the 'postmodern' view of public opinion that informs the following analysis and discussion of public opinion as it is used by the two opposing camps in the CSR debate: (neo-) liberal sceptics (section 4) on the one side and CSR promoters (section 5) on the other.

2. POLITICS AS SALVATION: ENTER DELIBERATIVE DEMOCRACY

As mentioned, a political conception of CSR can be guided by either a consensual or a conflictual understanding of democratic processes. Scherer and Palazzo (2007), strongly inspired by Habermas, opt for the former. They see a theory of deliberative democracy as a viable discursive and dialogic alternative to positivist economic approaches that merely provide an instrumental interpretation of corporate responsibilities, and monological business ethics solutions to the problem of providing a normative justification for CSR.

Scherer and Palazzo are not the first to come up with the idea of looking to democratic processes rather than philosophical principles (concerning virtues, duties, consequences, discourse, social contracts) in order to justify CSR. Another grand conceptual design has been proposed by Preston and Post, who, in their seminal book: *Private Management and Public Policy – The Principle of Public Responsibility* (1975), argued that the most significant impact that society exerts on business is through the realm of *public policy*. Importantly, they avoid a narrow and legalistic interpretation of the term 'policy' as they emphasize that public policy may be made explicit in law and other formal acts of governmental bodies, but that it can also manifest itself in implicit policies that are not formally articulated or enforced. Indeed, Preston and Post define public policy as an inclusive process through which 'the members of society – individuals, organizations, and interest groups – identify issues of public concern, explore conflicting view points, negotiate and bargain, and – if a resolution is reached – establish objectives and select means of obtaining them' (ibid., p. 2). Public policy is 'the means by which society as a whole articulates its goals and objectives' (ibid., p. 101), it refers to 'widely shared and generally acknowledged principles directing and controlling actions that have broad implications for society at large or major proportions thereof' (ibid., p. 56). The public policy process reflects 'general societal commitments and shared values' (ibid., p. 12). As Oberman (1996) points out, the implicit theme here is social control through value consensus. Building on a structural-functionalist paradigm, Preston and Post tend to emphasize integration and consensus while disregarding conflict and coercion.

Scherer and Palazzo follow in the footsteps of Preston and Post (even if they do not, actually, refer to them), as they propose deliberative democracy as a guiding force for CSR. An arguably even broader – and vaguer, one might add – notion than public policy. They nevertheless find that 'Habermas' theory of deliberative democracy is a very promising approach to appropriately define the social responsibilities of the business firm as a political actor in a globalized world' (2007, p. 1106). Scherer and Palazzo see deliberative democracy as a collaborative political process that calls for active participation from business in alternative modes of governance. In their view, '[a] deliberative concept of CSR embeds corporate decision making in processes of democratic will formation. These processes, driven by civil society actors and spanning a broad field of public arenas, establish a *democratic control on the public use of corporate power*' (ibid., p. 1109.

These grand designs are both examples of normative CSR using political means. They essentially substitute (monological) philosophical ideals with (discursive) democratic ideals – hoping to be able to rectify governance gaps and failures through the means of deliberative democracy. But the question remains whether there really is a fundamental difference between, on the one hand, philosophical normativity, and, on the other, democratic normativity. The political conception of CSR provided by Scherer and Palazzo is certainly wide open to the general criticisms that can be levelled at idealized notions of deliberative democracy: it remains strongly normative and procedural, more concerned with ideals and intentions than with reality and implementation, it pays little attention to corporate agency, it tends to overemphasize the potential role and significance of civil society organizations in regard to CSR while disregarding the legitimation problems their actions involve, and it relies too strongly on communicative rationality (the power of 'the better argument') in the face of massive noncommunicative (strategic) forces. Thus, it tends to separate rationality from power and rhetoric (cf. Flyvbjerg 1998).

3. POLITICS AS REFLECTION: THE AMBIGUITY OF PUBLIC OPINION

This chapter has a different ambition in regard to contributing to a politically enlarged conceptualization of CSR. Quoting Foucault (1984, pp. 375–6), and keeping in mind the suggested shortcomings of the grand normative designs proposed by Scherer and Pallazzo and Preston and Post, it can be argued that 'the forms of totalization offered by politics are always, in fact, very limited'. Paraphrasing Foucault, the aim here is not to produce alternative totalizing forms, but to open up problems, to approach politics from behind and cut across it on the diagonal (ibid.).

This calls for an open conception of public opinion, one that is not so much invested with normative value beforehand as it provides a lens that allows us to explore, empirically, on a second order level, how public opinion is invested with value in the CSR discourse. Peters (1995) provides the analytical point of departure. He argues that public opinion in modern society has no existence apart from mediated representations, and therefore always has an important textual or symbolic component. It is a rhetorical invention and in many uses appears more as a political or ideological construct than a discrete sociological referent. Its forcefulness often owes as much to its strength as a persuasive symbol as it does to being an actual social force. Although it may claim to be an expression of the popular will, public opinion is often, in fact, public only 'as a visible fiction before the eyes of the people' (ibid., p. 16). Peters speaks of 'the modern need to *imagine* the public' (ibid.). When the political public cannot be assembled in one place we look to substitutes, symbolic representations of the social whole, however they are mediated. Importantly, the imagined public is not *imaginary* in the sense that when we act upon symbolic representation of 'the public' it comes to exist as a real actor: 'Fictions, if persuasive, become material, political reality. In the region of politics, fact and fictions intermingle, often begetting one another' (ibid., p. 17).

Habermas similarly touches on the theme of fiction. He refers to public opinion as an institutionalized fiction that cannot be identified directly as a real entity in the behavior of the populace, but serves as a critical as well as a manipulative force in public communication (1991). He also refers to it as a normative postulate with empirical relevance (Habermas 1996). According to Habermas, public opinion is a *symbolic* expression of a constitutive ideal underlying the self-understanding of modern democratic societies: that the exercise of social and political power – in order to be or appear legitimate – must be subjected to the normative mandate of democratic publicity (Habermas 1991).

In contrast to the modernist aspirations of Habermas, whose view of public opinion is embedded in a normative theory of deliberative democracy, the fictionalized view of public opinion that informs the following analysis can be considered as 'postmodern' (Peters 1995, see also Ettema et al. 1991). In accordance with the tenets of postmodern/poststructuralist philosophy, the starting point is that there is no ultimate frame of reference, no ultimate truth, and no universal knowledge. As Scherer and Palazzo point out, postmodern thinking is non-foundational, which makes it a problematic source for the definition of the role of business in society (2007). This is, however, only a problem if your aim is to actually define this role in (authoritative) moral or democratic terms. Parallel to this, some writers on public opinion (see Splichal 1999) find the turn to a postmodern understanding too radical because it provides little leeway for making normative statements and convincing appeals to the democratic ideals inherent in the concept.

Importantly, the proposed understanding of public opinion as a robust fiction does not lead to a strategy for debunking the concept. As a conclusion this would be quite uninteresting, inconsequential and politically impotent. Rather it provides a point of departure for exploring how and by which rhetorical and symbolic means public opinion come to play a (real) role in the CSR discourse. In other words, it provides a *performative* view of public opinion.

Conceptually, public opinion has so far been neglected in CSR. While references to public interests and opinions are legion in this literature, no more thorough treatment of the concept as such is found (Vallentin 2009). To find conceptual developments and theoretical reflection we have to look for disciplines such as political philosophy, political science, mass communication and sociology (Glasser and Salmon 1995). The suggested analytical strategy makes it possible to show how theories and conceptions of public opinion are (implicitly) mobilized and come into play in the CSR discourse. Thus, the chapter will show how insights from the public opinion literature can be used to inform and broaden the language we use to make sense of CSR. Now, let us turn first to the question of how public opinion is performed in the (neo-)liberal opposition to CSR.

4. PUBLIC OPINION AS ENEMY OF REASON

The antithesis of public opinion in regard to CSR is spelled out very clearly in the classical statements against CSR made by prominent liberal economists. Milton Friedman famously begins his short chapter on social responsibility in *Capitalism and Freedom* (1962) by stating: '*The view has been gaining widespread acceptance* that corporate officials and labor leaders have a "social responsibility" that goes beyond serving the interests of their stockholders' (p. 133, emphasis added). To Friedman, of course, CSR is a subversive and fundamentally misguided doctrine. It is also self-defeating. The call for corporate managers to be more public-minded and concerned with societal matters beyond the purely economic does not lead to more responsible business but, in the long run, to a dangerous concentration of power in the hands of these very corporate managers. A development that must, ultimately, be circumvented by government. In other words, social responsibility is a recipe for more intrusive government – giving less sway to market forces and undermining the model of free enterprise. To Friedman, business is a private, not a public matter. The problem with public opinion is that it tends to disagree.

In 'The social responsibility of business is to increase its profits' (1970), Friedman speaks of '*the present climate of opinion* with its *widespread aversion* to "capitalism", "profits", the "soulless" corporation and so on', and of '*the already too prevalent view* that the pursuit of profits is wicked and immoral and must be curbed and controlled by external forces' (p. 159, emphasis added). To Friedman, CSR is nothing more than hypocritical window-dressing, but he cannot summon much indignation to denounce those corporate managers that respond to the call for more social responsibility as 'our institutions and *the attitudes of the public* make it in their self-interest to cloak their actions in this way' (ibid., emphasis added).

Friedrich A. von Hayek (1960) similarly speaks of '*the fashionable doctrine* that [corporate] policy should be guided by "social considerations"' (p. 225). He finds that '[i]t is perhaps only natural that management should desire to pursue values which they think are important and that they need little encouragement from *public opinion* to indulge in these "idealistic" aims' (p. 226, emphasis added). To Hayek (as well as Friedman), the fundamental problem with CSR is that it leads to the acquisition of arbitrary and potentially dangerous powers by private companies. He finds that the old-fashioned conception, which regards corporate managers as trustees of corporate shareholders, is the most important safeguard against this development. Nevertheless, '*public opinion*, and the traditions growing inside the corporations, have tended in the opposite direction' and have been 'directed toward making corporations act more deliberately in "*the public interest*"'. He continues: 'These demands appear to me to be radically mistaken and their satisfaction more likely to aggravate than to reduce the dangers against which they are directed' (ibid., emphasis added).

Even before Friedman made his first statement on CSR, Theodore Levitt (1958) made what is arguably the richest of the classical liberal statements against CSR. In 'The Dangers of social responsibility' he similarly picks up on the theme of fashion. According to Levitt, the business of business is to generate profits, but promoters of the corporation's profit-making function do not get invitations to speak at the big, prestigious business conferences 'where social responsibility echoes as *a new tyranny of fad and fancy*' (p. 42, emphasis added). Indeed, '[i]t is not fashionable for the corporation to take gleeful pride in making money. What *is* fashionable is for the corporation to show that it is a great innovator; more specifically, a great public benefactor; and, very particularly, that it exists to "serve the public"' (ibid.). In some respects, the talk about social responsibility is merely talk. But it is also more than that. What people say they can come to believe, and CSR is moving into the believing stage. It is becoming a design for change, and this constitutes a danger. Levitt pulls no punches: if the corporation becomes preoccupied with its social burden and invests itself with all-embracing duties, obligations and powers, it can gradually be turned into a twentieth-century equivalent of the medieval Church – with the corporate bureaucrat emerging as a new Leviathan. The result can turn out to be a form of business statesmanship, a corporate ministry of man leading to 'a monolithic society in which the essentially narrow ethos of the business corporation is malignantly extended over everyone and everything' (p. 46). To avoid this slippery slope, we need to keep functions separate. Corporations should have as their only goal to produce sustained high-level profits. Indeed, '[w]elfare and society are not the corporation's business. Its business is making money, not sweet music' (p. 47).

As should be apparent, it is characteristic of liberal critiques of CSR that they present themselves as being in opposition to general public opinion, and that they see public opinion not as a voice of democratic reason but as a fundamentally misguided anti-capitalist force. Social responsibility represents an eclipse of economic and political reason and to the extent that it supports this doctrine: so does public opinion. The main thrust of the argument is not that CSR is bad for business in terms of profits, but that it is bad for democracy in terms of pluralism. Thus, the authors are operating in the realm of political economy and using political arguments. Of course, their statements should not be taken at face value. They must be considered in terms of their symbolic content. Public opinion becomes a way of framing arguments (Goffman 1974). It is a rhetorical tool rather than a necessarily accurate and well-substantiated reflection of facts. To argue that one is in opposition to the dominant trend is, in this particular case, a way of softening the impression of hard economic reasoning. It is also a way of performing a reversal of fortunes: when you read Friedman, Hayek and Levitt you get the impression that CSR has been the dominant business philosophy for decades and has put traditional economic reasoning about corporate affairs to shame. They seem to suggest that making money is generally, however wrongly, considered to be a shameful pursuit. To less partisan observers this can, at best, be considered as an alternative representation of reality.

It may come as no surprise that economists, usually strong believers in technical rationality and expertise, tend to paint a two-dimensional picture of public discourse as a source of noise and distortion that stands in the way of sound economic reasoning and obstructs the free reign of market forces. The implied theory of public opinion is a negative one that associates publicity not with rationality, but with conformity, fashion, tyranny. This leads us to the view of public opinion presented by Elisabeth Noelle-Neumann (1995), who, indeed, makes a basic distinction between (1) public opinion as rationality, and (2) public opinion as social control (I return to the former conception in the next section). Public opinion as social control is not concerned with the quality of arguments. 'The decisive factor is which of the two camps in a certain controversy is strong enough to threaten the opposing camp with isolation, rejection, and ostracism' (pp. 43–4). In her theory of 'the spiral of silence', Noelle-Neumann (1984) suggests that people are equipped with a 'quasi-statistical' organ that allows them to perceive with great subtlety the development and climate of opinions in their social environment. Focusing on the fear of isolation as a social psychological force, she argues that it is more important for people to avoid isolation than to express their own judgments and concerns in public. Particularly when it comes to controversial, socially contested issues, people tend to conform to the majority opinion among their significant others. Public opinion can then be defined as those opinions 'in the sphere of controversy that one *can* express in public without isolating oneself' (Noelle-Neumann 1979, p. 150). Public opinion represents not the voice of reason, not a rationally formed consensus but the voice of the majority or the voice of a loud minority being perceived as the majority via mass media and other means of communication. This view of public opinion is thus closely related to notions of 'the tyranny of the majority' (Tocqueville 1969) and 'the silent majority' (Bryce 1995). Public opinion becomes similar to the concept of fashion. It creates conformity by silencing opposition to dominant ideas; it establishes priorities and confers legitimacy (Noelle-Neumann 1979).

Social control can be considered as the model of choice for CSR skeptics. It considers public opinion as a negative, controlling, if not even tyrannical presence, that limits the freedom of business as well as

individuals. Public opinion becomes an expression of political correctness, and sensible business leaders, who must per definition be opposed
to CSR, are presented as victims of a hostile opinion climate. This kind of
framing does, however, also give CSR skeptics an opportunity to present
themselves in a favorable light: as courageous fighters for reason and the
common good amidst a sea of perhaps well-intended but nevertheless
misguided public nonsense. According to this view, 'the chance to change
or mold public opinion is reserved to those, who are not afraid of being
isolated' (ibid., p. 155). Levitt uses exactly this kind of reasoning when he
argues that altruism, self-denial, charity and similar values, although vital
in other walks of life, are virtues that are alien to competitive economics,
and '[i]f it sounds callous to hold such a view, and suicidal to publicize it,
that is only because business has done nothing to prepare the community
to agree with it' (1958, p. 49). It seems as if the courage among business
people to go against the dominant stream of opinion in order to change it,
was missing in the 1950s.

Apparently, little has changed. Even if the classical liberal critiques of
CSR in many ways seem out of sync with current realities, the rhetoric
used by the liberal camp has, at least until recently, essentially remained
the same (although to some extent the historically specific theme of anti-
totalitarianism has been toned down). In the skeptical review of CSR
written by Clive Crook and published by *The Economist* in January 2005,
the promoters of CSR are still, however regrettably, declared as undis-
puted winners of the battle of ideas concerning CSR: 'According even
to middle-of-the-road *popular opinion*, capitalism is at best a regrettable
necessity, a useful monster that needs to be bound, drugged and muzzled
if it is not to go on the rampage' (p. 10, emphasis added). Crook even goes
as far as to claim that:

> [i]n public relations terms their victory is total. In fact, their opponents never
> turned up. Unopposed, the CSR movement has distilled a widespread suspicion
> of capitalism into a set of demands for action. As its champions would say,
> they have held companies to account, by embarrassing the ones that especially
> offend against the principles of CSR, and by *mobilising public sentiment* and
> an almost universally sympathetic press against them. Intellectually, at least,
> the corporate world has surrendered and gone over to the other side. (p. 3,
> emphasis added)

The other side being, of course, the wrong side, that is, the anti-capitalist
side. Crook, like his predecessors, tends to polarize matters. Supposedly,
you cannot be pro CSR and not be fundamentally opposed to capitalism. It is either/or. Once again, the competition that the promoters of
CSR are winning is not about reason and what is right and wrong in a

moral sense. It is only about popularity. They have been able to capture the public agenda and silence the opposition (vis-à-vis the model of social control). Fortunately, it is a hollow victory, as corporate CSR is mostly for show. The intellectual surrender of the corporate world is indeed only that, as corporate CSR-policies 'smack of tokenism and political correctness' (p. 4). CSR is little more than a cosmetic treatment, at best a gloss on capitalism that many, justifiably, see as 'a sham, the same old tainted profit motive masquerading as altruism' (ibid.). Does this give cause for concern? On the whole the answer is no because there is no need for fundamental reform. 'Better that CSR be undertaken as a cosmetic exercise than as a serious surgery to fix what doesn't need fixing' (ibid.).

The nonsense of public opinion stands in stark contrast to a sound business rationale. The positive and productive aspects of public opinion are not totally disregarded, however. Crook concedes to the promoters of CSR, that '[c]apitalism does function on top of, and one way or another is moulded by, *prevailing popular opinion*' (p. 10, emphasis added). 'Companies do operate in *a climate of opinion*. To be successful and profitable, they must take account of *how they are perceived*' (ibid., emphasis added). Public pressure is seen as a positive force in the sense that without it there would be no economic incentive for companies to behave decently:

> If nobody is paying attention, why worry about dealing honestly with people, or honouring a contract? This pressure of *outsiders' perceptions* is an indispensable force. Without it, companies in a private-enterprise system would be nasty, brutish and very short-lived. (ibid., emphasis added)

Having said that, it is important that this pressure is, if not well-informed, then certainly not utterly misguided. It needs to embody some basic economic understanding. 'To improve capitalism, you first need to understand it. The thinking behind CSR does not meet that test' (p. 4). In other words, public opinion cannot entirely be disregarded as a counterproductive and irrational force, but the publicity surrounding CSR for the most part can.

Crook concedes defeat but only in the most superficial and passive-aggressive sense that involves belittlement and ridicule of the victors and of the concept of CSR as such. It is, as we have seen, a tried and tested strategy. But lately new winds have been blowing from the liberal camp. Friedman died in 2006, and almost symbolically this is also the year that saw the publication of an important *Harvard Business Review* article by Michael Porter and Mark Kramer entitled: 'Strategy and society – the link between competitive advantage and corporate social responsibility'. This article reads as a programmatic statement of *strategic CSR*, which is about realizing that social responsibility can be much more than a cost or a constraint. 'It can be a source of opportunity, innovation, and competitive advantage' (Porter and Kramer 2006, p. 82). In tune with this statement, many recent contributions to the CSR literature focus on how attentiveness to social responsibility issues can lead to the development of new products and services providing new solutions to social and environmental problems. Instead of social responsibility being about passive and/or accommodating corporate responses to outside forces, it becomes a creative act of seeing or envisioning new market opportunities with a responsible edge. Indeed, Porter and Kramer suggest that value creation should be *the* guiding principle behind corporate engagement in CSR: 'The essential test that should guide CSR is not whether a cause is worthy but whether it presents an opportunity to create shared value – that is, a meaningful benefit for society that is also valuable to the business' (2006, p. 84).

With strategic CSR, former CSR skeptics are moving from a defeatist mode of reasoning (however *faux* the announced defeat may seem to be) to a more confident and proactive mode aiming to set a new, more economically inclined public agenda in regard to CSR, i.e. to establish a new and more politically correct (and therefore more politically sustainable) economic truth about CSR: that it is only 'only good' to the extent that it creates economic value. We are thus witnessing a transition from a liberal to a neo-liberal mindset. Whereas classic liberalism has called for a clear separation of business and politics, neo-liberalism dissolves the distinction between economy and society as it subjects all human action to economic rationality – with 'the social' being encoded as a specific instance of 'the economy' (Lemke, 2001). As a result, moral concerns become embedded in the rationality of markets. Moral problems and issues are recoded and re-emerge as business opportunities (Shamir 2008). According to this view, CSR is not about adhering to public interests, it is about optimizing business interests in ways that are also beneficial for society. The turn to strategic CSR indicates a change of tune. To illustrate, the special report on CSR written by Daniel Franklin and published by *The Economist* in 2008 is certainly critical, but not totally skeptical towards CSR. It is acknowledged that 'CSR has arrived' and has seemingly come to stay, and that it is now a matter of 'not whether but how' companies should engage in it (Franklin 2008, p. 8). It is concluded that done badly, CSR 'is often just a figleaf and can be positively harmful. Done well, however, is it not some separate activity that companies do on the side, a corner of corporate life reserved for virtue: it is just good business' (ibid., p. 6). The liberal camp is not so much surrendering to CSR (in its various, politically correct and publicly supported incarnations) as it is aiming to appropriate it by means of economic reasoning.

5. PUBLIC OPINION AS A DEMOCRATIC FORCE

The pro-CSR camp, in contrast, sees public opinion as a democratic and rational force for good and as a possible source of enlightenment. Whereas liberal economists are concerned with conditions of private ownership, free markets and free enterprise, CSR promoters are concerned with, using again the formulation by Scherer and Palazzo (2007), embedding corporate decision making in processes of democratic will formation. As mentioned earlier, public opinion has conceptually been neglected in the CSR literature, which is to say that we do not find a fully developed theory or normative conception of public opinion in this literature. Looking for references to public opinion we find bits and pieces here and there rather than a coherent body of work. Nevertheless, modern contributions to the CSR literature can arguably, if only implicitly, be said to subscribe to 'the idea of public opinion as a democratic legitimation' (Mills 1956, p. 299). Public opinion, in the positive sense, very much embodies the message of democracy in CSR, i.e. the need to uphold the principle of popular sovereignty as a guiding light for business. The positive argument does, however, have at least one thing in common with its negative opponent. It presents itself as being in opposition to mighty powers – not public opinion but the economic and political powers that be.

In spite of the defeatist claims made by the liberal adversaries, we do not find the CSR camp already celebrating its victory. CSR may increasingly appear fashionable and politically correct, but even today it hardly constitutes the dominant way of thinking about business, whether in academia, in politics or in private companies. Hence, CSR promoters tend to present themselves as a concerned opposition fighting a constant battle against all sorts of short-sighted economizing, philosophies of profit maximization, and economic performance indicators as the predominant measures of success in business. They are facing some mighty adversaries – not only the liberal skepticism of Friedman and others, but also theoretical dogma and the political, legal and economic ways of the world, so to speak. Economic theories of the firm, for instance, leave little room for any kind of democratic intervention in corporate affairs. Similarly, societal institutions and legal frameworks most often favor the rights of owners/shareholders at the cost of other stakeholders. Parliamentary politics are often (even when we are talking about political parties not devoted to the cause of deregulation) more concerned with competitiveness and growth than with democratizing business. And business is usually more concerned with the kind of public opinion we can speak of in economic market terms (in the language of market analyses), than with public opinion as a more politically significant non-market force (Mahon et al. 2004). Not to mention modern investor capitalism, in many instances short-sighted and/or excessively risk-taking, which often seem to operate beyond democratic control and to be far removed from any self-imposed restrictions that we may associate with adherence to the public interest.

But what kind of democratic, rational and progressive force for good is public opinion, then, in regard to business? And how can we speak of it? Liberal skeptics conjure up images of public opinion as a mighty and powerful beast glorifying CSR, putting capitalism to shame, and silencing the opposition. However, the hopes of CSR promoters in this regard generally fail to match the intensity of the misgivings of the adversaries. CSR promoters usually prefer to speak of stakeholders and stakeholder relations, or of regulatory measures related to public policy instead of public opinion, and this has to do with the political limitations of the latter notion. Public opinion lacks the materiality needed to push CSR through. Although it is an important influencer and a vital legitimizing force in the corporate sphere, public opinion is, strictly speaking, not a regulatory force. It can influence but not determine corporate decisions. As Habermas would have it: 'public opinion reigns, but it does not govern' (1991, p. 239). A discursively generated public opinion is an empirical variable that can make a difference, but public influence is transformed into communicative power only if and when it passes through the filters of actual decision making processes (Habermas 1996).

Keeping these limitations in mind, CSR promoters still see public opinion as a form of social control (although, obviously, in a positive sense). Ideally, it is a democratic or moral force serving the common good by subjecting business to general societal interests, demands and expectations. A lot of the drama (suggested, particularly, by Levitt and Crook) is taken out of the equation, however. Considering its inability to govern and directly control business, public opinion is not an effective harbinger of radical reform, but, at best, a moderator or corrective of all-out capitalism and free market economics. It is not an alien force, but rather represents an affirmation of democratic ideals that can be considered fundamental to business.

This is the argument made by Joel Bakan in his critical exposé of *The Corporation* (Bakan 2004). Bakan shows how corporate concerns about public legitimacy go back almost as far as the institution of business itself. The business corporation was originally conceived as a public institution with the purpose of serving national interests and advancing the public good. It was, and is, a creation of the state, a product of public policy. However, as the corporation has grown in size and power, it has attained considerable autonomy, becoming a private concern, a self-interested, profit-driven institution, which is today the dominant economic force in society. The process of business becoming more powerful, influential, self-sustained has been accompanied by increasing awareness of and demands for corporate social responsibility with the corporation increasingly being regarded not just as a private contract relationship between corporate managers and owners/shareholders but in terms of a social contract with society. Berle and Means (1968) were among the first to argue that corporations and their managers, due to the magnitude of their powers, are obliged to serve the interests of society as a whole and not just the interests of their shareholders (Bakan 2004). The call for business to reaffirm its original purpose of serving the public interest has been made countless times since then – in the CSR literature and elsewhere.

Bowen (1953) argued that '(t]he duty of business in a democracy is . . . to follow the social obligations which are defined by *the whole community*' (quoted from Preston and Post 1975, p. 1, emphasis added). Frederick (1960) spoke of '*the public responsibilities* of private businessmen' and of corporate managers who 'should voluntarily act as *trustees of the public interest*' (1960, pp. 54, 56, emphasis added). His definition of corporate responsibility prescribes

> that businessmen should oversee the operation of an economic system that fulfils *the expectations of the public*. . . . in the final analysis [it] implies *a public posture* towards society's economic and human resources and a willingness to see that those resources are used for broad social ends and not simply for the narrowly circumscribed interests of private persons and firms. (ibid., p. 60, emphasis added)

Similarly, it has been suggested that business functions by public consent and that business belongs to the people (Carroll 1999).

The positive, democratic ideal of public opinion that is brought to bear in these examples from the classical CSR literature has its origin in political philosophy (Splichal 1999). It has long been part of political theory 'that the prince's fortress lies in the hearts of his people', that the prince must heed the opinion of his subordinates, and that his virtues must always reflect the people's expectations (Luhmann (referring to Machiavelli's *Discourses*) 1990, p. 203). In modern times, public opinion has arisen as the 'secret' sovereign and the invisible authority of political society. It can be considered as 'the culminating idea of the political system' (ibid., p. 204). Indeed, it 'plays the same role as tradition in earlier societies: to offer something to which one can adhere in a way that saves one from reproach' (ibid., p. 215).

Keeping in mind the assumptions on which the present analysis is based, i.e. that public opinion is an institutionalized fiction that serves as a critical as well as a manipulative force in public communication, it is obvious that these ways of talking about public opinion have a high symbolic content. Although they may be inspirational, such assertions are also open to various sorts of manipulative abuses (as when business leaders pay lip service to democratic ideals without actually delivering on their promises). They evoke images of the public of classic democracy:

> based upon the hope that truth and justice will somehow come out of society as a great apparatus of free discussion. The people are presented with problems. They discuss them. They decide on them. They formulate viewpoints. These viewpoints are organized, and they compete. One viewpoint 'wins out'. Then the people act out this view, or their representatives are instructed to act it out, and this they promptly do. (Mills 1956, pp. 299–300)

As Mills laconically points out, this description must be recognized as 'a set of images out of a fairytale' (ibid., p. 300). It is 'not a description of fact, but an assertion of an ideal, an assertion of a legitimation masquerading – as legitimations are now apt to do – as fact' (ibid.). It is, however, also a description that allows CSR promoters to present themselves in a favorable and, indeed, legitimate light, as fighters for democracy and the common good against the evils of modern corporate capitalism. CSR promoters often evoke the spirit of civil society and seem to speak on behalf of 'the people' and represent 'the public interest'. This is no less a symbolic act and no less a reflection of rhetorical framing and strategizing than the statements made on the other side. It can always be questioned with what right and mandate self-appointed representatives of the public interest take it upon themselves to, indeed, speak on behalf of the social whole.

One way to counter the one-dimensional and ideologically tainted view of public opinion presented by CSR skeptics is, to put it bluntly, to replace ideology with fairytales. Another way, I would suggest, is to provide a broader and multidimensional view of all the, far from univocal, ways in which public opinion actually influences corporate approaches to CSR – and the ways in which companies actually influence public opinion. As argued elsewhere (Vallentin 2009), the concept of public opinion has meaning above and beyond the principles associated with the classical (fairytale) model of democracy. It embodies a variety of insights as to how companies respond to outside pressures. As a reflection of corporate social responsiveness, public opinion can be considered both as a market force (as reflected in corporate uses of surveys and various sorts of market analyses), and as a mobilization of civil society interests ('opinions of publics') (as reflected in stakeholder management). Also, in the realm of issues management, it can be considered not only as a form of social control (vis-à-vis section 4), but also as a mode of strategic enactment (vis-à-vis the manipulative aspects of the concept). In other words, a richer vocabulary of public opinion that is attuned to all the ways in which it does its work – while emphasizing the symbolic, rhetorical, socially constructed nature of the concept – is less prone to ideological manipulation – and therefore may prove an efficient weapon against CSR skeptics intent on reducing it to simply being an enemy of reason.

Speaking of ideology and manipulation, let us end the discussion by taking it back to where it began. What about the fundamental problem suggested by liberal economists: that the public-minded way of thinking about business implied by CSR is ultimately self-defeating as it, if put into practice, will lead to a dangerous concentration of power in the hands of corporate managers? How can this argument be countered from the CSR camp? This idea can be considered both as a hypothesis and as an ideological premise. If it is the former, it has certainly not been unequivocally confirmed over the last decades. Business has increasingly taken upon itself to help solve or alleviate social and environmental problems. But does that mean that corporate managers have become more powerful, or does it reflect that corporate managers are increasingly under public pressure to behave decently? Certainly, it can be argued that in today's globalized economy we are in a situation not unlike the scenario envisioned by Friedman, Hayek and Levitt: private companies, particularly multinational giants, control enormous resources and are gaining power and influence compared to governments. Few would, however, argue that CSR is the cause of this concentration of power. CSR may not be the solution to the problem, but it is certainly not the main cause of it.

Therefore, it may be argued, the problem with CSR that liberal commentators point to is not the most pertinent one. Private companies are already extremely powerful. The most pressing question is not whether CSR will, in some respect, make them marginally more powerful, but whether or how CSR and the winds of change blowing around this concept can serve to give some of that power back to society, so to speak.

6. CONCLUSION

The aim of this chapter has been to elucidate the political arguments made in regard to public opinion in the CSR discourse, not to establish a particular understanding of public opinion as being somehow truer or more sustainable than others. The argument has thus been made for a political understanding of CSR to embody a critical mode of reflection. The ongoing politization of business can be considered both as a blessing and a curse, and in this regard public opinion can emerge both as friend and foe. Instead of political efforts in CSR being preoccupied merely with finding new answers to the same old normative questions, they can also see it as their task to be attentive to problems, conflicts, tensions, ambiguities, and (seemingly) irreconcilable differences in the CSR discourse, and to provide a vocabulary allowing for a richer understanding of the political forces at play in this discourse. To focus on public opinion is one way to go about this agenda.

The proposed critical mode of reflection is not just about debunking the opposition to CSR. It also suggests a need for self-reflective attentiveness towards the blind spots established by the ways of seeing that constitute the modern CSR discourse. The point that has been made about public opinion being a rhetorical tool and a way of framing arguments, applies equally on both sides of the debate – and therefore we have to be attentive to the strengths and weakness of arguments on both sides.

Liberal skeptics have tended to frame CSR and capitalism as a matter of either/or (although the notion of 'strategic CSR' suggests a break away from this dichotomy), but to argue for the democratic value of public opinion in regard to business is not (necessarily) to argue against capitalism as such. It is to argue against a particular brand of capitalism that is morally blind and immune to democratic impulses; a brand of capitalism that, in today's world, can be considered not only democratically and morally suspect, but also as very risky (as strongly indicated by the current financial crisis). The debate goes on.

REFERENCES

Bakan, J. (2004), *The Corporation: The Pathological Pursuit of Profit and Power*, London: Constable.

Berle, A.A. and G.C. Means ([1932] 1968), *The Modern Corporation and Private Property*, New York: Harcourt, Brace & World.

Bowen, H.R. (1953), *Social Responsibilities of the Businessman*, New York: Harper & Row.

Bryce, J. (1995), *The American Commonwealth*, Indianapolis, IN: Liberty Fund.

Carroll, A.B. (1999), 'Corporate social responsibility – evolution of a definitional construct', *Business and Society*, **38** (3), 268–95.

Crane, A., D. Matten and J. Moon (2004), 'Stakeholders as citizens? Rethinking rights, participation, and democracy', *Journal of Business Ethics*, **53** (1–2), 107–22.

Crook, C. (2005), 'The good company – a sceptical look at corporate social responsibility', *The Economist*, January, pp. 1–18.

Dodd, E.M. ([1932] 1998), 'For whom are corporate managers trustees?', in M.B.E. Clarkson (ed.), *The Corporation and its Stakeholders – Classic and Contemporary Readings*, Toronto, ON: Toronto University Press.

Dubbink, W. (2004), 'The fragile structure of free-market society', *Business Ethics Quarterly*, **14** (1), 23–46.

Ettema, J.S., D. Protess, D.R. Leff, P.V. Miller, J. Doppelt and F.L. Cook (1991), 'Agenda-setting as politics: a case study of the press-public-policy connection', *Communication*, **12** (2), 75–98.

Flyvbjerg, B. (1998), 'Habermas and Foucault: thinkers for civil society?', *British Journal of Sociology*, **49** (2), 210–33.

Foucault, M. ([1984] 1991), 'Politics and ethics: an interview', in P. Rabinow (eds), *The Foucault Reader – An Introduction to Foucault's Thought*, Harmondsworth: Penguin Books, pp. 373–380.

Franklin, D. (2008), 'Special report: CSR', *The Economist*, January.

Frederick, W.C. (1960), 'The growing concern over business responsibility', *California Management Review*, **2** (4), 54–61.

Friedman, M. (1962), *Capitalism and Freedom*, Chicago, IL: University of Chicago Press.

Friedman, M. (1970), 'The social responsibility of business is to increase its profits', in W.M. Hoffman, R.E. Frederick and M.S. Schwartz (eds) (2001), *Business Ethics – Readings and Cases in Corporate Morality*, New York: McGraw-Hill, pp. 156–160.

Friedman, M. (1975), *Open Mind*, interview segment, transcript downloaded from http://capitalismandfriedman.wordpress.com/2009/04/15/friedman-calls-himself-a-liberal.

Glasser, T.L. and C.T. Salmon (eds) (1995), *Public Opinion and the Communication of Consent*, New York: Guildford Press.

Goffman, E. (1974), *Frame Analysis – An Essay on the Organization of Experience*, Cambridge, MA: Harvard University Press.

Habermas, J. (1991), *The Structural Transformation of the Public Sphere – An Inquiry into a Category of Bourgeois Society*, Cambridge, MA: MIT Press.

Habermas, J. (1996), *Between Facts and Norms – Contributions to a Discourse Theory of Law and Democracy*, Cambridge, MA: MIT Press.

Hayek, F.A. (1960), 'The corporation in a democratic society: in whose interest ought it and will it be run?', in I. Ansoff (ed.) (1969), *Business Strategy*, Harmondsworth: Penguin Books, pp. 225–39.

Lemke, T. (2001), '"The birth of bio-politics": Michel Foucault's lecture at the Collège de France on neo-liberal governmentality', *Economy and Society*, **30** (2), 190–207.

Levitt, T. (1958), 'The dangers of social responsibility', *Harvard Business Review*, **36**, 41–50.

Luhmann, N. (1990), 'Societal complexity and public opinion', in N. Luhmann, *Political Theory in the Welfare State*, Berlin: Walter de Gruyter.

Mahon, J.F., P.P.M.A.R. Heugens and K. Lamertz (2004), 'Social networks and non-market strategy', *Journal of Public Affairs*, **4** (2), 170–89.

Margolis, J.D. and J.P. Walsh (2003), 'Misery loves companies – rethinking social initiatives by business', *Administrative Science Quarterly*, **48** (2), 268–305.

Matten, D. and A. Crane (2005), 'Corporate citizenship: toward an extended theoretical conceptualization', *Academy of Management Review*, **30** (1), 166–79.

Matten, D. and J. Moon (2008), '"Implicit" and "explicit" CSR: a conceptual framework for a comparative understanding of corporate social responsibility', *Academy of Management Review*, **33** (4): 404–24.

Mills, C.W. (1956), *The Power Elite*, New York: Oxford University Press.

Noelle-Neumann, E. (1979), 'Public opinion and the classical tradition: a re-evaluation', *Public Opinion Quarterly*, **43** (2), 143–56.

Noelle-Neumann, E. (1984), *The Spiral of Silence – Our Social Skin*, Chicago, IL: University of Chicago Press.

Noelle-Neumann, E. (1995), 'Public opinion and rationality', in T.L. Glasser and C.T. Salmon (eds), *Public Opinion and the Communication of Consent*, New York: Guildford Press, pp. 33–54.

Oberman, W.D. (1996), 'Preston, Post and the principle of public responsibility', *Business and Society*, **35** (4), 465–78.

Peters, J.D. (1995), 'Historical tensions in the concept of public opinion', in T.L. Glasser and C.T. Salmon (eds), *Public Opinion and the Communication of Consent*, New York: Guildford Press, pp. 3–32.

Porter, M.E. and M.R. Kramer (2006), 'Strategy and society – the link between competitive advantage and corporate social responsibility', *Harvard Business Review*, **84** (12), 78–92.

Preston, L.E. and J.E. Post (1975), *Private Management and Public Policy – The Principle of Public Responsibility*, Englewood Cliffs, NJ: Prentice Hall.

Rorty, R. (1991), 'The priority of democracy to philosophy', in R. Rorty (ed.), *Objectivism, Relativism, and Truth: Philosophical Paper, Vol. 1*, Cambridge: Cambridge University Press, pp. 175–96.

Scherer, A.G. and G. Pallazzo (2007), 'Towards a political conception of corporate responsibility: business and society seen from a Habermasian perspective', *Academy of Management Review*, **32** (4), 1096–120.

Shamir, R. (2008), The age of responsibilization: on market-embedded morality', *Economy and Society*, **37** (1), 1–19.

Splichal, S. (1999), *Public Opinion – Developments and Controversies in the Twentieth Century*, Lanham, MD: Rowman & Littlefield Publishers.

Tocqueville, A.D. (1969), *Democracy in America*, New York: Doubleday.

Vallentin, S. (2009), 'Private management and public opinion – corporate social responsiveness revisited', *Business & Society*, **48** (1), 60–87.

Walsh, J.P. (2005), 'Book review essay: taking stock of stakeholder management', *Academy of Management Review*, **30**, 426–52.

6. Business ethics and the question of objectivity: the concept of moral progress in a dialectical framework

Samuel Mansell

1. INTRODUCTION

The purpose of this chapter is to explore the possibilities and limits of moral argument in informing the development of corporate legislation. Through a philosophical consideration of what is implied in the concept of a moral argument, a dialectical framework is outlined in which a moral basis for regulation can be conceived. This framework is built upon the idea that moral progress, as it applies to corporate regulation and more generally, is dependent upon the interaction of two contrary forces. These can be called 'continuity' and 'progression' (see, for example, Coleridge [1830] 1972). The latter refers to the distillation of moral argument that arises in a discursive space upon the need to solve a particular moral problem in the present, and the former refers to what may be called the historical sediment of moral convention, out of which a culturally specific value system has grown. Though these two forces may at times pull in contrary directions, the morally informed development of corporate legislation can be seen as dependent upon the mutual interaction of both.

With the proliferation of ethical concerns over the social conduct of business, arising from such issues as the accounting scandals of Enron, WorldCom, Parmalat, and Ahold, the exploitation of sweatshop labor by multinational corporations, the problem of environmental protection in an era of global capitalism, etc., many critics have urged that a tougher regulatory environment is required for the moral reform of business (see for example Mitchell and Sikka 2005 and Jones et al. 2005, p.132). If regulation requires a moral validity upon which its legitimacy depends, then one can ask what sort of justification is possible in establishing this validity and what limits there might be to its implementation. This chapter suggests the form that a possible answer might take.

First a range of recent criticisms of the idea of 'objectivity' in business ethics is engaged with. I consider what may be problematic in the way these concerns are stated, and an alternative view is presented of what 'objectivity' could mean in the moral critique of organization. This view is consistent with one important intention behind these various critiques, that of enabling a plurality of divergent arguments to be heard and upholding the value of free speech, while differing crucially in how 'objectivity' is understood as a concept.

Part of the argument is that if the possibility of obtaining 'objective' truth is inherent in any (rational) argument surrounding a disputed item of knowledge (whether concerned with ethics or not), and yet the knowledge a subject possesses of any object is generally assumed to be fallible (i.e. never beyond the possibility of error), then implications arise for how a discursive space can be conceived for the pursuit of knowledge. I will look particularly at the arguments for free speech and toleration proposed by liberal thinkers John Milton ([1644] 1886) and John Stuart Mill ([1859] 1991). However, it is fruitful also to explore what limitations there might be to the institutionalization of a moral position that might be agreed within the kind of discursive space advocated by these writers. To this end, I consider the 'procedural conservatism' of Edmund Burke ([1790] 1968), who emphasizes how inherited views of the good are embedded at a cultural and psychological level, which limits the effectiveness of any radical alternative to how a given society is organized.

It is within this dialectical framework of *continuity* and *progression*, the former being concerned with the embedded nature of moral convention (or tradition) and the latter with the development of morally informed legislation in an environment of free speech and thought, that a response can be envisaged to concerns about ethics and business. First, however, I turn to criticisms that have been made of the very possibility of 'objectivity' in the field of business ethics.

2.   SKEPTICISM CONCERNING THE 'OBJECTIVITY' OF ETHICAL KNOWLEDGE

To inquire into the possibilities of building a moral argument upon which the validity of legislation can stand, one might first consider the ontological status of ethical claims. Whilst there has been no shortage of debate on this issue amongst ethical philosophers of the past few decades, a useful distinction can be drawn between cognitivist and non-cognitivist understandings of ethical language (see Singer 1990; Darwall 1998; Rachels 1998 for useful overviews). The former holds that when ethical language is used an objective property of the world is being described, in the light of which the utterance made can be either true or false. Darwall gives the following account:

> The thesis that ethical convictions admit of truth and falsity in this way is called cognitivism. Cognitivists believe that claims made with ethical language, and the states of mind we call ethical convictions or beliefs, have propositional or cognitive content, that these concerns admit of literal truth or falsity, and that ethical claims or convictions are correct or incorrect if, and only if, the propositions they assert are true or false, respectively. (Darwall 1998, p. 71)

On the other hand, a non-cognitivist approach denies that ethical language actually refers to anything that could be true or false, and is instead the statement of a subjective preference, or merely the expression of an attitude or desire. This is the position taken by those writing in the tradition of logical positivism, such as Russell (1935) and Stevenson (1963). According to Darwall (1998, p. 71), non-cognitvism holds that 'no ethical facts exist of the sort that could make ethical claims true, but it denies that any ethical claims are strictly false either. Ethical claims are not "apt" for truth or falsity. They assert nothing propositional'.

For a non-cognitivist, moral argument consists entirely in persuading others to adopt a certain preference or attitude, while the cognitivist proceeds on the basis that one might arrange their reasoning and evidence so as to demonstrate the 'truth' of their ethical view. It is important to note that this distinction does not concern whether 'objective truth' about ethics can actually be acquired, but only whether this possibility is assumed in the ordinary language people use when expressing their moral convictions.

In the context of these considerations, it is worth examining some of the skeptical epistemological positions that have been advanced recently by various scholars in the field of business ethics. Willmott (1998, p. 77) states emphatically that '"good" and "evil" do not inhere within particular actions. Rather, certain actions are deemed to be morally defensible or repugnant within particular culturally and historically contingent discourses on ethics.' It is not clear whether this is consistent with the cognitivist or non-cognitivist position, as Willmott (1998) does not clarify whether ethical language admits of truth and falsity. His position would nonetheless have the implication for a cognitivist that all ethical claims are false, as according to him there are no objective ethical facts to be known. This skepticism regarding the possibility of ethical 'facts', is shared by Jones et al. (2005, p. 173) who ask 'what fixed points might we find on the human scale? The answer so far seems to be none. The very multiplicity of ideas about human nature, progress, utopia, beauty and so on . . . tells us something rather significant about the impossibility of certain human knowledge.' This leads them to suggest: 'Ethics no longer becomes the articulation of a good that is self-evident from a first or universal principle . . .' (2005, p. 174). Again, this is not to deny that ethical language can be propositional, but only that ethical 'knowledge' cannot be found in any objective fact that is independent of the subjective conditions of experience.

Brewis reaches a similar conclusion in elucidating a Foucauldian argument for a feminist business ethics. She writes: 'He [Foucault] has no notion of a better society in terms of the ways in which we live and relate to each other. Foucault's (1991, p. 79) notion of knowledge being contingent in its entirety means that we have no firm ethical grounds for judging particular practices' (Brewis 1998, p. 64).

This resonates with Parker's 'absolute insistence on the contingency of all identity thinking, including that which identifies itself as "for" or "against" Business Ethics' (2003, p. 209). Furthermore, Freeman and Philips (1999, p. 129) outline a 'pragmatic' and 'postmodern' business ethics: 'there is no Truth to be known. There are no 'foundations' to be found. Rather, Truth is the compliment we pay to ideas upon which there is relatively more agreement among intelligent creatures.' What these authors share with Jeanes and Muhr (this volume) as well as Rozuel (this volume) is a strong aversion to any presumption of there being a fixed, objective set of moral facts that could be discovered and used in moral argument.

However, when the implications of this are considered for the formation of ethical reasons that might be used to justify new legislation for business, difficulties arise. Given this 'non-objective' outlook, it is entirely unclear what status would be given to the role of argument and counter-argument in establishing a consensus on a particular issue. Few people, for example, would desire statutory legislation for business to be passed on the basis of nothing more than a single person's subjective attitude. Yet if there is no solid ground beyond one's own (culturally and historically conditioned) subjectivity, then what merit would there be in taking a plurality of perspectives into account? It seems that if there are no 'facts' to be acquired through moral argument, then the existence of a discursive space wherein competing views of the good can be articulated would seemingly lack support. If I happen to say that I prefer apples to pears, and a friend says s/he prefers pears to apples, it does not follow that we need a discursive space in which to articulate our rival views on the taste of fruit. So what is the difference with ethics? Is ethics nothing more than a question of preference? Or might there be objective reasons for why we ought to act in a certain way, independent of our subjective inclination?

If we return again to the critics of objectivism, a strong normative stance can often be found which appears to be at odds with any supposedly contingent view of the good. Often it can be seen that the moral values of toleration and pluralism, in the sense that multiple ways of living and knowing *ought* to be allowed, stand as an implicit justification for their non-objective epistemology. This can be seen in the following examples. Alvesson and Willmott (2003, p.17) write of 'counteracting discursive closure' and that problems of objectivism 'freeze the social order'. They go on to argue that 'when informed by poststructuralism, studies of management strive to open up representations in a way that has unsettling and potentially emancipatory consequences' (2003, p. 19). Here the moral view that a frozen social order is bad and 'emancipatory consequences' are good seems to be used as part of the justification for their non-objective epistemology. In similar fashion Parker (2003, p. 207) argues for the contingency of all ethical claims: 'To take a position, a stance, on a particular matter is immediately to concede the ground to a rapacious form of philosophy which seeks to close things down'. The normative position that this *ought* not to happen becomes intertwined with his claim for the contingency of ethics.

Willmott (1998) makes this trend explicit, writing that poststructuralist thinking contributes to an ethics with a '*non-specific normative purpose* as it unsettles our comfortable sense of there being authoritative descriptions of ethics' (1998 p. 79, emphasis in original). He goes on to state that 'Poststructuralist analysis is . . . perhaps best characterized as involving *a commitment to a mood of restlessness*' (1998, p. 90, emphasis in original). For Willmott (1998), the normative and epistemological appear as inseparable. This is again evident in Parker (1998, p. 294), who tells us: 'I want the madness to remain, to acknowledge the impossibility of ethics if I am to live my life well' and furthermore: 'It would be better to embrace the paradox – that being ethical requires giving up on ethics and doing justice requires giving up on the search for the law' (1998, p. 295). The impossibility of ethical knowledge, which by itself is a strictly epistemological position, is here justified by what is required by ethics, what is required by justice, and what is required for Parker to live his life well. The epistemological is again intertwined with the normative.

As a final example, Freeman and Philips (1999, p. 136) say that 'the role of the Business Ethics scholar is neither to prescribe nor describe business, but one of putting together narratives which describe the best and the worst of business as we know it'. How can the business ethics scholar avoid being prescriptive if s/he is to distinguish the 'best' from the 'worst' of business? The difficulty with the position taken by all these theorists, is that if their normative view of how business and society ought to be (e.g. that society *ought* to tolerate a multiplicity of ethical perspectives) becomes part of their argument for the epistemological contingency of ethical knowledge, then clearly a normative ground is being assumed that is independent of this contingency. As the philosopher and poet S.T. Coleridge put it:

> If there be nothing infallible in nature, if honour, if honesty, if to do to others as you would be done by, are not infallible, what becomes of your own modesty, of your own tolerance? Nothing remains for you to tolerate, there remains no distinction, no criterion upon earth. (Coleridge [1819] 1949, p. 172)

The complete contingency of all moral positions, and the denial that there exists any such thing as a moral 'fact', becomes in practice difficult to sustain. One cannot from this position advocate toleration, multiplicity, pluralism, difference, or even human rights, as overriding moral values; nor can one promote a toleration of different perspectives because this will lead to a more 'complete' view of the good. However, as can be seen, a support for toleration and pluralism and an aversion to rationalization and closure are central ideas for many of these authors. As Parker (1998, p. 289) writes, 'The means–end rationalization that ends in the practice now known as business ethics . . . seems to be destroying the very possibility of ethics itself'. Willmott (1998, p. 93) asserts that the contribution of post-structuralism 'dwells in *the subversion of closure*' (emphasis in original) and Jones et al. (2005, p. 139) state emphatically that 'ethics is about justice and about goodness and both are *always* debatable and contestable' (emphasis in original).

However without any ethical 'facts' that can be known, one might wonder what basis remains for arguing that ethics is 'contestable' or that we ought to 'subvert closure'. If one takes the non-cognitivist view that ethics is just a subjective attitude, or a cognitivist view that all propositional ethical claims are false because there are no ethical 'facts' to be known, it becomes difficult to see why ethics should be debated and contested. What is it that we are trying to discover in a debate about ethics? What is it we are trying to show when we contest the ethical standpoint of another person? Of course, one might equally posit that if there is an objective ethical 'Truth' that we can discover once and for all, then there would be no reason to debate and contest it once it has been found. To assume that we can possess objective ethical knowledge might be said to lead to the very rationalization and closure of debate, which is feared by the authors quoted above. So, if there ought to be a discursive space within which ethics can be contested, then what epistemological assumption is consistent with this? This question shall now be explored.

3. COGNITIVISM AND THE ASSUMPTION OF FALLIBILITY

If the experience of ethical conviction is considered phenomenologically, then considerations arise which suggest that ethical language generally has a propositional use. If we hear on the news that a group of children has been kidnapped and are being tortured so as to extract money from their parents, we would probably feel moral outrage. Imagine we now hear someone being interviewed who is trying to justify the torture of the children because of the overall goal of the kidnappers. If after hearing and considering all the justifications, we still feel the same moral outrage as before, would we feel that compared to the interviewee we had merely a difference in attitude, or that as Darwall (1998, p.18) puts it, '[our] respective convictions appear to vie for a space that, logically, no more than one can occupy'? Would we not feel the conviction of the interviewee to be not merely different from ours, but also *incorrect*? As Darwall argues:

> It is not unusual to hear people say, in one moment, that ethics is no more than opinion, taste, or preference and then vehemently express, in the next moment, some strong ethical view. In the latter instance, it certainly *looks* as if they are committed to the correctness of their view. Surely it looks that way to their interlocutors. (Darwall 1998, p. 19)

It therefore seems that ethical convictions differ from the mere tastes or attitudes that people have. There does appear to be a role for argument and counter-argument, which suggests that ethical language carries a propositional weight, which goes beyond what is entailed in stating an attitude or preference. R.M. Hare (1963, p. 53) outlines what he sees as 'three necessary ingredients' of moral argument, which allow us to reject alternative propositions. These are (1) facts; (2) logic; and (3) inclination. With regard to the second of these, he writes:

> When we are trying, in a concrete case, to decide what we ought to do, what we are looking for . . . is an action to which we can commit ourselves (prescriptivity) but which we are at the same time prepared to accept as exemplifying a principle of action to be prescribed for others in like circumstances (universalizability). If, when we consider some proposed action, we find that, when universalized, it yields prescriptions which we cannot accept, we reject this action as a solution to our moral problem – if we cannot universalize the prescription, it cannot become an 'ought'. (Hare 1963, p. 51)

What Hare has identified here is that there are mechanisms of reasoning which people ordinarily use to test the validity of their moral arguments. This lends weight to the notion that people aspire to *correctness* in their judgments, and feel that others who differ from them can be 'wrong'. It may be objected that even if we can trace a certain objectivism in the way people express their convictions, it by no means follows that there really exist objective ethical facts that can be known and which categorically bind us to a certain course of action. Mackie (1977, p. 79), for example, suggests that this can be explained by 'patterns of objectification' where people internalize socially conditioned demands and desires, which come to represent categorical imperatives in the imagination, whereas in fact they are only hypothetical.

This view may be correct. Even if we assume a cognitivist understanding of ethical conviction, which seems to have been suggested from what has gone before, it does not follow that people actually do grasp subject-independent facts when they express their moral convictions. However on this point, Thomas Nagel ([1980] 1998) provides an important intervention, which is worth quoting at length. He argues that this skepticism regarding the possibility of objective facts, or what Jones et al. (2005) call 'fixed points' on the human scale, is due to an inappropriate allocation of the burden of proof – where unless something can be *demonstrated* its existence is called into doubt. He writes:

> No demonstration is necessary in order to allow us to *consider* the possibility of agent-neutral reasons: the possibility simply *occurs* to us once we take up an objective stance. And there is no mystery about how an individual could have a reason to want something independently of its relation to his particular interests or point of view, because beings like ourselves are not *limited* to the particular point of view that goes with their personal position inside the world. They are also . . . *objective selves*: they cannot *help* forming an objective conception of the world with themselves in it; they cannot help trying to arrive at judgements of *value* from that standpoint. (Nagel [1980] 1998, pp. 120–21; emphases in original)

It follows that despite the difficulty of *proving* the existence of objective ethical values, the propensity to consider ethics from an *objective standpoint* is such that a denial of the existence of ethical facts would run counter to the way that people actually experience ethics. There is of course a great deal more which could and has been said on the question of ethical objectivity. The intention here has merely been to suggest that a cognitivist understanding of ethics, which is to say that ethical language carries with it an aspiration to objective truth, is consistent with how people experience ethics. Therefore, the denial of any facts to be known in ethics, which is the common thrust of the various critiques of objectivity in business ethics, seems to undermine an indispensable part of ethics: namely, how people experience it, which seems to include an aspiration to correctness of judgment from a standpoint which is independent of one's class, race, culture, etc.

A belief in the possibility of ethical truths can therefore be a starting point for framing a discursive space in which debates about corporate legislation might occur. However, there is still the objection that if there are fixed ethical truths, which can in theory be discovered once and for all, then why is a discursive space needed in which a plurality of views can be articulated? Why listen to other voices once the Truth has been found? This may be why Alvesson and Willmott (2003, p. 17) relate objectivism to 'taken-for-granted assumptions and ideologies that freeze the contemporary social order'.

However, the idea that 'objectivity' necessarily has anything to do with closing down debate might be a mistaken assumption. This objection would be convincing if one took 'objectivity' to entail omniscience and hence *infallibility*. However the role of logical argument in establishing the validity of an ethical opinion, which was considered above, would suggest that the sense in which the word 'objectivity' might be used certainly does not entail infallibility (that is, that we cannot be in error). That we are prone to error is suggested by the fact that we seek evidence and reasoning to support our views – if we were infallible there would be no need for this. As suggested earlier, we may in practice inevitably assume a lack of fallibility with regard to some ethical positions, as could be seen in the explicit normative intent behind much of the 'post-structural' insistence on contingency noted above. Nevertheless, to the extent that moral argument is felt to require a basis in logic and evidence, it is sensible to assume that this also entails a person's fallibility with regard to truth.

4. THE FALLIBILITY OF ETHICAL KNOWLEDGE ENTAILS A DISCURSIVE SPACE FOR PLURALIST DEBATE

If the possibility of obtaining ethical knowledge is admitted as a sensible presumption, then it follows as an implication that one can speak of the 'moral progress' of a society, culture, individual, or nation, etc. If there is no moral yardstick or reference point that is independent of our subjective conditions of experience, then literally there could be no standard to which progress can be made, or by which progress could be measured (see Frederick 1999). By admitting an independent ethical standard, it becomes possible to speak of progress (for example, through the passing of corporate regulation) toward a more ethical state of affairs. If fallibility with respect to ethical truth is also admitted, it follows that in the disposition to do good we are inclined to seek out all the relevant factors that might alter our viewpoint – given sufficient time to acquire this information and deliberate upon it (see Aristotle 1980, pp. 125–6). It would seem unwise to act in accordance with what one deems to be right, whilst knowingly failing to consult evidence that might lead to a different perspective.

If we consider a concept of moral progress where the limits of moral argument can be outlined for a reform in corporate legislation, it might be asked what role should be given to a discursive space of public debate and enquiry, following what has been said above. Merely because someone is fallible with regard to the truth, it doesn't necessarily follow that a plurality of different perspectives should be listened to in reaching an ethical judgment. For example, if I try to compute in my head the answer to 56 squared, it is highly likely that I shall arrive at the wrong figure. With respect to the answer of 56 squared, I can consider myself fallible. However, if I really want to arrive at the answer, I should either get a calculator or work harder to figure it out mentally. It is not strictly necessary that I should consult a multiplicity of perspectives on what the answer might be. So is it likewise with moral judgments? If a legislative response is made to the ethical controversies surrounding business, should a single entrusted legislator simply sit down and work out, on the basis of all available evidence, what the 'objectively correct' legislation should be?

For John Stuart Mill ([1840] 1980, [1859] 1991), truth in ethical questions is not of the same order as in mathematics or science, where a fully correct answer can be discovered by a single person. Mill argues that 'truth' in ethics must be looked for in a plurality of competing perspectives, where moral progress can occur only through the collision of divergent views. This seems to rest on the assumption that it is impossible or highly unlikely that all the factors relevant in an ethical judgment could be possessed by one person at any one time. He writes: 'All students of man and society . . . are aware that the besetting danger is not so much of embracing falsehood for truth, as of mistaking part of the truth for the whole' ([1840] 1980, p. 105). According to Mill, a partial truth might be contained in even those doctrines that appear obviously false overall. In his famous essay 'On liberty' ([1859] 1991) he argues that there is a common case in which 'the conflicting doctrines, instead of being one true and the other false, share the truth between them; and the nonconforming opinion is needed to supply the remainder of the truth, of which the received doctrine embodies only a part' ([1859] 1991, p. 52).

If it is assumed that human beings are not merely fallible (i.e. prone to error) in their pursuit of truth, but in non-scientific subjects one must harness a plurality of viewpoints, it would seem that a discursive space is necessary in which as great a range of arguments as possible might be heard. This basic requirement can be seen as vital in the pursuit of a morally informed legislative response to the ethical crises of the contemporary corporate world, or to any other matter of moral concern for which regulatory intervention is considered necessary. 'Truth' and the notion of 'moral progress' can then be seen to arise in a dialectical fashion, through the collision of contrary yet complementary positions. The seventeenth century poet and political writer John Milton argues in a similar spirit in his 1644 essay 'Areopagitica: a defence of the liberty of unlicensed printing'. He writes: 'all opinions, yea, errors, known, read, and collated, are of main service and assistance toward the speediest attainment of what is truest' ([1644] 1886, p. 30); and this rests in part on the fact that 'we bring not innocence into the world, we bring impurity much rather: that which purifies us is trial, and trial is by what is contrary' ([1644] 1886, p. 32).

If the suggestion here is that truth is best attained through a collision of contrary opinions, no matter which opinion is preconceived as right, then further support is added by Mill ([1859] 1991, p. 41), who writes 'on every subject on which difference of opinion is possible, the truth depends on a balance to be struck between two sets of conflicting reasons'. Mill is keen to emphasize how the suppression of dissenting opinions is injurious not merely to the dissenters but to those whose view is held in the majority. This is because the rational assurance held by a person that their view is as free as possible from error, is altogether lost if no views to the contrary are permitted. He declares:

> the peculiar evil of silencing the expression of an opinion is, that it is robbing the human race; posterity as well as the existing generation; those who dissent from the opinion, still more than those who hold it. If the opinion be right, they are deprived of the opportunity of exchanging error for truth: if wrong, they lose, what is almost as great a benefit, the clearer perception and livelier impression of truth, produced by its collision with error. (Mill [1859] 1991, p. 21)

This is essentially an argument for free speech and thought, and the toleration of opinions that differ from those of the status quo. In short, it is an epistemological justification for hearing all sides of an argument. Milton ([1644] 1886, pp. 32–3) sees the attainment of virtue as being dependent on the survey of vice, and the scanning of error necessary for the confirmation of truth. Therefore, he asks: 'how can we more safely and with less danger scout into the regions of sin and falsity, than by reading all manner of tractates, and hearing all manner of reason?' (ibid.)

Contrary to the understanding that 'objectivity' of truth leads to discursive closure, where all debate would cease if a single Truth was believed, it can instead be said that truth has the right to be called *objective* only to the extent that it continues to fight off contesting opinions, on its own merit, through free and open discussion. Objectivity requires a spirit of pluralism with respect to truth. As noted earlier, this toleration of competing views on the basis of our own fallibility makes little sense if there is no subject-independent truth to be known in the first place. Mill articulates what seems a sensible position:

> There is the greatest difference between presuming an opinion to be true, because, with every opportunity for contesting it, it has not been refuted, and assuming its truth for the purpose of not permitting its refutation. Complete liberty of contradicting and disproving our opinion, is the very condition which justifies us in assuming its truth for purposes of action; and on no other terms can a being with human faculties have any rational assurance of being right. (Mill [1859] 1991, p. 24)

Mill goes on to argue that the confidence an individual may place in their own judgment where conflicting opinions are possible, can follow only from their efforts to acquaint themselves with the full range of available argument. He asks how it is that a person's judgment can be deserving of confidence: 'Because he has kept his own mind open to criticism of his opinions and conduct. Because it has been his practice to listen to all that could be said against him. . . . No wise man ever acquired his wisdom in any mode but this; nor is it in the nature of human intellect to become wise in any other manner' ([1859] 1991, p. 25). In accordance with this, Mill makes the poignant insight that one cannot really know the strength of an idea without knowing how to defend it against all the ideas that conflict with it. For this, one needs a thorough knowledge of the competing ideas:

> He who knows only his own side of the case, knows little of that. His reasons may be good, and no one may have been able to refute them. But if he is equally unable to refute the reasons on the other side; if he does not so much as know what they are, he has no ground for preferring either opinion. (Mill [1859] 1991, p. 42)

The progression of moral ideas over time might then be conceptualized as occurring within a discursive space, which allows for the free expression of thought and ideas. There is of course the important question of where to draw the line, of whether a particular view that is thought to possess dangerous consequences for society should still be allowed full expression, or should be curtailed on moral grounds more pressing than any right to free speech. I will return to this point later, yet for now it is sufficient to remark that the necessity for a maximized space in which the collision of contrary opinions can occur is implied by the pursuit of ethical truth and the assumption of fallibility. If this argument is valid then 'progress' in the domain of ethics might ideally proceed along these lines. As Milton poetically describes it:

> Well knows he who uses to consider, that our faith and knowledge thrives by exercise as well as our limbs and complexion. Truth is compared in Scripture to a steaming fountain; if her waters flow not in perpetual progression, they sicken into a muddy pool of conformity and tradition. A man may be a heretic in the truth; and if he believe things only because his pastor says so, or the assembly so determines, without knowing other reason, though his belief be true, yet the very truth he holds becomes his heresy. (Milton [1644] 1886, p. 57)

As regards the various calls for the moral reform of business through regulation, for example as articulated by Sikka (2002) and Mitchell and Sikka (2005), the implication is that all manner of disputing voices must be heard in the formation of a morally justified policy. Those who are responsible for legislation must try to base their arguments on as wide a pool of opinion as possible, listening to the arguments of shareholders, trade unions, members of affected communities, workers, managers, the press, government advisers, business school academics inter alia, etc. This is not to say that each of these groups should be entitled to a say in the final policy decision, but only that where they wish to make a relevant argument they should be given this chance wherever possible.

It can of course be added that in a climate of skepticism about the possibility of objective answers to ethical questions, the epistemological necessity to hear a diverse range of views collapses. As Thomas McCarthy (1994, p. 21) writes, 'context-transcendent claims to validity are permanently exposed to criticism from all sides' and serve the 'ongoing *critique* of dogmatism, error, and self-deception in all their forms' (ibid., emphasis added). The extent to which a viewpoint advances a truth that reaches beyond its own context is, logically, the extent to which it can be critiqued from outside that context. This notion of being 'open to criticism' is necessary in any assumption of fallibility, and without this it is difficult to see any argument for tolerant and pluralist debate.

However, to say that as wide a range of viewpoints should be heard 'as possible' is of course a rather imprecise statement. What determines the boundaries to what can and cannot be said? Should there be any boundaries at all? If, for example, a discussion takes place regarding the rights of people to glorify acts of terrorism, then as part of the 'tolerant and pluralist debate' should Muslim clerics be allowed to preach anything they choose to anybody who will hear, as part of this very debate? The question, of what moral limits there should be to the expression of thought and opinion, is an impossible one to answer here. However, I wish to suggest the outline of a consideration that may be relevant, and space permitting, to link this to questions of business regulation.

5.   THE POSSIBILITY OF MORAL PROGRESSION ENSURED THROUGH THE COUNTERWEIGHT OF MORAL CONTINUITY

The classical liberal argument for the limits of free expression is provided by J.S. Mill in *On Liberty* (1859), who argues that where harm is directly caused by the public actions of a person, then society is justified in restraining that person's liberty. He writes: 'Acts, of whatever kind, which, without justifiable cause, do harm to others, may be, and in the most important cases absolutely require to be, controlled . . . by the active interference of mankind' (Mill [1859] 1991, p. 62). However, Mill does not argue that this simple idea is an a priori moral truth that must apply equally to all civilizations of all ages. He states: 'Liberty, as a principle, has no application to any state of things anterior to the time when mankind have become capable of free and equal discussion' (1859, p. 15). The historical development of a civilization is therefore a factor that cannot be overlooked in judging the context in which a discursive space can operate for the free exchange of ideas. In short, a discursive space cannot exist in a historical vacuum.

It follows that the effectiveness of a discursive space in facilitating moral progress is dependent upon its historically inherited legitimacy as a source of legislative power. The extent to which an institution for public debate is considered a legitimate source of power by all those subject to its decisions, cannot have been produced *ex nihilo* out of the very debates taking place in it. The British House of Commons, for example, does not hold a right a priori to exercise its legislative and policy making powers without limit. Its legitimacy depends on its existence within a framework of moral conventions, which can be called a constitution (even if unwritten), and over the bounds of which it cannot step. It can be argued that no matter how correct, reasonable and justified a proposed policy may seem to all those who advocate it (who may indeed be a majority), the assumption of fallibility implies that there be limits to its powers.

What limitations might be implied by the assumption of moral fallibility? It can be argued that greater weight should be given to inherited values and laws which have undergone years of interrogation and critique, and have proved their usefulness to society, than the most finely calculated argument drawn from the diversity of perspectives to be heard on a present issue. It is instructive on this point to consider the position Mill attributes to S.T. Coleridge, whom he regarded as a 'Romantic conservative':

he considered the long or extensive prevalence of any opinion as a presumption that it was not altogether a fallacy; that, to its first authors at least, it was the result of a struggle to express in words something which had a reality to them, though perhaps not to many of those who have since received the doctrine by mere tradition. The long duration of a belief, he thought is at least proof of an adaptation in it to some portion or other of the human mind; and if, on digging down to the root, we do not find . . . some truth, we shall find some natural want or requirement of human nature which the doctrine in question is fitted to satisfy. (Mill [1840] 1980, p. 100)

If there is some merit in this position, we can assume there will always be a residue of tradition and moral convention surrounding any policy initiative or new regulation, and this residue will not easily lend itself to rational explanation or objective proof. This is not to suggest that moral decisions and the values they depend upon cannot be justified objectively, but that if we assume fallibility on our part then there are limits to what we can reasonably expect to achieve with moral argument. A significant weight might then be given to the moral values that are inherited by tradition, and a legislative power to the institutions that purportedly represent them. This might be a justification for the House of Lords in Britain as a counteracting power to the Commons (though whether the House of Lords represents such values is of course debatable).

It can be envisaged that given the fallibility of all attempts at moral *progress*, a counterweight, which can be called a force of *continuity,* is needed to complete the framework within which moral development can occur. Edmund Burke, in *Reflections on the Revolution in France* (1790) in which he launches his famous denunciation of the French Revolution, argues that if an importance be granted to the inheritance of moral rights, then certain institutions must also be inherited in parallel. If we expect to pass on our rights to free speech, freedom of association, freedom of religious expression, etc., to our descendants, then there is no assurance of this if the question of these rights is to be decided afresh with every change of government. This is what Burke has in mind when he declares: 'No experience has taught us, that in any other course or method than that of an *hereditary crown,* our liberties can be regularly perpetuated and preserved sacred as our *hereditary right*' (Burke [1790] 1968, p. 109; emphasis in original). Furthermore, he states 'from Magna Carta to the Declaration of Right, it has been the uniform policy of our constitution to claim and assert our liberties, as an *entailed inheritance* derived to us from our forefathers, and to be transmitted to our posterity . . .' (Burke [1790] 1968, p. 119; emphasis in original).

Burke explicitly derives this emphasis on the hereditary nature of liberty from the limitations of human reason and what he calls 'moral competence'

([1790] 1968, pp. 104–5). He writes 'to fortify the fallible and feeble contrivances of our reason, we have derived several other, and those no small benefits, from considering our liberties in the light of an inheritance' ([1790] 1968, p. 121). If a counterweight of inherited values can be considered as a limit to the possibilities of reform and public policy making, then the existence of a discursive space out of which moral progress arises depends on the existence of a dialectical framework. The thesis is a force of progression, the articulation of multiple competing viewpoints in a discursive space of public debate, the antithesis a force of continuity, the limitations set upon the power of progression by the inherited values, which are specific to a given culture. Burke gives an excellent account of the benefits arising from such a framework when describing how the constitutional balance of France stood before the Revolution of 1789:

> These opposed and conflicting interests . . . interpose a salutary check to all precipitate resolutions. They render deliberation a matter not of choice, but of necessity; they make all change a subject of *compromise*, which naturally begets moderation; they produce *temperaments*, preventing the sore evil of harsh, crude, unqualified reformations; and rendering all the headlong exertions of arbitrary power, in the few or in the many, for ever impracticable. Through that diversity of members of interests, general liberty had as many securities as there were separate views in the several orders. (Burke [1790] 1968, p. 122, emphasis in original)

Today in the UK, the frequent clashes of opinion (a notable example being the proposed legislation for detaining terror suspects without charge) between the House of Commons and House of Lords illustrate the necessity for compromise that Burke refers to. It could be conjectured that toleration for dissenting opinions is most seriously threatened by the imposition of a single ideology that has overwhelming popular support, where what is aimed at is a total upheaval of existing society – without the 'checks and balances' of a system aimed at producing compromise. The 'popular' revolutions that have occurred through history often seem to enjoy a substantial level of popular support – the sentiments behind the social upheaval of France in 1789, China in 1949, Russia in 1917, and even Germany in 1933, were not confined to a small minority. The point is that where a sweeping change of values and institutions is desired by a great number of the people, in any public debate – however open – the revolutionary mindset may well be the dominant one. However, what concerns writers such as Burke ([1790] 1968), is that the will of the popular majority at any one moment is not 'morally competent' to affect drastic changes to the institutions around which a society is organized.

Earlier I looked at how various critics of business ethics are concerned by how a single ideology can 'rapaciously' close down debate, and 'freeze' the social order. History gives us many examples of this being achieved through the workings of ideologies, which hold, or have held, tremendous popular support. The force of progression, even where distilled and sublimated through a process of public debate and the free exchange of ideas, needs a counterweight if this process itself is to remain intact. It can be concluded that the protection of the discursive space, which is so clearly desired by those critics of business ethics who fear the closure of ideas, is best ensured by the existence of contrary forces (which I have here called continuity and progression) which through their collision produce compromise and moderation.

In considering the implications for a moral reform of corporations, as regards their regulation, there is not the space here to enter into particular detail. However, plenty of general examples can be brought to mind where the rational argument of academic debate may conflict with the traditional moral norms of organizational life. For example, at least since the late 1980s there has been a 'stakeholder vs. shareholder debate' about corporate responsibility. Stakeholder theorists such as Donaldson and Preston (1995) and Blair (1995) have called into question the assumption that shareholders have inviolable property rights over the corporation's assets. However, regulation could not be passed which removed the property rights of shareholders without a clear consideration of the role played by the idea of property rights, however justifiable (or not), as a moral norm in society. This is not to say that moral convention should always have priority over improvement – indeed as Burke remarks: 'A state without the means of some change is without the means of its conservation' ([1790] 1968, p. 106). Rational argument can of course bring about a change in convention over time, but if the process of improvement is to be considered legitimate for those subject to it, it is sensible to see balance as a necessity.

A further example might be found in countries where there may be a perfectly rational argument for gender equality in the workplace (that is, equal pay for equal work, equal opportunity for promotion, etc.) but the social equality of men and women is not recognized. However justifiable a law may look in rational terms, unless it strikes a balance with the preconceived opinions and traditional views of those subject to the law, it is unlikely to be found fully acceptable. Equally, a law, which obligated companies to adopt a two-tier board structure with worker representation at board level, would be problematic in cultures with no precedent for worker control. From personal conversation with managers who have dealt with the sudden implementation of works councils in business, I have been told that constructive dialogue was impossible due to the totally divergent agendas preconceived by the workers and management.

6. CONCLUSION

It can be said in conclusion that the idea of 'objectivity' and the rational pursuit of ethical 'truth' does have a role to play in the progress of new ideas in the field of business ethics and corporate legislation. The idea of an 'objective' truth to which argument can aspire has met with much skepticism from various authors. I have tried to show that 'objectivity' need not be considered as the dogmatic imposition of an ideology, which closes down all space for discussion. Indeed, the very notion of contesting an idea by providing better reasoning and evidence in support of an alternative, which according to Hare (1963) is inseparable from the practice of ethical justification, is inconsistent with the denial that one may be 'correct' or incorrect' in the assertion one makes. Furthermore, if an assumption is made that we are fallible and hence prone to error in our truth claims, an idea can be called 'objective' only to the extent that it has successfully contested all available arguments to the contrary. One of Mill's ([1859] 1991) central arguments is that our surety of an idea can never be so strong that we put it beyond all means of contestation. So a tolerant pluralism of ideas where prevailing dogmas are free to face critical examination is implied by the very idea of objectivity – *not* by its denial.

The progression of moral ideas can be considered as a dialectical movement of competing opinions that collide with one another in the practice of open and rational debate. I call this 'rational' because of the role of reason and evidence in moral argument. A morally informed legislative response to a given issue can be said to depend upon this dialectical collision of contrary viewpoints, where ideally the new regulation passed takes account of all the available arguments that have been heard and discussed.

If this dialectical movement of rational argument and counter-argument is desirable for arriving at new ideas, then this is only so at an ideal and abstract level. It cannot however exist in a vacuum, and the very existence of a discursive space for debate depends on the powers it yields being limited by the culturally specific moral norms that surround it. The institutions and powers that represent this context of moral convention may be called forces of *continuity*, as opposed to the forces of *progress* that arise out of a discursive space for rational debate, as a moral response to a given concern. It can be conjectured that the protection of this discursive space against a 'rapacious' (Parker, 2003, p. 207) ideology that seeks to close it down, is best ensured through a delicate balance between the implementation of fresh argument and ideas, and the historical context of moral convention. There is not to say that there is an essential conflict between the abstract ideals people strive toward in thought, and the habits and traditions around which their life is practically based. However, the number of social revolutions based upon a set of intellectual ideas, such as the 'Rights of Man', Marx's communist Utopia, or the Western liberal-democratic ideals perpetuated around the world today which have led to disastrous outcomes the very opposite of what their progenitors intended, suggests something fundamental about the delicate balancing act of continuity and progression.

With the multiplicity of ethical controversies that have enveloped business (especially large corporations) in recent years, and with a new Companies Act coming into force in the UK in 2008, the limits and possibilities of ethical argument are of contemporary importance. If a moral reform of the world of business is what is desired, then the dialectical notion of truth emerging through the contestation and rational argument of rival moral views, with the moral conventions that exist around business as a limit on the implementation of these ideas – in short, a framework which finds a place for both continuity and progress – can be a useful outline and starting point for theorizing how this development can proceed.

REFERENCES

Alvesson, M. and H. Willmott (2003), 'Introduction', in M. Alvesson and H. Willmott (eds), *Studying Management Critically*, London: Sage, pp. 1–22.

Aristotle ([c. 350 BC] 1980), *The Nicomachean Ethics*, New York: Oxford University Press.

Barrell, J. (1972), 'Introduction', in S. Coleridge ([1830] 1972), *The Constitution of Church and State*, London: Everyman, pp. *viii-xxxii*.

Berlin, I. (2002), *Liberty*, New York: Oxford University Press.

Blair, M. (1995), *Ownership and Control: Rethinking Corporate Governance for the Twenty-First Century*, Washington, DC: Brookings Institution.

Boatright, J. (1994), 'Fiduciary duties and the shareholder–management relation: or, what's so special about shareholders?', *Business Ethics Quarterly*, **4** (4), 393–407.

Brewis, J. (1998), 'Who do you think you are? Feminism, work, ethics and Foucault', in M. Parker (ed.), *Ethics & Organization*, London: Sage, pp. 53–75.

Burke, E. ([1790] 1968), *Reflections on the Revolution in France*, London: Penguin Classics.

Coleridge, S. ([1819] 1949), *Philosophical Lectures*, London: Pilot Press.

Coleridge, S. ([1830] 1972), *On the Constitution of Church and State*, London: Everyman.

Darwall, S. (1998), *Philosophical Ethics*, Boulder, CO: Westview Press.

Donaldson, T. and L. Preston (1995), 'The stakeholder theory of the corporation: concepts, evidence and implications', *The Academy of Management Review*, **20** (1), 65–91.

Foucault, M. (1991), 'Questions of method', in G. Burchell, C. Gordon and P. Miller (eds), *The Foucault Effect: Studies in Governmentality*, Brighton: Harvester Wheatsheaf, pp. 73–85.

Frederick, R. (1999), 'An outline of ethical relativism and ethical absolutism', in

R. Frederick (ed.), *A Companion to Business Ethics*, Malden, MA: Blackwell, pp. 65–80.

Freeman, R. and R. Phillips (1999), 'Business ethics: pragmatism and postmodernism', in R. Frederick (ed.), *A Companion to Business Ethics*, Malden, MA: Blackwell, pp. 128–38.

Gray, J. (2000), *Two Faces of Liberalism*, New York: New Press.

Hampsher-Monk, I. (1987), 'Introduction', in *The Political Philosophy of Edmund Burke*, Harlow: Longman, pp. 1–43.

Hare, R. ([1963] 1998), 'A moral argument', in J. Rachels (ed.), *Ethical Theory 1: The Question of Objectivity*, New York: Oxford University Press, pp. 51–7.

Hoy, D. and T. McCarthy (1994), *Critical Theory*, Malden, MA: Blackwell.

Jones, C., M. Parker, and R. ten Bos (2005), *For Business Ethics*, London: Routledge.

Laclau, E. and C. Mouffe (1985), *Hegemony and Socialist Strategy*, London: Verso.

Mackie, J. ([1977] 1998), 'The subjectivity of values', in J. Rachels (ed.), *Ethical Theory 1: The Question of Objectivity*, New York: Oxford University Press, pp. 58–84.

McCarthy, T. (1994), 'On the idea of a critical theory and its relation to philosophy', in D. Hoy and T. McCarthy (eds), *Critical Theory*, Malden, MA: Blackwell, pp. 7–30.

Mill, J. ([1840] 1980), 'Coleridge', in J. Mill, *On Bentham and Coleridge*, Cambridge: Cambridge University Press pp. 99–168.

Mill, J. ([1859] 1991), 'On liberty', in J. Mill, *On Liberty and Other Essays*, New York: Oxford University Press, pp. 5–128.

Mill, J. ([1861] 1991), 'Considerations on representative government', in J. Mill, *On Liberty and Other Essays*, New York: Oxford University Press, pp. 205–467.

Milton, J. ([1644] 1886), 'Areopagitica', in *Famous Pamphlets*, London: George Routledge & Sons.

Mitchell, A. and P. Sikka (2005), *Taming the Corporations*, Basildon: Association for Accountancy and Business Affairs.

Nagel, T. ([1980] 1998), 'Value', in J. Rachels (ed.), *Ethical Theory 1: The Question of Objectivity*, New York: Oxford University Press.

Parker, M. (1998), 'Against ethics', in M. Parker (ed.), *Ethics & Organizations*, London: Sage, pp. 282–95.

Parker, M. (2003), 'Business, ethics and business ethics: critical theory and negative dialectics', in M. Alvesson and H. Willmott (eds), *Studying Management Critically*, London: Sage, pp. 197–219.

Rachels, J. (ed.) (1998), *Ethical Theory 1: The Question of Objectivity*, New York: Oxford University Press.

Russell, B. ([1935] 1998), 'Science and ethics', in J. Rachels (ed.), *Ethical Theory 1: The Question of Objectivity*, New York: Oxford University Press, pp. 19–27.

Sikka, P. (2002), 'Wall Street rues accounting scandals', accessed 15 July 2008 at www.abc.net.au/lateline/stories/s595990.htm.

Singer, P. (ed.) (1990), *A Companion to Ethics*, Malden: Blackwell.

Stevenson, C. ([1963] 1998), 'The nature of ethical disagreement', in J. Rachels (ed.), *Ethical Theory 1: The Question of Objectivity*. New York: Oxford University Press, pp. 43–50.

Willmott, H. (1998), 'Towards a new ethics? The contributions of poststructuralism and posthumanism', in Martin Parker (eds.), *Ethics & Organization*, London: Sage, pp. 76–121.

7. The self as a moral anchor – applying Jungian psychology to managers' ethics

Cécile Rozuel

To be ethical is work, and it is the essential human task.

(Stein 1995, p. 10)

1. INTRODUCTION

The emergence of modern moral philosophy corresponds to the undermining of the traditional assumption that there exists an 'authoritative source outside of human nature' such as God, on the content of right and wrong (Schneewind 1993, p. 147). The question of man's free will and the origin of our moral knowledge were then brought to the center of the debate to which not only philosophers but also psychologists would soon take part. Recent calls for an interdisciplinary approach to ethics are reflected by Kaler's statement:

> Instead of looking to a separate realm of ethical theory, ethical investigation looks to theories drawn from the social and natural sciences: theories that help the ethical investigation determine what is and is not good for human beings by illuminating the nature of human nature and the effects of particular sorts of social arrangements upon human beings. (1999, p. 212)

Moral psychologists have concerned themselves with enhancing our comprehension of moral development processes and stages of ethical decision making. However most of these studies have failed to apprehend the individual as a whole. They have focused instead on the roles endorsed by people, or they have investigated the morality of people through the lenses of cognition, rationality or emotions. Rarely do these studies account for the complexity and unity of the individual being. Yet morality is strongly connected to the realization of being a self, that is, the realization that one is a complex but whole being with physical, rational, emotional and spiritual dimensions.

The self emerges as a central element of one's relation to moral goodness. The self actually participates in the articulation and implementation
of moral judgments (Bergman 2002). Blasi (1984, 1993) in particular,
grants the self a central role in the morality of a person, in so far as the
person will be motivated to act according to their ideals that constitute
their sense of moral self, or their self-identity. People aspire to consistency between their actions and their aspirations, because their self is key
to who they are. Colby and Damon's studies of the personality of moral
exemplars (1993 and 1995) emphasize the importance of cohesion between
one's moral judgments and one's sense of self in fostering moral behavior.
In fact, 'when there is perceived unity between self and morality, judgment and conduct are directly and predictably linked and action choices
are made with great certainty. . . .Thus, when moral and personal goals
are a central component of self, moral goals are central to the self' (Colby
and Damon 1993, p. 150). Conscience, to that extent, might be viewed
as the self's tool to remind us of who we really are, to recall the personal
autonomy that seems to suffer in situations of moral dilemma (Killen and
Nucci 1995; Lovell 2002).

Carl G. Jung's psychology has a distinctive ethical dimension, which
articulates around the concept of conscience and the archetype of the self.
Knowing oneself and becoming an individual are purported to be moral
tasks. However Jung's moral view has not been examined extensively,
maybe because Jung did not provide a clear moral framework; rather his
reflections on morality are spread across his numerous works. Although
Jung's ideas sometimes significantly evolved over the years, his perspective
on the moral implications of the individuation process and the nature of
conscience remained fairly stable. This chapter proposes to examine this
contribution in detail, and to illustrate how a Jungian framework can contribute to understanding the moral experiences of managers.

The concepts of self and ego are first generally defined, and the concept
of compartmentalization is introduced to outline the importance of the
self in moral behavior. Jung's view of the psyche is then presented with
a particular focus on the conceptualization of conscience and the moral
significance of individuation. The final part of the chapter reviews the
implications of a Jungian analysis of two managers' moral experiences.

2.   DEFINING THE SELF

The meaning of self is manifold. Colloquially, the notion of self is used
to distinguish one person from others and it identifies one's personality
or most essential character. Psychologically, the self is given different

meanings according to the school of thought to which one belongs. Thus American ego-psychology associates self with a construction of the ego, that is with the 'I' or the subject, whereas English tradition is inclined to consider the self as the locus of the whole psychic activity, and the product of dynamic processes that foster the unity of the person (Doron and Parot 1991, pp. 670–71). Layder assimilates self with 'personal identity' and contends that the self is 'how a person regards themselves and how they, and others, relate to, or behave towards themselves' (2004, p. 7). For Layder, the self is both sociological, that is part of a social context, and psychological in that it is independent of the social world. The self is also defined as essentially, though not exclusively, emotional and as flexible and capable of evolution over a life-span. Furthermore, Layder depicts the self as the center of awareness but also as the bearer of something of a spiritual nature to which people commonly refer as 'the higher self'. Hubback uses the metaphor of 'layers of insight' to explain how 'the personal self is potentially in touch with the healing energy of the greater self' (1998, p. 283).

The self is therefore a complex entity, both stable and dynamic. Colman describes the self as 'the overall process of the organism as a whole' (2008, p. 353) and stresses that 'the totality of our being is made up of the totality of our action in the world' (2008, p. 355). He distinguishes between being a self, knowing we are a self and having a self. If every living being can be said to be a self, only creatures capable of self-reflexivity can develop a sense of self and then claim that they have a self, in the sense of having a soul. The sense of self is in Colman's view the result of our knowledge that we are a self. The fact of having a self however depends on the others first attributing a self to us in their mind. In other words, according to Colman (2008, p. 359) we come to have a self by the recognition others make that we are just like them, which leads them to treat us 'as beings' like themselves and vice-versa. In that respect, Colman defines the self as partly personal and partly collective.

The ego is held as the necessary counterpart to the self. The ego usually identifies the person as an entity (Doron and Parot 1991), but the terms are often mistaken for one another. For example we usually associate self with selfishness or selflessness, whereas psychologists would argue that selfishness in the sense of egoism is a matter of the ego. Self-awareness, self-knowledge or self-realization are concerned with the self; however self mastery or self control actually imply the mastery of the ego, in so far as the purpose is to control some aspects of our personality rather than the essence of our being.

The self encompasses the ego yet the ego is itself composed of multiple ego-pieces, which may contradict one another (Aïssel 2005). White argues that we are split into 'interacting subsystems', which have 'their own beliefs, goals, plans, and strategies' (1991, p. 193). Self-deception takes place when we identify with a particular subsystem and think that it represents our wholeness whilst in reality we remain a fragmented being (Chakraborty 2004, p. 41). The spiritual aspiration of wholeness implies overcoming the misleading influence of these subsystems in order to express our full potential as a human being (Guillory 2001; Ashar and Lane-Maher 2004; Forman 2004). This achievement, which brings about a growing perception of an interrelatedness of everything, is important not only for spiritual progress but also to maintain a psychological balance which itself influences our ability to make appropriate moral decisions. Repression of the self by holding on to the ego (or the ego-pieces) can lead to extreme or adverse emotional states through which individuals project onto others their own repressed personality (King and Nicol 1999).

3. COMPARTMENTALIZATION AS A THREAT TO THE WHOLE SELF

The self plays a central role in the process of consciously acknowledging and confronting particular aspects of our personality. In fact, being connected or unconnected to the self shapes our moral capability (Terestchenko 2007). Connectedness to self ('*présence à soi*') characterizes the person who remains deeply loyal to their feelings, beliefs and values whereas the person unconnected to their self ('*absence à soi*') yields to the collective and betrays their individuality and what their conscience says to comply with the rules of a sometimes unjust and unethical system (Terestchenko 2008, p. 15). Whoever lacks a conscious connection to their self equally lacks a more acute perception of their values and the strength to stand by their values in adversity.

Unconnectedness to self eases the compartmentalization of the person in so far as the self is bracketed off whilst other aspects of the personality take over. Compartmentalization thus probably represents the greatest threat to the realization of a whole self (Gotsis and Kortezi 2008). The compartmentalized person may consciously or unconsciously cut off the moral values, aspirations, feelings and emotions that are deemed inappropriate and irrelevant to a certain context, for example in the workplace. Compartmentalization also happens when we distance ourselves from the values, aspirations and feelings we hold but do not wish to or cannot confront. Through this process, individuals actually become unconscious of parts of themselves and lose sight of their self as a unified whole. Ultimately, people can develop psychopathologies, although more generally the symptoms take the form of the general unrest that can be observed amongst organizational members in Western economies (Gotsis and Kortezi 2008).

In their study on spirituality in organizations, Mitroff and Denton (1999) highlighted how managers do not wish to split themselves up according to the demands of the context or even pretend that it is possible to do so. Yet compartmentalization is often perceived as a necessity for success, especially business success (Lovell 2002). Ashar and Lane-Maher (2004) argue that this is symptomatic of the old business paradigm, as opposed to a more integrative, holistic model we are supposedly developing now. Figler and Hanlon (2008, p. 619) also denounce this 'psychological fragmentation' resulting from an excessive attention to rationality and logic, and the subsequent demise of subjectivity and the unconscious sources that inform human relationships. According to these authors, acknowledging and accepting that the unconscious has a strong influence on our behavior paves the way for more fruitful, psychologically smarter and more mature work relationships (Figler and Hanlon 2008). Other studies have suggested that spiritually open workplaces, which recognize intuition and emotions as elements of decision making, foster greater creativity, trust, honesty and organizational commitment (Guillory 2001; Krishnakumar and Neck 2002).

In order to achieve wholeness, the person must tackle their tendency to compartmentalize. Whilst role-playing, excessive rationalization, extreme empathy, compartmentalization or self-delusion widen the gap between our perception of who we are and our self, the ability to bring our consciousness back to our being (experienced as both physical, mental, emotional and spiritual) constitutes an essential step towards self-completion in a holistic perspective. In return, self-completion, or what Jung calls individuation, nurtures a greater awareness of shared values, a deeper respect for the other as part of the shared humanity and a more solid ground to enact our moral values.

4. THE JUNGIAN PERSPECTIVE ON THE SELF AND THE PSYCHE

Howard and Welbourn (2004, p. 49) underline that psychologists in general, and Carl Jung in particular, help bring a new perspective on the self, on the significance of the conscious and the unconscious, and on the spiritual and moral dimension of the self and self-discovery. It is argued that Jung's conceptualization of the psyche around the ego-consciousness on the one hand and the archetypal self on the other hand provides a clear, useful and practical framework to explore the morality of individuals. In particular, the process of individuation symbolizing the conscious realization of self can be likened to an inner expression of the pursuit of the virtuous life through the realization of one's life-purpose. Developing self-knowledge, in the sense of developing the knowledge of the archetypal self, is enlightening so that self-knowledge becomes a vehicle for moral knowledge. Equally, the individuation process becomes both morally tainted and a moral achievement in itself.

According to Jung, the psyche is central to our life and our perception of the external world. He believed the psyche is composed of two parts, the conscious and the unconscious. The conscious part is the domain of the ego whilst the unconscious part is twofold. The personal unconscious is composed of our hidden memories or those ideas we rejected and that remain on the edge of consciousness, whereas the collective unconscious contains the footprint of humanity and emerges in the form of archetypes amongst other things. The study of the personal unconscious would allow the identification of complexes that are nothing but personal representation of archetypes. An archetype is an image, 'an unlearned tendency to experience things in a certain way' (Boeree 2006) or 'a fundamental and universal matrix' (Sédillot, 2005, p. 336). Figure 7.1 schematizes the layers of the psyche.

Jung (2005, p. 464) had noticed that people tend to display 'traces of character-splitting' through which we adopt a particular attitude to suit a particular milieu (see also Lennerfors this volume for a different analysis of character splitting). This phenomenon corresponds to the process of compartmentalization which was discussed earlier and which varies according to the ego's degree of identification with 'the attitude of the moment'. The mask we present to suit the societal expectations is called the persona. The persona is who we pretend to be and how we want to be perceived by others, like an outer personality or a 'false self' (Hill 2000, p. 211). Identification with the persona constrains the expression of our true individuality and personality, therefore the ego must disengage from the persona to allow for individuation to occur (Hill 2000). The persona is by essence collective, the personal interpretation of collective expectations, hence alien to the expression of each person's individuality. Consequently an overwhelming persona constrains our ability to use that '*libre arbitre*' so constitutive of moral responsibility. In Jung's terms (1977, p. 153) 'every man is, in a certain sense, unconsciously a worse man when he is in society than when acting alone; for he is carried by society and to that extent relieved of his individual responsibility'.

On its own, the ego is defined as 'a complex of ideas, which constitutes the center of [the] field of consciousness and appears to possess a high

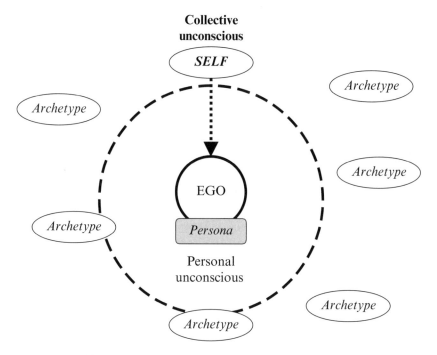

Source: Compiled by author.

Figure 7.1.   Layers of the psyche

degree of continuity and identity' (Jung 2005, p. 425). The ego is actually a complex, that is an associated group of ideas (Hill 2000, p. 38) that
emerges during childhood. It is key to the development of our personality
especially since we first need to familiarize with the collective rules before
we can differentiate from them (Jung 2005, p. 449). The ego gives us and
helps us maintain the sense of who we are through our life changes and
experiences, acting as 'a sort of initial nucleus around which a distinctive
individual personality can form' (Chakraborty 2004, p. 34). The ego is
necessary for our mental health and the manifestation of our will (Sédillot
2005, p. 113). However it is only secondary to the self who is the subject of
the whole psyche and actually prefigures the ego (Jung 1973, p. 259).

The Jungian self is 'the archetype of wholeness and the regulating center
of the psyche; a transpersonal power that transcends the ego' (Sharp
1991). Jung (2005, p. 460) explains that 'the self designates the whole
range of psychic phenomena in man. It expresses the unity of the personality as a whole.' The self is a postulate in that it is 'potentially empirical'

but consists in 'the experienceable and the inexperienceable (or the not yet experienced)' that is conscious elements as well as unconscious hence unknown factors (Jung 2005, p. 460). The self is also transcendental in so far as it unites opposites or dualities and 'represents the integration of all the disparate parts of ourselves [so that] in accepting all the different aspects that make up our personality, we become who and what we really are' (Crowley 1998, p. 38). Crowley (1998, p. 37) further notices that Jung derived his concept of self from the Hindu idea of 'Atman – the divine Self within'; therefore the self may be likened to a divine presence in us. Self-knowledge thus consists in 'widening and deepening' our awareness to uncover the 'mysterious and divine' aspect of the self so that 'the self can be understood as both the source and goal of human life' (Brooke 1991, p. 18). Wholeness is attained when self and ego work together in harmony (Sharp 1991). Indeed, self and ego are complementary and a reflection of one another in some way. Colman summarizes this clearly: 'It is not the ego that is the agent of our lives but the self – the agency of free will is initiated by something that is beyond our conscious awareness, albeit our conscious awareness is a crucial element in the process' (Colman 2008, p. 356).

5.   MORAL CONSCIENCE AND ETHICAL CONSCIENCE

The Jungian self operates at an inherently moral level. Robinson stresses that: 'For Jung, the psyche, as the locus of conscious agency, was the necessary and essential factor for actualizing ethical goods. . . . Yet the psyche is itself the locus for the realization of the individual personality – an ethical good, for Jung, second to none. Psyche is thus both means and, often, the end for the realization of moral goods' (2005, p. 91). More specifically, Jung articulated his moral vision around the concept of conscience. Conscience is viewed as 'a complex phenomenon consisting on the one hand in an elementary act of the will, or in an impulse to act for which no conscious reason can be given, and on the other hand in a judgment grounded on rational feeling' (Jung 1978b, p. 437).

Conscience has three aspects for Jung. It is represented alternatively 'as an inner agency outside of the ego's sphere, as an intrapsychic dialectic between the ego and this unconscious agency, and as the form of knowledge that results from this dialogue' (Robinson 2005, p. 19). As an inner agency, conscience is similar to a 'numinous archetype' that puts moral demands on individuals in spite of them (Robinson 2005, p. 18). These demands are imperious and influence the sense of personal balance the individual has. Indeed for Jung: 'Conscience – no matter on what it is based – commands the individual to obey his inner voice even at the risk of going astray. We can refuse to obey this command by an appeal to the moral code and the moral views on which it is founded, though with an uncomfortable feeling of having been disloyal' (1978b, p. 445). This unconscious agency, which is sometimes likened to the 'vox Dei', brings forward its moral judgments to the ego (as the center of consciousness) and engages in a dialogue with it in order to determine a final moral judgment, which consists in the moral knowledge we work with (Jung 1978b).

Individuals are inevitably influenced by the moral codes *en vigueur* in the community in which they have grown up and lived. But the content of the moral codes is assumed to have emerged throughout time from an initial and fundamental 'moral reaction' that arises from the unconscious and constitutes 'a universal factor of the human psyche' (Robinson 2005, p. 20). Conscience is thus anterior to the moral codes. In fact we generally feel happy to abide by the moral codes because they partly reflect the conscience that is the 'inner voice' in every individual. Instances when we experience a conflict between what our conscience dictates and what customary moral or social codes claim we should do are evidence that codes are not essentially formative of our moral values. When we feel uncomfortable with what the moral code prescribes, we actually experience what Jung calls a 'conflict of duty' (Jung 1978b, p. 454). For this reason, Jung distinguishes between 'moral conscience' and 'ethical conscience'. Whereas the former is about conforming with the social norms (what Jung calls the 'mores'), the latter emerges when the individual is experiencing a conflict of duty and requires consciousness of the inner voice.

Conflicts of duty refer to situations where after having rationally examined various moral options the individual still doubts which course of action to take because both options seem acceptable. Furthermore, invoking moral codes does not provide any help in deciding which way to go. Consequently, the deciding factor, which cannot emerge from the moral codes proceeds 'from the unconscious foundation of the personality' and will eventually lead to:

> a creative solution . . . which is produced by the constellated archetype and possesses that compelling authority not unjustly characterized as the voice of God. The nature of the solution is in accord with the deepest foundations of the personality as well as with its wholeness; it embraces conscious and unconscious and therefore transcends the ego. (Jung 1978b, pp. 454–5)

To summarize, moral conscience is about conformity to moral codes whilst ethical conscience is concerned with establishing a dialogue between the unconscious and the conscious ego in order to produce a 'creative

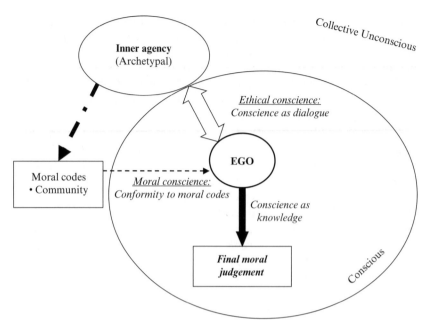

Source: Compiled by author.

Figure 7.2.   The structure of conscience

(moral) solution' that will reflect the self of the individual. Developing the ability to listen and trust that inner voice is thus essential for moral practice. A schematic representation of the structure of conscience is proposed in Figure 7.2.

Located in the collective unconscious, the inner agency is accessible to everyone and is essentially the same for everyone. Thus we potentially have got the same morality, though our actual morality will depend on our degree of consciousness and self-knowledge. Ethical conscience reflects a shared essence, the collective unconscious. To obey ethical conscience somehow means to be connected to our collective heritage, hence to other human beings in a spirit of a shared humanity, or even a shared beingness. Similarly the impulse one feels towards obeying ethical conscience is at the source of our striving for the ideal of being ourselves (Knobe 2005). It may also explain the nature of the actions of moral exemplars (Colby and Damon 1993, 1995).

Conscience is nevertheless dual. We are all endowed with a right and a wrong (or false) conscience, the 'angel' and the 'devil' who more often than not have an equal power of influence (Jung 1978b, p. 447). Consequently, 'the ambivalence of conscience radically complexifies the task of discernment and raises basic questions about the meaningfulness – the very intelligibility – of the concept of conscience' (Robinson 2005, p. 24). Strength of character, spiritual awareness and consciousness of self become determining factors in our ability to make moral decisions. Jung explains:

> Were it not for this paradox the question of conscience would present no problem; we could then rely wholly on its decisions so far as morality is concerned. But since there is great and justified uncertainty in this regard, it needs unusual courage or – what amounts to the same thing – unshakable faith for a person simply to follow the dictates of his own conscience. (Jung 1978b, p. 442)

We can and we should develop such courage to follow the right call of our conscience by increasing our conscious awareness of the content of our psyche, in particular the ego's tricks to shift our consciousness from the self onto the shadow.

6. THE MORAL SIGNIFICANCE OF INDIVIDUATION AND THE SHADOW

Integration of the archetypal shadow is a particularly important step in moral development (Ketola 2008). The shadow can be likened to our dark side, which we should acknowledge and confront rather than reject or ignore. Jung explains clearly the importance of such recognition: 'Unfortunately there can be no doubt that man is, on the whole, less good than he imagines himself or wants to be. Everyone carries a shadow, and the less it is embodied in the individual's conscious life, the blacker and denser it is' (Jung 1973, p. 76). King and Nicol (1999, p. 237) underline that integration of the shadow enables the person to develop 'an awareness of his/her connection to other human beings, providing a basis for communication, understanding and respect'. Recognition of the shadow means acknowledging our imperfection and authorizes a more conscious relationship with others to be developed (Jung 2002, p. 73).

The shadow is not bad in itself since our instincts, insights and impulses also originate from it. In fact, it appears dark in contrast with the bright image we project of ourselves in the persona. The persona actually inhibits the necessary coming-to-consciousness of the shadow. Jung makes this point explicit: 'The shadow is a moral problem that challenge the whole ego-personality, for no one can become conscious of the shadow without considerable moral effort' (Jung 1978a, p. 8). Recognizing the shadow is thus a moral action that requires courage but it is also the first and necessary step towards self-knowledge and greater moral knowledge and moral strength. If we fail to acknowledge our shadow, the psychic energy is nevertheless absorbed by the shadow and nourishes our hidden violence, our primitive animal nature inherited from and carried within the collective unconscious. For Jung, we all carry within our unconscious 'humanity's black collective shadow' of which we should become aware to prevent its manifestation at our expense and that of others (2002, p. 68).

As we integrate the shadow and become closer to our self, we approach individuation. According to Sharp (1991): 'Individuation involves an increasing awareness of one's unique psychological reality, including personal strengths and limitations, and at the same time a deeper appreciation of humanity in general.' The process of individuation is key to personal development; yet to become distinct one must have grown out of the collective and must have comprehended the rules of the collective. Individuation is therefore clearly different from individualism in that individuation nurtures a moral dimension and a respect for the community even when the individual has drifted apart from it (Sharp 1991). Jung approached the issue of individuality in a critical manner: 'Individuation, therefore, leads to a natural esteem for the collective norm, but if the orientation is exclusively collective the norm becomes increasingly superfluous and morality goes to pieces. The more a man's life is shaped by the collective norms, the greater is his individual immorality' (Jung 2005, p. 449). This would be so because the individual somehow has not confronted his own moral responsibility but relies on and hides behind the collective instead. Von Franz (1968) insists that individuation requires a 'coming-to-terms' with one's individuality, which may be a great hardship and requires the moral courage to see things as they are and to see oneself as one is.

Figure 7.3 proposes a summary of a Jungian framework of morality through self-knowledge. The persona is at the forefront of ego-consciousness and interacts with society. It is therefore the first element of which we must become conscious. As long as the ego identifies with the persona, our consciousness cannot be directed elsewhere, for instance towards archetypes such as the shadow or the self. On the moral level, the ego is influenced by moral conscience which itself is partly a by-product of social norms.

Conflicts of duty emerge whenever people find themselves unable to solve the dilemma with what moral conscience advises them to do. The person thus needs to turn to their ethical conscience. Our awareness of ethical conscience grows as we become further acquainted with the content of our unconscious. We first have to become familiar with our personal unconscious whose content will give us an insight into the collective archetypes that influence us. The shadow is almost inevitably one of the first archetypes one will have to confront and to consciously integrate. Little by

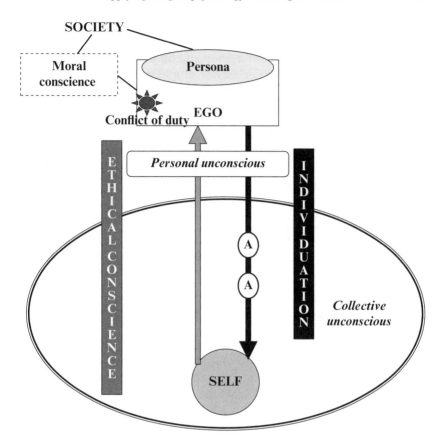

Source: Compiled by author.

Figure 7.3. A Jungian framework of morality

little we nevertheless approach the self. Ethical conscience takes its roots in the inner agency, which we can assimilate to the self as both a source and recipient of the 'vox Dei'. Moral knowledge springs from the confrontation of moral conscience with ethical conscience. Besides, moral behavior depends on the degree to which our ego collaborates with or obeys the self. If our ego remains strongly dependent on the persona, ethical conscience will not have as great an influence on our moral behavior as on someone who is more individuated.

Self-knowledge and the life-enlightening process of individuation thus emerge as the essential groundwork to establish a more solid and more comprehensive moral knowledge. This requires detaching oneself from the stifling security of the community's norms, and reaching for a transcendental principle, which illuminates the reality of our shared humanity. By all means individuals must exist as individuals and not stand as products of the mass liable to poor ethics because of a lack of consciousness, even if the process is painful (Jung 1978b, p. 447). Individuation, as Robinson insists, bears an intrinsically high moral value:

> The point Jung was making is that the inwardly directed individual is more likely to be creative and energetic in his contribution to society, ultimately benefiting it more, than the person governed solely by external factors. . . . Yet Jung believed that individuation was conducive to the betterment of society not simply for practical reasons regarding social performance, but rather because individuation leads to a strengthened sense of identification with others, which in turn benefits the collective. This identification with others would, presumably, make one less inclined to dehumanize them, to project upon them one's own shadow, and to place them outside one's moral community. A self-identity grounded on the conviction of a shared nature with others is, according to Jung, the basis of harmonious relations with oneself and others. (Robinson 2005, p. 106)

7.   A JUNGIAN FRAMEWORK OF MORALITY

A Jungian framework of morality articulated around self-knowledge and individuation is relevant to explore the moral experiences of managers. It points in the direction of self-reflection to assess the degree of consciousness of individuals. It also highlights the moral significance of archetypal influences in our relationships with others and provides a practical way to deal with them. As Hart and Brady explain: 'By contrast, the best managers confront their managerial shadow. They realize there is a tension between managing and simply being a person, a friend, a neighbor, etc. Confronting the shadow is the first step in backing away from inhumane control and moving toward a perspective that balances organizational and individual interests' (Hart and Brady 2005, p. 419).

With a view to assessing the relevance of the Jungian framework of morality discussed in this chapter, a study was designed whose purpose was to collect accounts of moral experiences that managers have had. The aim was to analyse these moral experiences and interpret them through the Jungian concepts highlighted in the framework so as to gain a better knowledge of managers' moral behavior. The study adopted an interpretivist perspective. Interpretivism acknowledges a multiple-voice approach where researchers want to understand social reality through the experiences of its actors. The purpose is sense-making by capturing the meaning people give to social reality as they perceive it (Symon and Cassell 2006). Knowledge is neither value-free nor objective but rather subjective.

Researchers in the interpretivist tradition must empathize with the subjects to understand the phenomenon (Schwandt 2003).

Consequently, the focus of the case-based study was to understand the lived experience of various individuals who work as managers and to relate their experience of morality and their perception of self to a Jungian framework of self-knowledge and individuation. Each manager was considered a single case within which their experience of self and morality was set to be explored. Twenty-five managers in France and Britain were interviewed in the first quarter of 2007. A selected number of interviews were later transcribed and analysed with a particular focus on the concepts presented in Figure 7.3.

8. JUNGIAN ANALYSIS OF MORAL EXPERIENCES

Each manager interviewed was analysed as an individual case. The cases of Martin and Deborah are used here to illustrate the process of analysis and the findings emerging from the Jungian interpretation of their experiences. Martin has been working for five years as Regional Director for real estate operations for a French bank. Trained in business, he worked for a couple of banking institutions prior to his current position. Deborah, on the other hand, works as lead technical architect and staff manager for a UK-based IT engineering company. Although her background is in computing and her responsibilities involve technical supervision, she also acts as a career counselor and Human Resources manager for 12 employees. She has been working at her current company for more than 15 years.

Martin and Deborah have very different characters and experiences of their work environment. Martin typifies a case where the persona is used as a protection against the inadequacy between his personal expectations and those associated with his managerial role. He is aware of playing a part but feels he needs to if he wants to continue doing his job. On the contrary Deborah appears to have successfully integrated her personal values into her professional role so that she can be herself and avoid compromising her moral standards whilst performing well on a business basis. Actually Deborah seems more in line with her ethical conscience whilst Martin appears to struggle with his moral discomfort, which results from the tension between moral conscience and ethical conscience.

8.1 Persona and self-image

Martin seems constantly in contradiction with himself, which shows in his perception of a persona. Martin likens his job to that of a merchant and describes himself as a comedian. He believes he has to wear the banker's uniform and seems to accept it as a means to detach himself from his job. Yet Martin pays great attention to his relationships with his clients not just because it is good for business but also because he might come to personally like the client as a person. Hence Martin is not as detached as he wants to believe he is. Rather Martin wishes to be a 'banker persona' when at work because somehow he feels he does not really play a part but is his actual self, a fact that worries him. Consciously constructing a persona becomes Martin's means of defense against his own self, as shown in the following excerpt:

> I always try to maintain a barrier between me and my clients. I know very well that some clients would like to go further, I would like so too, some clients – these are clients, at some point, you feel you really get on well, but there's a time when a signal lights up and says 'No, you shouldn't go too far because if you do, you won't be able to tell the difference between professional and personal matters'. . . and this, there's nothing worse than that. . . . Similarly, from a strictly familial viewpoint, you come home in the evening, you close the door, you don't expect a client to phone you on the grounds that he's a friend. What will he talk about – do you think he will talk about the 'friend stuff' or the 'work stuff'? The work stuff, right! No, to be careful, it's better not, erm, as much as possible, this is something – if we should meet up, have a drink and all that, there are cafés, restaurants to do that. Better to stay within a 'purely business' relationship.

If Martin seems to have found ways to accommodate his persona, he nevertheless has got issues with what we may identify as his shadow. For example Martin explains that he could never be nasty yet he later says that he could 'act nasty' if people were to cause him trouble at work. He also states that in his opinion being honest is not very good to advance one's career yet according to him one can reach the top of the ladder whilst being honest. These contradictions in Martin's view of himself suggest that he does not really know who he is, what he wants or even which image he wants to present to others. This ambivalence may pinpoint at Martin's inability to integrate his shadow.

Deborah does not present a strong persona. She seems to have clear ideas of what she can do and what she cannot do as well as what she is good at and bad at doing. She praises straightforwardness and honesty and she strongly dislikes organizational politics and the requirements of playing a part, which itself influences the development of a persona. The statement below illustrates how she rejects elusiveness and pretence:

> Politics. I hate having to say the right thing to the right person to achieve what you want. I don't like pretending, I don't like acting. I like – in my perfect

world, everybody would just be themselves, and I would say what I think, and he would say what he thinks, and we would understand each other, but it's not like that. . . . Because . . . people expect you to behave in certain ways and they react differently to different things. So I know now how I need to approach certain people, I know what I have to say to them, I know how I have to say it to them. But I just think it's wrong that I should have to do that – they should just know what I mean when I say something [laugh]. And they shouldn't have to act the part for me either. I'd like to know what they really think, I don't care what veneer they have to put on it, you know, how they should say something . . . you know, if somebody says 'Yes', I would like them to mean 'Yes'; or if they say to me 'No' I just want them to mean 'No'. I don't want them to mean 'Yes, but', 'No maybe'.

8.2 Moral conscience and ethical conscience

Martin also demonstrates contradiction in his approach to morality. His view of ethics mainly based on a respect for the law would at first evoke moral conscience rather than ethical conscience. He declares that trust and honesty are core values for him but suggests that he does not act so much out of personal integrity as out of personal interest.

> I'll be completely honest, either it goes against my values, or it goes against my interests. Erm, I haven't told you that tomorrow, accepting a bribe would go against my values. You're the one who concluded that. At the moment, it actually also goes against my interests. It's clear that for the time being it's more in my interest to keep doing my job than accept a sum of money. Let's be clear. It's not, it's not because we are talking about deontology that those people who tell you they would not accept a bribe do it for deontological reasons. It's maybe only because they calculate faster than others and say 'It is not in my interest to do so.' And personally, I haven't told you – and you've got evidence – I haven't told you it would go against my values. I've only said it would go against – now, I tell you maybe it would also go against my interests. What's the significance of both? I won't answer for I don't know. Honestly, I don't know whether it's a question of values or of interest. Isn't it the same eventually? And, in the end, the fact that I say 'No', we call it deontology and it reassures everyone.

Actually, Martin needs to be reassured that his actions are indeed moral whilst he personally doubts they are. This again points towards a daunting shadow that makes him sense his darker side, that is, what he mentions as his potential for 'falling on the other side of the fence'. This in turn makes him frantically question his own motivations and his ability to do the right thing. Martin's reliance on rules or the law to analyse moral issues emphasizes his need to cling to a non-personal framework so as to avoid confronting his own feelings. However in as much as he wishes to make decisions on purely objective facts, he also regrets that more personal factors of decision-making such as intuition, emotion and experience are nowadays discarded. It could be that his attachment to intuition reflects a sensitivity to ethical conscience which Martin does not wish to investigate further.

Deborah's ethos appears very strong and well integrated in her behavior, as a contrast to Martin's indecisiveness. Deborah has set clear boundaries to guide her conduct. However she sometimes lack the confidence to trust her gut feeling of what is right and wrong, as if she wanted to convince herself she is wrong whilst she personally feels she is right. Nevertheless Deborah makes her decisions based not on codes or rules of conduct but on what she feels capable of doing or what she feels confident doing. She relies on her gut feeling which sets the limits she cannot cross, not just morally but almost physically: 'If inside you feel "No" then how can you say "Yes"? You don't believe it, you can't work with it.' Deborah thus clearly relies on her ethical conscience to make decisions that are in accordance with who she feels she is whilst being aware that she benefits from it as well. Deborah seems to have managed to build a business credibility from her very personal sense of morality. The fact that she cannot blatantly lie 'because you see it in her face' could be considered an unconscious defense system to prevent her from being entangled into a situation that makes her feel uncomfortable from her values perspective, as the following quote illustrates.

> I was working with this bid, a proposal to a company. . . . Then it came to a point when we had to make a presentation to summarize what we had written, and the sales guy wanted to say something that I knew was wrong, was false. But it sounded good, and it would have made the customer think that we were clever, we're good and all that. And I couldn't do it. So I said 'No'. And he said 'You have to'. And I said 'No. I can't. You'll see when I say something that I don't believe, you'll see it in my face. You'll hear it in my voice. I cannot do that.' And we had a discussion for two or three days. And in the end . . . somebody else had to do that. . . . I don't know if it was the right thing to do. I could see why he wanted to say that. But I think for me, I knew I couldn't say that with any credibility, so it was quite an easy decision for me, cause I would have been letting the company down even if I agreed to say that. Because I'm 100% sure that I would have, something would have given it away in the way that I'd have said it, because – I think that my strength in presenting something, standing up in front of an audience is that people believe me because I don't do the bullshit thing, I don't lie, I don't, you know, make things flowery or anything like that, I'll say what I think.

9. DISCUSSIONS AND IMPLICATIONS

The persona and its correlate the self-image appear to be primary in making sense of our moral experiences. The persona is often at the root of a person's relationship to the world, and more specifically to his or her perceived obligations as a manager. For example Martin is attached to a 'business persona', which in his view carries out the features necessary to perform well in a somewhat ruthless and short-termist world. In this respect, the persona plays up a stereotypical view of what a good business person is expected to be: ambitious, results-oriented, pragmatic, rational instead of emotional, able to favor the organization's interests over the individuals' interests. As long as the persona controls our consciousness, the ego lacks psychic space to turn to the more authentic self. Martin's acting up simply provides him with the illusion he can cope in an environment that maybe does not suit him entirely.

To reject the persona paves the way for a stronger sense of self. However it demands that the person extricates him or herself from the anesthetic but reassuring collective. Deborah seems to have made hers. Jung's cautious statement that '[f]ar too much of our common humanity has to be sacrificed in the interests of an ideal image into which one tries to mold oneself' (1977, p. 157). By rejecting the persona that the corporate culture expects her to wear and by enacting what she feels is right, she manages to nurture a greater moral consistency and personal integrity.

Compartmentalization is an equally important indicator of our degree of self-awareness and an element of our morality. Deborah exemplifies a person who does not compartmentalize but rather brings her values to her workplace, cultivates and takes advantage of her moral strengths and acts so as not to compromise her sense of self. Compromising is not an option because it would damage her professional image and capabilities, which would in turn damage the company's image and interests. Deborah seems very confident in affirming her individuality, suggesting that she is connected to herself and able to listen to and to act upon these gut feelings that tell her what to do.

On the other hand, Martin unsurprisingly compartmentalizes his life tightly as a means to self-preserve and keep doing his job well. Martin apparently aspires to feel confident in himself and to affirm his right to exist as an individual yet he fails to acknowledge what he stands for. He has a sense of his shadow, his shortcomings and his weaknesses, but he has not managed to accept them and integrate them so that he does not dare to trust himself. His growing anxiety about his future, which he mentioned at the end of the discussion, partly reflects his great uncertainty about his self.

Morality in practice is also a matter of choice. Jung's conceptualization of moral and ethical conscience helps understand the underpinnings of our moral choices. Actually moral conscience is by definition limited by the rules and customs of a given social group, whilst ethical conscience draws from an archetypal source of knowledge. As a consequence, ethical conscience enables us to find 'creative solutions' when we face a dilemma, which we cannot solve by calling upon the moral rules and customs we commonly use. Ethical conscience thus becomes a way to free oneself from the bounds of customary morality in order to find a new path of moral action.

10. CONCLUSION

Business ethics studies have begun to adopt a more interdisciplinary scope. The study outlined in this chapter follows this call and suggests that Jungian psychology has much to offer to apprehend the moral experiences of managers. The process of self-knowledge and individuation is necessarily personal but organizations could and should encourage initiatives that enable their managers to understand the inner motives and archetypal mechanisms behind their behaviors. Indeed complete individuals contribute more fully to society than parted beings.

The cases of Martin and Deborah demonstrate how the Jungian framework of morality can bring new insights to understand why people behave the way they do. The sense both managers have of themselves plays a significant part in their respective confidence when they make moral decisions and enact those decisions. The concept of compartmentalization and connectedness to self are central elements to make sense of managers' moral experiences, because the self is the core component of our moral system, the anchor, which preserves our moral integrity as individuals. To echo Bankwala's statement (2004, p. 162) that understanding behavior implies looking at what we value in life, we shall conclude that in understanding moral behavior it is important to see that we behave the way we do depending on how we value our self; if we lack clarity of our self, any moral attitude will do (whether right or wrong).

REFERENCES

Aïssel, S. (2005), *La Nouvelle Psychologie Spirituelle*, Barr, France: Spiritual Book France.

Ashar, H. and M. Lane-Maher (2004), 'Success and spirituality in the new business paradigm', *Journal of Management Inquiry*, **13** (3), 249–60.

Bankwala, Y.J. (2004), 'Organizational transformation through human values', in L. Zsolnai, (ed.), *Spirituality and Ethics in Management*, Dordrecht, the Netherlands: Kluwer Academic Publishers, pp. 159–67.

Bergman, R. (2002), 'Why be moral? A conceptual model from developmental psychology', *Human Development*, **45** (2), 104–24.

Blasi, A. (1984), 'Moral identity: its role in moral functioning', in W. M. Kurtines and J.L. Gewirtz (eds), *Morality, Moral Behavior, and Moral Development*, New York and Chichester: John Wiley and Sons, pp. 128–39.

Blasi, A. (1993), 'The development of identity: some implications for moral functioning', in G.G. Noam and T.E. Wren (eds), *The Moral Self*, Cambridge, MA: MIT Press, pp. 99–122.

Boeree, C.G. (2006), 'Carl Jung', accessed 5 July 2007 at http://webspace.ship.edu/cgboer/jung.html.

Brooke, R. (1991), *Jung and Phenomenology*, London: Routledge.

Chakraborty, S.K. (2004), 'Spirit-centered, rajarshi leadership', in L. Zsolnai (ed.), *Spirituality and Ethics in Management*, Dordrecht, the Netherlands: Kluwer Academic Publishers, pp. 33–50.

Colby, A. and W. Damon (1993), 'The uniting of self and morality in the development of extraordinary moral commitment', in G.G. Noam and T.E. Wren (eds), *The Moral Self*, Cambridge, MA: MIT Press, pp. 149–74.

Colby, A. and W. Damon (1995), 'The development of extraordinary moral commitment', in M. Killen and D. Hart (eds), *Morality in Everyday Life – Developmental Perspectives*, Cambridge: Cambridge University Press, pp. 342–70.

Colman, W. (2008), 'On being, knowing and having a self', *Journal of Analytical Psychology*, **53** (3), 351–66.

Crowley, V. (1998), *Principles of Jungian Spirituality*, London: Thorsons/HarperCollins.

Doron, R. and F. Parot (1991), *Dictionnaire de Psychologie*, Paris: Presses Universitaires de France.

Figler, R. and S. Hanlon (2008), 'Management development and the unconscious from an analytical psychology framework', *Journal of Management Development*, **27** (6), 613–30.

Forman, R. (2004), *Grassroots Spirituality: What it is, Why it is There, Where it is Going*, Exeter: Imprint Academic.

Gotsis, G. and Z. Kortezi (2008), 'Philosophical foundations of workplace spirituality: a critical approach', *Journal of Business Ethics*, **78** (4), 575–600.

Guillory, W.A. (2001), *The Living Organization – Spirituality in the Workplace*, 2nd edn, Salt Lake City, UT: Innovations International.

Hart, D.W. and F.N. Brady (2005), 'Spirituality and archetype in organizational life', *Business Ethics Quarterly*, **15** (3), 409–28.

Hill, R.D. (2000), *Self Discovery – The Spiritual Psychology of C.G. Jung*, Baltimore, MD: AmErica House Book Publishers.

Howard, S. and D. Welbourn (2004), *The Spirit at Work Phenomenon*, London: Azure.

Hubback, J. (1998), 'The dynamic self', *Journal of Analytical Psychology*, **43** (2), 277–85.

Jung, C.G. ([1969] 1973), *Psychology and Religion: East and West – The Collected Works of C.G. Jung Vol.11*, 2nd edn, London: Routledge & Kegan Paul.

Jung, C.G. ([1966] 1977), *Two Essays on Analytical Psychology – The Collected Works of C.G. Jung Vol.7*, 2nd edn, Princeton, NJ: Princeton University Press.

Jung, C.G. ([1969] 1978a), *Aion – The Collected Works of C.G. Jung Vol. 9 Part II*, 2nd edn, Princeton, NJ: Princeton University Press.

Jung, C.G. ([1970] 1978b), *Civilization in Transition – The Collected Works of C.G. Jung Vol.10*, 2nd edn, Princeton, NJ: Princeton University Press.

Jung, C.G. ([1958] 2002), *The Undiscovered Self*, London: Routledge.

Jung, C.G. ([1971] 2005), *Psychological Types – The Collected Works of C.G. Jung Vol. 6*, London: Routledge.

Kaler, J. (1999), 'What's the good in ethical theory?', *Business Ethics: A European Review*, **8** (4), 206–13.

Ketola, T. (2008), 'Taming the shadow: corporate responsibility in a Jungian context', *Corporate Social Responsibility and Environmental Management*, **15** (4), 199–209.

Killen, M. and L.P. Nucci (1995), 'Morality, autonomy, and social conflict', in M. Killen and D. Hart (eds), *Morality in Everyday Life – Developmental Perspectives*, Cambridge: Cambridge University Press, pp. 52–86.

King, S. and D.M. Nicol (1999), 'Organizational enhancement through recognition of individual spirituality – reflections of Jaques and Jung', *Journal of Organizational Change Management*, **12** (3), 234–42.

Knobe, J. (2005), 'Ordinary ethical reasoning and the ideal of "being yourself"', *Philosophical Psychology*, **18** (3), 327–40.

Krishnakumar, S. and C.P. Neck (2002), 'The "what", "why" and "how" of spirituality in the workplace', *Journal of Managerial Psychology*, **17** (3), 153–64.

Layder, D. (2004), *Social and Personal Identity – Understanding Your Self*, London: Sage.

Lovell, A. (2002), 'Moral agency as victim of the vulnerability of autonomy', *Business Ethics: A European Review*, **11** (1), 62–76.

Mitroff, I.I. and E.A. Denton (1999), *A Spiritual Audit of Corporate America: A Hard Look at Spirituality, Religion and Values in the Workplace*, San Francisco, CA: Jossey-Bass.

Robinson, D.W. (2005), *Conscience and Jung's Moral Vision – From Id to Thou*, Mahwah, NJ: Paulist Press.

Schneewind, J.B. (1993). 'Modern moral philosophy', in P. Singer (ed.), *A Companion to Ethics*, Malden, MA: Blackwell, pp. 147–57.

Schwandt, T.A. (2003), 'Three epistemological stance for qualitative inquiry', in N.K. Denzin and Y.S. Lincoln (eds), *The Landscape of Qualitative Research – Theories and Issues*, 2nd edn, Thousand Oaks, CA: Sage, pp. 292–331.

Sédillot, C. (2005), *ABC de la Psychologie Jungienne*, Paris: Grancher.

Sharp, D. (1991), 'Jung Lexicon – a primer of terms and concepts', accessed 5 July 2007 at www.cgjungpage.org.

Stein, M. (1995), *Jung on Evil*, London: Routledge.

Symon, G. and C. Cassell (2006), 'Neglected perspectives in work and organizational psychology', *Journal of Occupational and Organizational Psychology*, **79** (3), 307–14.

Terestchenko, M. (2007), *Un Si Fragile Vernis d'Humanité – Banalité du Mal, Banalité du Bien*, Paris: La Découverte/Poche.

Terestchenko, M. (2008), 'On s'y habitue', *La Chronique* (*mensuel d'Amnesty International France*), **254**, 15.

von Franz, M.L. (1968), 'The process of individuation', in C.G. Jung (ed.), *Man and His Symbols*, New York: Dell Publishing–Random House, pp. 157–254.

White, S.L. (1991), *The Unity of the Self*, Cambridge, MA: Bradford Books/MIT Press.

8. The impossibility of guidance – a Levinasian critique of business ethics

Emma Louise Jeanes and Sara Louise Muhr

1. INTRODUCTION

Conventional approaches to understanding and promoting business ethics most often rely on utilitarian, deontological or virtue-based ethics (see, for example, Hartman 2005). Whilst adopting different perspectives, and often leading to contrasting ethical prescriptions, in all cases these approaches rely on being able to define the 'right' behavior – distilling the philosophy of ethics into principles of guidance. Such attempts to formularize ethics, found in most standard texts on business ethics, attempt to help the decision-maker define and respond to ethical issues. Often through a series of steps informed by one of these prescriptive approaches, conventional business ethics attempts to assist the decision-maker to make the 'right' (moral) decision. In this chapter we question these conventional perspectives and consider the 'possibility' of ethics in business.

Here we argue that the ethical implications of these formulae for action need further consideration. The typical response of organizations to the potential risk of unethical behavior is to develop codes of conduct that give guidance as to the appropriate behaviors, drawing on these utilitarian, duty-based or virtue-based ethics – providing rules to follow, or qualities to aspire to (typically focusing on one's integrity as a moral actor). However, we argue in this chapter that this mechanism poses two challenges to ethical behavior. First, whilst the guidance goes some way towards encouraging 'good' behavior, in doing so it also takes away individual responsibility for behaving ethically: it does people's thinking for them and replaces it with a bureaucratic procedure – follow these rules and you can't go wrong (or at least you can't be held responsible for the outcome). Second, and more crucially, is the possibility – we will argue impossibility – of knowing what 'good' behavior is, if not at all, then certainly prior to the ethical encounter. In exploring this im/possibility, we take a Levinasian perspective, which places ethics at the heart of social relations – an ethics without a system of judgment, but an ethics by which one experiences a calling into question in the face of others. Our argument is explored through the narrative of a lead consultant involved in the new justice policy in South Africa.

2.   A CRITICAL APPROACH TO CONVENTIONAL BUSINESS ETHICS

Almost all books on business ethics contain chapters on three basic perspectives on business ethics: utilitarianism, deontology and virtue ethics. Utilitarianism is based on the assumption that moral decision making should provide the greatest amount of happiness/pleasure for the greatest number of people; deontology (or duty based ethics) preaches a universalism where the ultimate imperative is that you should only do to others what you would want to be done to you and that this imperative is categorical; and finally virtue ethics defines virtuous characters constituting a moral person (for reviews of business ethics literature see, for example, Des Jardins and McCall 1999; Hartman 2005; Shaw 1998). In this chapter, we question these conventional approaches, and show how a Levinasian ethics identifies the impossibility of the conventional approaches' emphasis on finitude. Instead we suggest an ethics of infinity as the constant interruption of conventional practice.

Business ethics, following these conventional lines of thought, has taken the role of a rulebook, which provides guidance for 'right' and 'good' behavior. These perspectives are then used to generate instructions on how to behave and act in a proper manner, both within the organization and when engaging with different actors outside the organization (see, for example, Warren 1993; Stevens 1994; Jackson 2000). The conventional approaches to business ethics call for the involvement of 'objective moral experts' in the organizational process of constituting moral guidelines – whether these guidelines prescribe ways of calculating and prioritizing actions, defining ethical rules or identifying virtuous characters and ideals. These 'codes' provide justification as well as guidance for the behavior of managers and employees of organizations – a set of rules that, if followed, show individuals how to be on the side of what is recognized as 'right'. As a consequence, codes and guidelines give protection of rights and duties for organizational members as well as for the stakeholders outside the organization.

Inherent within these rule-based approaches is the promise that such determined codes ensure the objective and rational 'solution' to moral issues and potentially problematic or precarious situations (see Cummings 2000, p. 217). The goal for business ethics has in this way been to reduce undecidability in decision-making (Jones et al. 2005, p. 8). It suggests that if we know the right rules, we will be able to make the right moral decisions. Ethics becomes a codified system in which independence of thought is largely removed, or as du Gay (2000) argues, organized more positively in favor of a bureaucratic ethos, where the agent can become impartial or distanced from the object of morality. Such an approach enables (or aspires to enable) the explication of clear and consistent guidance for appropriate behavior, and enables good governance to be demonstrated.

Rule following under this approach appears to be the highest moral achievement. Organizations seek to control the behavior of its employees as it – and not just the individuals – are held responsible for the actions of those within the organization, 'almost as if organizations allow people to disclaim personal responsibility for things that they have done' (Jones et al. 2005, p. 82). This approach can be justified by arguing that these guidelines and virtues are more considered, a sign of higher levels of moral reasoning (Kohlberg 1981), and by the need for consistency and for standards to be maintained where an individual's ethical reasoning may differ from that of the organization's (or more accurately, its key decision-makers), particularly in a climate in which businesses are scrutinized by society for their 'trustworthy' credentials (Lunau and Wettstein 2004) despite the limited evidence of the effectiveness of codes (Doig and Wilson 1998). The shift in emphasis to hold organizations, and not just individuals, responsible for their actions has led to modes of organizing (such as through codes of conduct) that no longer place the individual as solely, or sometimes even significantly, responsible for their actions. The documentation of due process at the same time demonstrates good governance on the part of the organization, and enables the individual to avoid personal responsibility for their actions if due process has been followed. Yet it is the individual who decides and acts in ethical or unethical ways. Indeed, the following of rules without deviation and flexibility has been a tactic of trade union resistance – a means of disruption rather than improvement of process.

The desire to be ethical, or crucially to appear to be ethical, is not necessarily driven by an inner call to be ethical – good ethics has become good business. What can be recognized in the practice of most business ethics is the idea of reciprocity. This idea implies there is a strategic component inherent in responsible action. In many cases decisions are not made on the basis of one of these prescriptions, but out of recognition that certain groups are useful to the organization. As Jones et al. (2005, p. 122) remind us: 'we care about the Other because the Other is useful for us'. In this sense, the ethical consideration is not what Derrida (1992, p. 7) would call a pure gift – a giving without expectation or desire of a return, but is instead of circular economic self-interest. The attempt is to present oneself and one's social activities as good as is possible – a behavior that can be labeled as strategic or as conditional ethics. One's 'ethics' is based not on what is right, but what will be rewarded – behavior is undertaken strategically or conditionally on the reciprocity of others. We therefore argue that what many organizations currently do in the name of business ethics is to define sets of codes and formulate principles and guidelines for organization members. This procedure is considered good governance where the defined rules are designed to assure responsible behavior. Yet here we argue that following codes and guidelines does not necessarily ensure responsible behavior since responsibility and ethics cannot be prescribed. Instead, it must always include a space for singularity. In this sense, calculating or controlling behavior does not obtain responsibility. Instead, responsibility always implies a relation to a contingent Other, to the unknown and unmanageable. It means to respond to the other person or group and thereby to respond according to the singularity of that moment (see also Jones et al. 2005).

It is not the 'reality' of behavior, descriptive rather than prescriptive ethics, which is at stake here. It is well documented that these ethical approaches offer no guarantee that they will be followed. What we argue here is that the lack of ethics is predicated on the false premise these approaches employ. In this chapter we question the guidelines of utilitarian, deontological and virtue ethics, and consider whether it is *possible* to determine what the appropriate rules and virtues are for ethical behavior. We ask if it can ever be ethical to predetermine what an individual should be or do. This follows a recent call in the field of business ethics to alter the traditional and limited perspectives adopted, questioning the foundations of conventional business ethics (see, for example, Kjonstad and Willmott 1995; Jones 2003; Jones et al., 2005; ten Bos and Willmott 2001; Knights and O'Leary 2006; Muhr 2008b). To explore the impossibility of ethics in conventional business ethics, we turn to Emmanuel Levinas.

For Levinas there can be no finitude to responsibility. Instead, Levinas demonstrates how we can never be responsible enough and that there can be no formula for prescribing how we respond to this call for responsibility. It is this infinity in our responsibilities that is beyond measure and calculation. In doing so we ask the inevitable question – if there is no finite responsibility, how is ethics then possible?

3. LEVINASIAN ETHICS – A DIFFERENT APPROACH

We have suggested that following codes and guidelines does not necessarily ensure responsible behavior, and that responsibility and ethics cannot be prescribed. Such prescriptions, we argue, fail to acknowledge singularity – the very nature of difference that is beyond comprehension (see also Muhr 2008a). In this sense, calculating or controlling behavior does not achieve responsibility. Instead, responsibility needs to be understood as that which always implies a relation to a contingent other, to the unknown and unmanageable – it is the giving of a response to the singular other. In Levinasian ethics, the encounter with the Other always comes first and overrules all ethical guidelines. Ethics is about one's personal responsibility to the Other.

Levinas was a post-war French philosopher concerned with difference, whose work was influenced by his Jewish heritage, and his time in German concentration camps. Levinas was born in Lithuania in 1906, but lived in France for most of his life and became a French citizen in 1930, which is also why he is often referred to as a French philosopher. Levinas was taken prisoner by the Germans in World War II, but because he was a soldier in the French army, he was sent to a military prison camp, instead of a concentration camp. Unlike most of his family, Levinas and his wife and daughter survived the war. After the war he became director of a school that educated teachers. Strangely enough considering his later philosophical importance, he didn't hold a university position before 1964, when he was appointed Professor of Philosophy at the University of Poitiers (Critchley and Bernasconi 2002). Despite his gruesome life experiences, his work is not about anger and retribution but compassion and humility for others. Though Levinas always claimed not to build an ethical theory (for this would return us to a 'prescription' of some kind), his writings involve what Cohen (1998) calls an ethical vision, based on his concern for the Other. Levinasian ethics is, therefore, not a normative prescription of how to live one's life. It is better described as an inquiry into the meaning of ethics understood as an infinite openness to the Other's difference (Jones et al. 2005). At the heart of Levinas' writings lies the irreducible ethical proximity of one human being to another – morality, and through that encounter a relation to all others – justice.

Although Levinas was a student of both Husserl and Heidegger, his work expresses a position that is opposed to Husserl's intentionality as well as to Heidegger's philosophy of being. Whereas Husserl believes that every action is directed towards something that is intentional, Levinas argues for ethics in the non-intentional act. Heidegger, inspired by Husserl, formulates the similar argument that experience is always situated in being but Levinas believes that there is a sphere before being, which is the true ethical relation. For Levinas it is in the encounter with the ungraspable Other that one finds ethics (Bernasconi and Critchley 1981, see also Davis 1996). Levinas asks us to appreciate ethics as an encounter with the Other – an encounter that acknowledges the Other as an infinite Other. In this way, Levinas moves the encounter with the Other beyond being, beyond ontology, to where he finds ethics. Levinas' insistence on the non-ontological character of ethics is therefore directed against the contemporary ontology and existential phenomenology of Heidegger (Levinas 1969, p. 45) and the intentionality of Husserl – for the ethical relation is not chosen by us, but is there, always and already.

According to Levinas, the Other can never be reduced to the ontological characteristics of a person. The Other for Levinas, can therefore not be contained – a mere object to be included in one of my categories. Due to the irreducible strangeness of the Other, the relationship with the Other is never an 'idyllic and harmonious relationship of communion' (Levinas 1987b, p. 75), and as such 'he and I do not form a number. The collectivity in which I say "you" or "we" is not a plural of the "I"' (Levinas 1969, p. 39). If that were not the case, it would mean that the Other was reduced to the Same, a reflection of oneself. Seeing another person as Other (which Levinas argues we have no choice but to do) means acknowledging that person's fundamental difference to us – what makes them Other to us is their difference. Ethics arises in letting that difference interrupt our own world (Levinas 1969, p. 43).

4.   ETHICS AS FIRST PHILOSOPHY

For Levinas, meaning emerges from the face-to-face encounter as an ethical event. The encounter with the Other thereby calls the Self into responsibility. This responsibility is 'an assignation of extreme urgency, prior to every engagement and every beginning: *anachronism*' (Levinas 2000, p. 173, original emphasis). Every relation is therefore always 'before being'; one is always already in a social world. The relation to the Other comes before being, and consequently Levinas posits the primacy of ethics over ontology.

Ethics is therefore not a simple branch of philosophy, but first philosophy, that is, an ethics without an ethical system (Jones et al. 2005, p. 74), and a relation that is always there. Before cultural expression, before the said, lies the universal but deformalized humanism of the Other. 'Only the humanism of the *other man* is human' (Levinas 2000, p. 182, original emphasis). A humanism of the Other is an expression of the other as Other, as another irreducible different human being. As a consequence, before does not simply mean before as an epistemological condition, but rather before as 'better' (Levinas 2000, p. 224), as an unconditional ethical imperative (Cohen 2003). The ethical relation does not presuppose ethical behavior. Levinas instead describes the reality of the relation between the Same (self) and the Other in which the face ordains the Self to serve the Other, even though this responsibility may be accepted or refused (Levinas 1985). The moral Self comes into its own through its ability to rise above being, through its defiance of being. As Bauman inspired by Levinasian ethics states: 'Ethics does not have an essence, its "essence" so to speak, is precisely not to have an essence' (Bauman 1993, p. 72).

In an ethics that comes before being, there is nothing to justify the responsibility of the Self, and nothing to determine whether the Self is indeed responsible – that responsibility belongs alone to the Self. It is this 're-personalization' that makes it ethical. Ethics has nothing to do with rules, it can never be codified. It is not possible to determine by reason whether an action is moral; the Self remains uncertain as to whether the responsibility has been fulfilled – always left with the possibility that more could be done, and nothing given to the Other is ever enough. It is the awareness of this uncertainty and the awareness that our responsibility is limitless and infinite that makes us capable of ethics. After all, we can never know the needs of the Other and thus never do enough. The Other refutes my egoism, makes me shameful and gives me conscience, but also meaning. Responsibility does not have a purpose or reason; instead it is the impossibility of not being responsible to the Other, which forms my moral capacity (see also Bauman 1993). Consequently, Levinas rejects the Kantian and Utilitarian attempts to establish reason as the foundation of ethics. If reason is the foundation for consensus among all rational human beings then there is no dialogue in it (although there may be an ontological dialogue about it). Such an ethics does not presume an encounter with the Other, and therefore presents an uninterrupted Sameness – it is my view and my understanding of the world that makes the foundation of my ethical reasoning. Reason limits us to what is known – what is the same – and not that which is different and ungraspable. The failure of conventional methods to find reason that can prescribe always and unequivocally exactly demonstrates that which is beyond reason – that which is different, that which is unknown – and thus the impossibility of its ethics.

Levinas' claim of ethics as re-personalized and not based on reason also makes practical sense. After all, few of us would be ready to explain, if asked, what the principles that guide us are (Bauman 1993). We rarely explicitly consider the foundations, which are believed to form our ethical understanding of the world. We would not necessarily be able to explain our ethical 'calculation' – ethicality is not something we can explicate in codes or rules. Ethical questions are separate from ontological concerns as the concept of 'good' transcends essence. In this sense ethics is not something that can belong to a person as a set of guidelines to be applied when appropriate. Ethics cannot be managed, or 'totalized' (see, for example, Levinas 1969, pp. 23–4). Only general rules and principles can be universal and organized, not the specificity of the here and now. One may legislate universal rule-dictated duties, but ethical responsibility exists in the ethical call of another person, at this time, at this place – in this encounter. Crucially for Levinas, therefore, is the ultimate imperative of acknowledging any Other human being as an Other. The Other is not to be thematized or categorized, the other is always radically Other. In a Levinasian sense, conventional business ethics has no ethical foundation. As conventional business ethics tries to manage ethical behavior and formulate guidelines, it goes against the ultimate ethical imperative to acknowledge another as an irreducible Other.

It is the face of the Other that calls us into question. It is this responsibility that is the 'essential, primary and fundamental structure of subjectivity' (Levinas 1985, p. 95). And yet the face-to-face isn't an empirical event (though we may meet face-to-face) but is that 'which always overflows thought . . . [an] experience in the fullest sense of the word' (Levinas 1969, p. 25). The Levinasian face is therefore not the plastic face or the physical appearance of a human being. Rather, the face is an expression of otherness, it is the way the Other calls me into question. The face, in expressing the other as Other, always surprises me and exceeds my idea of what this Other might conceal. The expression of the face identifies the Other as a unique responsible human being, infinitely different from the Self. The face is present in its refusal to be contained and can never be comprehended or encompassed. It is neither seen nor touched (Levinas 1969, p. 194). The alterity of the Other does not therefore depend on any distinct quality that would distinguish the Other from me, for a distinction like this would imply a relation of knowledge which immediately would nullify alterity.

> The face of the Other at each moment destroys and overflows the plastic image it leaves me, the idea existing to my own measure and to the measure of its ideatum – the adequate idea. It does not manifest itself by these qualities, but καθ'αύτό [is in itself]. It expresses itself. (Levinas 1969, p. 51 original emphasis)

It is the emergence of the Other that founds and justifies the freedom of the Self – calling it to responsibility (Levinas 1969, p. 197). The Other, therefore, is necessary for the Same to be called into question – such a calling into question cannot occur spontaneously. It is precisely this strangeness of the Other, and the Other's irreducibility to the Same, that accomplishes ethics – the interruption of conventional ethics (Levinas 1969, p. 43).

5. IMPOSSIBLE ETHICS?

Demanding the re-personalization of responsibility, Levinasian ethics easily leaves the impression of being an impossible ethics (see also Bevan and Corvellec 2007; Jones 2003). In this section we will therefore consider the possibility, or impossibility of ethics. To be 'ethical' in an organization – that is to be recognizably ethical either within or outside of the organization – requires behaviors and characteristics that follow the guidelines of what is 'right', 'good' and 'just'. Yet, as we have argued, this fails to respond to the immanent nature of the ethical relation. A Levinasian perspective reformulates the ethical question. It is for me to respond to the calling into question of myself by the Other. No formula for action is possible. Indeed any attempt to formulate such rules merely serves to demonstrate the inability of those designing the ethical code to understand the nature of the ethical relation. Yet this ethical relation – always and already – does not assume I will behave ethically, nor does it assume there will be no 'calculation' – for it is not just the Other who calls me into question, but all others (what Levinas calls the third party) in the eyes of the Other. It is the face of the Other that opens me to all humanity (Levinas 1969, p. 213), thus it is on the relation of the face-to-face that justice is founded.

Responsibility starts from the encounter with the Other, but Levinas accepts the unavoidability of relying on the law to achieve justice in the encounter with the many. The moment the third party enters, an economy of responsibility is required to respond to the call of all others. The challenge in ethics, therefore, is not only the unknowable Other, but also the existence of the third party. Societies do not consist of isolated relationships between the Self and the Other; there are always others involved, who may not have a voice, but nevertheless are there – somewhere – and are affected by my actions. There are always other Others so we must compare; and this very comparability makes justice possible (Levinas 1998, p. 202). What Levinas accomplishes is thinking a justice that may require judgments, but that is founded in the responsibility to the Other: 'We wanted to describe the man to man relationship. Justice does not constitute it; it is what makes justice possible. Justice is rendered to the totality' (Levinas 1987a, p. 44). At the heart of Levinas' writings 'lies the irreducible ethical proximity of one human being to another, morality, and through that encounter a relation to all others, justice' (Cohen 1998, p. xi).

Responsibility for the Other, therefore, is also a responsibility for the third party, and the face of the Other does in this way not only signify its own otherness, but it also immediately reminds me of every other Other. As such, the radical asymmetry in the ethical call of the Other reminds me of the symmetrical claim for justice that I am Other for other Others (see also Byers and Rhodes 2007; Introna 2007). However, the contribution of such a justice lies not in its search for the universal categories and beliefs in equality and fairness, but in its irreducible willingness to be interrupted by the proximity of the Other. 'We need the law to give our judgment force, and yet when we face the [O]ther, in its singularity, it shatters the law, making the law seem perverse' (Introna 2007, p. 268).

In this sense, the universal for Levinas is constituted in the singular. The singularity of the face of the Other relates us with the third party, because the Other reminds us of every other Other. The multiplicity of multiple demands places 'limitations' on (or at least tempering of) the capacity of the Same to respond, which is overcome by the dimension of universal justice by which all others are served: the third party is not just interested in good intentions but also good deeds, therefore there must be some economy of action. Yet, at all times the relationship of the Same to the Other remains primordial and the responsibility infinite. This allows for universal justice, but a justice not justified by the universality of demands (or totalization), but always on the face-to-face, where some administration (which necessarily includes totalization) will be necessary (Peperzak 1995, p. 182). But justice must always come from the primacy of this face-to-face relation.

> How is it that there is justice? I answer that it is the fact of the multiplicity of men and the presence of someone else next to the Other, which condition the laws and establish justice . . . It is consequently necessary to weigh, to think, to judge, in comparing the incomparable . . . from whence comes justice. Justice, exercised through institutions, which are inevitable, must always be held in check by the initial interpersonal relation. (Levinas 1985, pp. 89–90)

Levinas cannot answer for the practicality of how we make these judgments—for that would be reintroducing a universal (and totalizing) ethics. The primacy of the ethical encounter no more excludes injustice than universalized laws, the possibility of violence to others will always remain. In that respect Levinas retains political realism and should not be seen as utopian: 'the work of justice is as consistent with the acknowledgement of the war implied in peace as the peace implied in war' (Caygill 2002, p. 96). Or as formulated by Critchley (2007, p. 13) 'if ethics without politics is empty, then politics without ethics is blind'. Thus, justice works in the space between ontology and ethics.

A Levinasian ethics, therefore, positions us with an uneasy balance between a calling into responsibility for the Other – an unknowable Other – and all others that demands a calculative aspect, the very basis of utilitarian ethics that we have argued must be rejected. In seeking justice Levinas acknowledges such a balance has to be struck – but always with the calling into question as the foundation for this relation. Levinasian ethics is in this way not a total rejection of the calculation found in business ethics. It is rather a questioning of its absoluteness and its search for finite solutions. Levinas does not suggest a new alternative theory to 'obey', nor does he claim the world will become more just. Levinasian ethics is instead a reminder that business ethics is not founded in ethics but in reason and calculability, and that setting up rules and definitions does not give us a better understanding of ethics or lead us to good (more 'moral') decisions. The lesson from Levinasian ethics is instead that we should accept the impossibility of determining correct ethical behavior, instead allowing our selves to be interrupted by the unknowable Other.

Levinas reminds us of the importance of experiencing ethics not in rules, but in a sense of personal responsibility – responsibility arising in the acknowledgement of the Other's otherness and in allowing the difference between me and the Other to haunt me. The everyday encounters with otherness and the sensibility towards this otherness is what makes me a moral person capable of questioning the ethical guidelines by which I am supposed to live. Rules and guidelines do not in themselves bring justice or make organizations responsible; ethics are founded in the encounter with the Other. Levinas reminds us that even though law and guidelines are important in the field of business ethics, they must never stand alone – justice, well ordered, begins with the Other.

6. 'AND JUSTICE FOR ALL' – THE CASE OF POST-APARTHEID SOUTH AFRICA

This section will, through an empirical example, illustrate how an international human rights consultant managed to go beyond conventional rule-guided ethics and practice an ethics for the Other. The case is based on stories from South Africa as told by a senior consultant from the Danish Institute of Human Rights. The consultant, highly ranked within the Danish Institute of Human Rights, was the lead consultant of the team that tabled the justice policy in South Africa after apartheid. The stories were collected through six semi-structured interviews (varying from long in-depth interviews to short probing follow-up telephone calls), which were conducted over a six-month period. The consultant subsequently read the case notes to verify the accuracy of the recording made, and adjustments were made in response to his comments. The stories thus rest on qualitative interviews with the consultant, which according to Alvesson (2003, p. 13), stand in contrast to so-called 'talking questionnaires'. The qualitative interview tries to establish a more genuine human contact in the interview situation, where trust, openness and interpersonal connection are important factors. This is done, not to get access to an objective truth, but to enter an inner world that can provide valuable deep insight about feelings, attitude, meanings and intentions (Alvesson 2003, p. 14). The case rests on the experiences of one person, but these stories are contextualized through an analysis of internal documents from the Danish Institute of Human Rights as well as academic articles on the post-apartheid period. It is to the context of our case that we now turn.

After Mandela was elected president in South Africa in 1994, the new government faced the task of building a new justice department. The Danish Institute of Human Rights was appointed the task of teaching this process, and the consultant of this study was the leader on this project with responsibility for setting up – and teaching – a planning unit consisting of both the former leaders of South Africa and the former opposition. During the years the process was underway, the consultant was primarily located in South Africa. The unit was established as an interim structure in the absence of the justice department's management team that was still to be defined. It was placed outside the premises of the justice department, but referred directly to the minister of justice, Dr Omar – a lawyer and member of the former opposition – who was the first non-white minister of justice. Under the apartheid system a 'race classification' was defined, which divided South Africans into four main groups: White, Black, Asian and Colored making it impossible for anyone but 'whites' to hold governmental positions (Burman and Schärf 1990). Thus, not only was the department solely staffed by white male Afrikaners, the justice department had an additional 11 sub-departments similarly staffed. Besides the main justice department, mentioned above where the ministry was based, there was one in each of the ten black homelands. The goal of the human rights team was therefore to coach the tabling of a justice policy and the building of a justice department that reflected the population. Before justice could be dispensed, the unit however had to build one representative department – transforming and merging South Africa's 11 apartheid-based justice departments into one unified structure (Lindsnæs et al. 2008). After two and a half years of the project period, the document 'Justice Vision 2000 – and Justice for All' was tabled and approved in parliament (Justice 1997).

Of the many lines of narrative, we will focus here on those in which the consultant recounts how, through the planning unit's role as a decentralized and empowered entity, he called upon his personal ethics to attain just decision-making. We start with a story, which begins in the latter stage of the project period (though it is informed by earlier encounters), where the justice vision had been tabled and where it was necessary for the planning unit to negotiate international aid and development projects for South Africa.

Given the international significance and delicacy of the situation, South Africa received many offers of financial support, particularly from the West. Yet the consultant taught the planning unit to make the decision to decline many of the international offers, as they did not correspond to or directly support the vision they had agreed upon, which was designed to bring South Africa towards a more just system.

> In South Africa we had tons of these project suggestions running in, and it became a problem because it took away focus from our actual task at hand. And we had to take action upon this. We [the planning unit] communicated that we were happy to receive money. But we would only run projects that fitted the strategy we were building up. And if the projects did not fit, we would not run them.

This meant that they declined a lot of projects, which seemed to be more or less only in the interest of the international society.

> The international donors have of course an international agenda. And this agenda is all about telling a given 'receiver-country' what they, internationally, think is right and wrong; in fact often without considering the context in the given country, or what that given country wants politically itself.

As the consultant explained, international projects are often accepted due to the fact that they follow the guidelines for international donation and have been approved by national agencies. The situation in South Africa was, as far as the consultant knew, the first time the 'powerful international society' had experienced a country declining funding.

> That was the first time people had experienced that we from a developing country said 'no thank you' to money. It caused both the justice department and us [the planning unit] major international pressure, and in fact made us pretty unpopular.

What we argue is significant here is not only the rejection of the funding from the international community, but the ethics that led to these decisions being made. The planning unit, coached by the consultant, down-prioritized the guidelines from the international society – guidelines that might be considered as internationally recognized as fair and just – because of the responsibility to the Other. This calling to responsibility came from the consultant's long-term engagement in South Africa and in the countless encounters he had with its people.

> Meeting the people in the planning unit made a great impression on me. Especially the stories of the former opposition, the blacks were incredible. They

have such strong personalities. These people come from terrible conditions, grew up in townships, and have been in exile and the like. These people really have some scars on their souls. And they are tough; they have survived. But these people also really have potential. To be able to survive the experiences they had, had made them tough.

The consultant is clearly marked by working closely with these people. Their strong character, and belief in justice after years of apartheid, especially impressed him. But also meeting the former white leaders made an impression on him. On the surface, they were powerful people, with importance and political influence, yet the consultant noticed that they were struggling with some difficult dilemmas around their power and their conscience. In this way they appeared powerful and strong on the surface, but were at the same time very vulnerable and aware of the unjust nature of the regime under which they had governed. Even though the apartheid regime was officially terminated, the two groups still experienced conflict.

> The group of 'non-whites' had very little trust left for the white leaders; many of these most likely responsible for the torturing or liquidation of family members and friends. But also the white group felt that they had to stick together, because they saw the 'non-whites' as a threat. The white group was very much aware of the fact that what they had done was not pretty. And due to that, they felt great insecurity of where this would end.

As the consultant was tasked to make these two groups of people work together, these conflicts were central to his work. His compassion and openness to the two groups was therefore crucial. His encounters with both 'whites' and 'non-whites' moved him and affected him – they interrupted his understanding, experience and assumptions. At the start of the project he saw them as two groups, but in time he realized that they were not as homogeneous as he (and they) thought. He didn't see blacks and whites, he didn't see their histories; instead he experienced the call to responsibility in his encounter with them. He saw them as Others towards whom he has a responsibility.

> It then suddenly occurred to me that I was not dealing with people who were mean or deluded or anything like that. I was dealing with *people*; wonderful people, who just had very different backgrounds. They all grew up 'learning' that the others were different and as a consequence 'worse' people. The non-whites saw the whites as 'stupid bastards' who could do basically what they pleased and the 'whites' saw the non-whites as people without real rights as such. But they were just people.

By engaging and working closely with both groups in the planning unit, they made a significant impression on him, but it was not as blacks and whites; freedom fighters or crooks, but as people, 'wonderful people' as he says. It is through these Others that he was opened up to the call of all others – to the people of South Africa.

> Already when I ran my first project down there, something happened to my attitude. When I started to talk about something, I got so caught up in it that I forgot who I was talking to. I talk to the eyes I see, and whether they are placed in the face of a man or a woman or a black or a white doesn't really mean anything to me. And it had that fortunate advantage that I quickly take a professional approach and always keeps the communication so to speak at an adult level. I very quickly got the nickname 'color blind'. When the situation is critical and cramped with conflicts, this attitude really pays out. By having this reputation, people rarely question our agenda no matter how delicate the situation becomes.

The consultant looked beyond what he called the plastic face of the person, seeing instead the call in their eyes, not the face in which they are placed. In this way it is the Levinasian face of the Other with which he communicates – responding to its call – not the plastic (or 'real') face of the person. Through his engagement with individuals in the planning group, he was able to see beyond the symbolism of their plastic face and was reminded of his responsibility to every other Other – to the South African people, when teaching the unit in their funding decisions. It was to the people of South Africa, with whom he had the encounters, that he was called into question – not to the international guidelines with which he worked. Through encounters with the Other, he was opened up to see all other South Africans as other Others. Responsibility for the Other turned into responsibility for the Levinasian third party. In the singular encounters, he saw the history, the conflicts, the tensions of the South African people, which made it possible for him to ignore international pressure and expectation. It enabled him to coach the unit towards making decisions that responded to their needs, not to the desires of the international community.

> This fact that we handled the international situation as we did made us have a rather significant impact on the situation in South Africa. Because when we came back to talk about human rights and law reforms, people listened because they knew that we did what we did to get success in the partnership we had; a partnership which was all about carrying out visions for the South African people. We did not have an alternative agenda.

A publication from the Danish Institute of Human Rights quoted the South African Minister of Justice, Dr Omar, as saying the following about their partnership:

> South Africa entered into many agreements with other countries for various issues, but on fundamental transformation issues we stuck with the Danes, because we knew that they had no other agenda. The Danes come from a broad progressive European culture, but they were sensitive to our diversity and history and there was never an occasion when the cultural differences between us affected our work adversely. (Lindsnæs et al. 2008, p. 21)

What we observe here is an international community founding the justification for their actions on internationally recognized guidelines. Yet this guidance has a purpose – an ethics not founded on the Other but on a vision of a greater (world) happiness. In following these guidelines countries (usually Western) were mandated to do what they recognized as the 'right' thing to do. But what is this greater world happiness? Who has made this calculation and codified it to instruct all future action? Following a Levinasian ethics, the actions of the donees are questionable since they donate money in the calculated interest of the Same; and not in the interest of the Other, for it is only through an understanding (possible only of the Same and not of the Other) that such a calculation can be made. In order to be ethical in a Levinasian sense, the moral self cannot be controlled by rules and calculation, nor, as we have also shown, can a decision be based on the expectation of getting something in return – it has to have a certain level of disinterestedness to be ethical (Levinas 2007, p. 205). Therefore even though this exchange is made according to international legislation, it is not ethical in a Levinasian sense. The funding for South Africa should come out of the response to the call, the desire to meet a sense of responsibility for the Other and not for the purpose of reaching higher international political goals. It is for me to respond to the call of the Other, not to consider what they can do for me. Yet the guidelines for funding are not founded on the call of the Other, but on mutual self-interest for a particular formulation for (and of) world peace. International funding is far from selfless-giving but funds that are given in respect of certain aims, formulated on the expectation of a return. For the response to be ethical in a Levinasian sense it needed to be founded in the encounter, and its calling into question – its interruption of the Self, not the following of predetermined rules far removed from the here and now.

In contrast the consultant from the Danish Institute of Human Rights was faced with the Other, he responded to its call, and allowed himself to be interrupted, and through him the planning unit were also opened to the call of other Others. In this way his response to the circumstances was not, in first instance, based on the conventions but on a personal response to this call. The situation in South Africa, and the challenges the consultant had ahead of him, had a powerful impact on him. The consultant was of course running a human rights project implementing a new justice policy, but he always kept a sense of responsibility for the Other as that upon which the policies were founded. Coached by the consultant, the planning unit therefore ended up not only implementing justice, but implementing a sense of justice, which in Levinasian terms originated in responsibility for the Other. The basic principle was human rights and the respect for the individual that originated in his long-term personal involvement with the people in the planning unit. The universality of justice came from the singularity of the respect for another human being as Other.

7.   CONCLUSION

If we take Levinas seriously, then 'ethics' cannot be achieved through rules of engagement or the exhibition of virtuous qualities, for the 'right' behaviors are unknown and cannot be known because the Other (and their needs) are unknowable, with any attempt to try and understand merely resulting in a reflection of the views of the Same (essentially putting yourself in the shoes of the Other and in doing so only considering your own perspective, your own needs). Yet this does not distract from a responsibility to the Other – the Other still commands me and calls me into question. Nor do we have to consider whether we have a responsibility to the Other. Our responsibility to the Other is there – always and already.

Thus by taking a Levinasian approach we argue that ethics is found in our response to the Other, rather than the calculation of the right consequences, the application of a 'moral' rule or an embodiment of a predetermined virtue or value. For Levinas, the ethical relation is founded on the primacy on the relation of the Same and the Other, yet the response of the Same to the Other, the nature of their responsibility is undefinable, uncodifiable, unknowable. This makes calculations, rules and virtues redundant in the Levinasian ethical relation. As the Other is absolutely other, and thus unknowable, it is not possible to know 'what is right' as such an understanding is impossible. No calculations or rules can be applied or appropriate virtues selected to ensure the ethical response. But nor is the relation devoid of ethics – it is the calling into question that *is* the ethical relation. It is this ethical moment of uncertainty that is the interruption of the Same, but also the interruption of a conventional perception (Critchley 1992). A Levinasian approach cannot be 'bureaucratized' in the way of conventional ethics, as it is exactly this process that requires knowledge of the Other – a reduction of the Other to the Same – a totalization of the Other. Levinas points to the limits of our knowledge, and thus the limits of using reason as a basis of our ethics. He argues that we should leave room for being awakened by the Other instead of trying to encapsulate it.

Levinas offers no easy practitioner-orientated means of ethical application – there is no Levinasian 'model' of ethics that can be codified and implemented, indeed such a thing would be counter to the very understanding of the Levinasian ethical relation. Nor does Levinas offer any easy answers to organizations that need to demonstrate their ethics in a world where a code of ethics is increasingly seen as the norm. No guidance is given as to how justice can be achieved. Instead Levinas suggests a form of disinterestedness:

> In this disinterestedness, when, as a responsibility for the other, it is also a responsibility for the third party, the justice that compares, assembles and conceives, the synchrony of being and peace takes form. (Levinas 1981, p. 16)

Levinas thus does more to disrupt our understanding of business ethics than to offer any ways of ensuring ethics (that is responding to the calling into question) in practice. Such an approach also questions the very possibility of a business-led, or strategic approach to ethics where self-interest and expectation of reciprocity are implicit. Therefore, whilst Levinas explores the possibility of justice, the primacy of the face-to-face relation remains primordial. Whilst the institutions of justice (rules and regulations) are necessary, to start with these would fail to ground justice in this ethical relation. To start with 'universal' justice would mean that the '"small" goodness of most people, the infinitude of the Other, and the ultimate meaning of the subjectivity would not count at all' (Peperzak 1993, p. 191). Indeed, the responsibility not only is primordial in founding justice, but surpasses universal justice by being urged to a moral creativity and limitless dedication that goes beyond (but not against) the political and technical conditions of justice (ibid., p. 192).

Ethics arises in the encounter with the Other, which interrupts my knowledge. This encounter depends upon my willingness to be changed by the Other's critique. Indeed, ethics demands that I let myself be changed; it demands that I am willing to take the perspective of the Other. This 'taking' does not imply an appropriation of the Other's perspective, but is a calling into question of the Self, an interruption called upon me by the acknowledgement of the Other's difference. In this way, Levinas offers no place for a 'rationalization' or assurance of ethics, but through the third party offers us a way of returning to some level of reasoning that can be implied to balance interests. Ethics is about letting the Other be other and different from me, and letting this difference interrupt my thoughts. It is by these means, we hope, that our work with Levinas itself may disrupt established understanding of business ethics.

REFERENCES

Alvesson, M. (2003), 'Beyond neopositivists, romantics, and localists: a reflexive approach to interviews in organizational research', *Academy of Management Review* **28** (1), 13–33.

Bauman, Z. (1993), *Postmodern Ethics*, Oxford: Blackwell.

Bernasconi, R. and S. Critchley (1981), *Re-Reading Levinas*, Bloomington, IN: Indiana University Press.

Bevan, D. and H. Corvellec (2007), 'The impossibility of corporate ethics: for a Levinasian approach to managerial ethics', *Business Ethics: A European Review*, **16** (3), 208–19.

Burman, S. and W. Schärf (1990), 'Creating people's justice: street committees and people's courts in a South African city', *Law & Society Review*, **24**, 693–744.

Byers, D. and C. Rhodes (2007), 'Ethics, alterity, and organizational justice', *Business Ethics: A European Review*, **16** (3), 239–50.

Caygill, H. (2002), *Levinas and the Political*, London: Routledge.

Cohen, R.A. (1998), 'Foreword', in E. Levinas (ed.), *Otherwise Than Being or Beyond Essence*, Pittsburgh, PA: Duquesne University Press.

Cohen, R.A. (2003), 'Introduction: humanism and anti-humanism – Levinas, Cassier, and Heidegger', in E. Levinas (ed.), *Humanism of the Other*, Champaign, IL: University of Illinois Press.

Critchley, S. (1992), *The Ethics of Deconstruction – Derrida and Levinas*, Oxford and Cambridge, MA: Blackwell.

Critchley, S. (2002), 'Emmanuel Levinas: a disparate inventory', in S. Critchley and R. Bernasconi (eds), *The Cambridge Companion to Levinas*, Cambridge: Cambridge University Press.

Critchley, S. (2007), *Infinitely Demanding: Ethics of Commitment, Politics of Resistance*, London: Verso.

Cummings, S. (2000), 'Resurfacing an aesthetics of existence as alternative to business ethics', in S. Linstead and H. Höpfl (eds), *The Aesthetics of Organization*, London: Sage.

Davis, C. (1996), *Levinas – an Introduction*, Cambridge: Polity Press.

Derrida, J. (1992), *Given Time*, Chicago, IL: University of Chicago Press.

Des Jardins, J.R. and J.F. McCall (1999), *Contemporary Issues in Business Ethics*, Belmont, CA: Wordsworth.

Doig, A. and J. Wilson (1998), 'The effectiveness of codes of conduct', *Business Ethics: A European Review*, **7** (3), 140–49.

du Gay, P. (2000), *In Praise of Bureaucracy – Weber, Organization, Ethics*, London: Sage Publications.

Hartman, L.P. (2005), *Perspectives on Business Ethics*, Singapore: McGraw-Hill.

Introna, L. (2007), 'Singular justice and software piracy', *Business Ethics: A European Review*, **16** (3), 264–77.

Jackson, T. (2000), 'Management ethics and corporate policy: a cross-cultural comparison', *Journal of Management Studies*, **37** (3), 349–69.

Jones, C. (2003), 'As if business ethics were possible, "within such limits". . .', *Organization*, **10** (2), 223–48.

Jones, C., M. Parker, and R. ten Bos (2005), *For Business Ethics: A Critical Text*, New York: Taylor & Francis.

JUSTICE (1997), 'Justice vision 2000 . . . and justice for all', five-year national strategy for transforming the administration of justice and state legal affairs, South Africa Department of Justice.

Kjonstad, B. and H. Willmott (1995), 'Business ethics: restrictive or empowering?', *Journal of Business Ethics*, **14** (6), 1–20.

Knights, D. and M. O'Leary (2006), 'Leadership, ethics and responsibility to the Other', *Journal of Business Ethics*, **67** (2), 125–37.

Kohlberg, L. (1981), *Essay On Moral Development: The Philosophies of Moral Development*, San Francisco, CA: Harper & Row.

Levinas, E. (1969), *Totality and Infinity – an Essay on Exteriority*, Pittsburgh, PA: Duquesne University Press.

Levinas, E. (1981), *Otherwise Than Being or Beyond Essence*, Pittsburgh, PA: Duquesne University Press.

Levinas, E. (1985), *Ethics and Infinity: Conversations with Philippe Nemo*, Pittsburgh, PA: Duquesne University Press.

Levinas, E. (1987a), *Collected Philosophical Papers*, Dordrecht, the Netherlands, Boston, MA, Lancaster: Matinus Nijhoff Publishers.

Levinas, E. (1987b), *Time and the Other*, Pittsburgh, PA: Duquesne University Press.

Levinas, E. (1998), *Entre Nous: On Thinking-of-the-Other*, New York: Columbia University Press.

Levinas, E. (2000), *God, Death and Time*, Stanford, CA: Stanford University Press.

Levinas, E. (2007), 'Sociality and money', *Business Ethics: a European Review*, **16** (3), 203–7.

Lindsnæs, B., T. Martin and L.A. Pedersen (2008), 'Partners in progress: human rights reform and implementation', in B. Lindsnæs (ed.), Copenhagen: The Danish Institute for Human Rights.

Lunau, Y. and F. Wettstein, F. (2004), *Die Soziale Verantwortung Der Wirtshaft. Was Bürger Von Unternehmen Erwarten*, Vienna: Haupt Verlag.

Muhr, S.L. (2008a), 'Othering diversity – a Levinasian analysis of diversity management', *International Journal of Management Concepts and Philosophy*, **3** (2), 176–89.

Muhr, S.L. (2008b), 'Reflections on responsibility and justice – coaching human rights in South Africa', *Management Decision*, **46** (8), 1175–86.

Peperzak, A. (1993), *To the Other. An Introduction to the Philosophy of Emmanuel Levinas*, West Lafayette, IN: Purdue University Press.

Peperzak, A. (1995), *Ethics as First Philosophy – the Significance of Emmanuel Levinas for Philosophy, Literature and Religion*, New York: Routledge.

Shaw, W.H. (1998), *Business Ethics*, Belmont, CA: Wordsworth.

Stevens, B. (1994), 'An analysis of corporate ethical code studies: "where do we go from here?"', *Journal of Business Ethics*, **13** (1), 63–9.

ten Bos, R. and H. Willmott (2001), 'Towards a post-dualistic business ethics: interweaving reason and emotion in working life', *Journal of Management Studies*, **38** (6), 769–93.

Warren, R (1993), 'Codes of ethics: bricks without straw', *Journal of Business Ethics*, **2** (4), 185–91.

9. The creature comforts of management – on morality and empathic response in economic exchange

Alf Rehn

1. INTRODUCTION

Can there be such a thing as a moral foundation of management, and what would it in such a case look like? And what, to begin with, would be a moral foundation in the case of management? This issue, which might seem like a most abstract one, only of interest to people with a distinct philosophical bent, might however be exceedingly practical and tell us a lot about the way in which the complex field of 'management' as a set of human practices is enacted and made meaningful, but it also forces us to consider what it is we mean by such a field. The notion of a foundation implies the existence of a certainty, while the notion of morality implies the existence of a judgment – which would mean that we could say a lot of very defined things about a thing that has a moral foundation.

Are we even prepared to accept something like this for this strange business of ours, one we are conditioned to think of as emerging *ex nihilo nihil?* Looking at how business ethics has been discussed, there is often little heed paid to the historical and anthropological constitution thereof (see however, Argandona 2007; Gordon and Thietart 2007), to the point where much of what is written in the field implicitly seems to assume that ethics comes to the economy a posteriori, as an addendum to an assumed Hobbesian state. As a consequence, relatively little attention has been paid to the way in which long-term cultural figurations in the field of social feelings affect contemporary management (cf. Newton 2001), and how moral notions may in fact be understood as a constant traveler to and with enterprise. In the same vein, there exists an implicit assumption that business ethics is intimately tied to the historical contingency that created the legal construct of the modern corporation in the latter part of the 19th century (although there were similar forms existing in Britain (and other countries) before this, I here take the American understanding of the corporation as a major sea-change in the field of management), which has led to a relative lack of discussion regarding the ethics of the economy, a concept that is much wider-ranging than that of business ethics, and also to a dearth of anthropological viewpoints in the debate thereof.

In this chapter I will argue that in order to develop the thinking of morality and management we need to revisit the very roots of human economies, and maybe even go beyond this historical limit. By bringing in notions from economic anthropology and even primatology I want to show that notions such as empathic response and honor – concepts that have tended to be either ignored completely or discounted as archaic or too trivial – in fact can be used to query the very notion of a business ethics, and also suggest an actual moral foundation of management. Here, I want to problematize the notion that we can point to any clear historical moment from which moment on we can talk of management, and thus challenge the epistemological assumptions I see existing in much of con-temporary business studies. In so doing, I want to argue that the power/ knowledge regime of management studies suffers from an ethical problem, namely the necessity to limit the discourse to things that can be managed within the framework that constitutes its identity project. By bringing in themes that break with both the modernist and the postmodernist tradi-tion in organization studies, I want to raise the issue of epistemological comfort as a necessary part of ethics – but also as a very dangerous thing in research. As a consequence, we need to ask ourselves whether the limita-tions we are imposing on our field of study needs to be studied as a form of ethics, and whether the comfortable tag of 'business ethics' might in fact make us both less ethically aware and less capable of discussing the wider ethics of exchange.

This is to a great deal influenced by the work of both anthropologists such as Marshall Sahlins, but also by the work by primatologists such as Frans de Waal, and the robust attack on 'veneer theory' (de Waal 2006). The latter is not necessarily a theory as such, but rather an implicit assump-tion in much of what is written on the issue of morality and ethics, where one treats these dimensions as a thin coat of civilization applied on the brutish and animal 'true nature' of man (and in extension other, related animals). De Waal challenges this, claiming that we can find behaviors in the large primates that fit well with notions of morality, and that further casts doubt on the idea that ethics would be a mark of progress, in the modernist sense. For business ethics this posits an interesting dilemma, for isn't the way we normally describe the field also a case of 'veneering' an assumedly brutish natural state of business? To extend the metaphor, the field of business ethics might thus be a case of a 'two coats'-fallacy, the veneering of a field assumed to be populated by people veneered by civilization . . . This is the dilemma my chapter will address.

2.   THE WORDS WE USE

In order to analyse the notion of management, I want to start by pointing to some problems of vernacular. Simply put, words such as 'management' and 'business studies' are fundamentally contingent, not only historically but also within specific language regimes. For instance, this chapter is written in English, even though this is my second or third language, and this phenomenon (i.e. the predominance of English) is rarely questioned. In Swedish, my main language, the word management might be translated into '*företagsledning*', or possibly just '*ledning*'. Business studies is normally translated into '*företagsekonomi*', but none of these terms represent perfect translations. In Chinese, the world's de facto major language, the terms are in all likelihood different yet again. Consequently, we are always already, even in management studies, trapped by language and our assumptions about our contingent words representing specific things in the world.

But as Ludwig Wittgenstein (1953/2001) so aptly pointed out in his philosophy of language, the important aspect of a word or words is not necessarily its definition but its use, and its use can be queried through the company it keeps. More to the point, he argued that an understanding of language use must take into consideration something he called 'family resemblances', i.e. the way in which words and concepts have overlapping characteristics and familiarities (cf. Rehn 2008a). As not all of these characteristics need to apply to every concept in the 'family', it becomes possible for us to understand, for example, both football and archery as sports, even though they share few or no characteristics. In the context of studying the moral foundations of management, we might start by considering what family 'management' belongs to. We might imagine something like:

Management – business – exchange – economy – enterprise – organization – leadership – and so on.

Such a list might also make us think about the different ways we might portray the field-intersection of management and ethics, so that we might make a second list:

Management ethics – business ethics – exchange ethics – economy ethics – enterprise ethics – organization ethics – leadership ethics – and so on.

Some of the concepts on this list are familiar (Numbers 1, 2, 6 and 7, for instance), whereas one (enterprise ethics) seems fairly redundant. The interesting thing for me here is the two logical but rarely used concepts of an exchange ethics and an economic ethics. The latter has seen some usage, normally in connection with the academic discipline of economics, or as a more general term of ethics in the economic space (see, for example, Koslowski 2000). The former, however, is very rarely used. Even though some might see this kind of linguistic analysis as a form of sophistry, I contend that it might in fact show us an important avenue of inquiry into how the notion of business ethics can be understood in the context of human history and culture.

Of special interest here is the relation between exchange and management. Oddly enough, the concept of exchange, which is widely used in the discourse of management studies, remains under-theorized. Exchange is one of those things we simply assume to exist. In fact, the concept of exchange might seem almost trite to try and analyse, so ingrained does it seem to be in all our dealings. Specifically, it might seem too basic a concept in studies that deal with management and organization, as these phenomena are assumed to exist in a market society (Slater and Tonkiss 2001) and therefore permeated by market exchange. Still, concepts such as interaction, agency, culture and interpretation are also similarly general, but nevertheless vehemently discussed and analysed within the literature. So why has the concept of exchange received so little interest?

Were we to look towards economic anthropology, we would find that exchange is in fact a central concept, perhaps the most important one of all in understanding economic behavior (see Davis 1992), and also a key form of enacting the social. As an example, in a footnote in his seminal *Stone Age Economics* Marshall Sahlins (1972, pp. 185–6) states that for his purpose in writing the book he was not interested in how a particular individual uses what little she has to achieve a goal chosen among alternatives and that he would instead conceive of economy as 'a component of culture rather than a kind of human action'. In the following footnote (ibid., p. 187) he went on to define economy as 'the process of (materially) provisioning society', and remarked that this definition is helpful since it does not necessarily refer to any individual provisioning. Instead, many exchanges may be strictly worthless as ways of bringing anything material to an individual, but they can still be very efficient ways of provisioning society: 'they [exchanges] maintain social relations, the structure of society, even if they do not to the least advantage the stock of consumables'.

In other words, one of the foundations of economy, and thus management, is ongoing exchange. This might seem self-evident, but it addresses a central issue in trying to address the moral foundations of management. As Sahlin's points out, exchanges are interesting not because they necessarily create profits, but because they provision the society/community/culture they exist in through creating patterns and figurations of social relations, i.e. they create the lattice of social acts and understandings we call culture. Inversely, exchange isn't necessarily a function for creating profit and/or improving the status of any one actor, but might in fact be described in its original guise as something akin to a grooming function, the scratching of a particularly social itch. This would be well in line with how economic anthropology (see, for example, Godelier 1972; Wilk 1996) has discussed exchange behaviors in early societies – not as a distinct function, but rather as an institutionalized behavior. For instance, exchange patterns in gift economies – such as the potlatch and the *kula* ring (see Mauss 1924/1950; Malinowski 1922, 1927; cf. Rehn 2001) – might be understood as emerging organically from micro-level behaviors and becoming functional only after the fact. This is for instance the argument in Claes Gustafsson's (1994) regrettably untranslated *Produktion av allvar* [*The Production of Seriousness*], where the usual teleological explanations for economic institutions are mercilessly criticized as having no analytical basis. Rather, Gustafsson argues, we should adopt an anthropological understanding of the economic world, and accept that the institutionalized patterns we can now observe may well have emerged quite spontaneously, and that the reason for them created *post hoc*. This is of course completely in line with the argumentation in Sahlin's (1972) brilliant essay *The Original Affluent Society* (published as the first essay in *Stone Age Economics*), in which he shows that the birth of structured economic behavior in all likelihood did not originate out of a need to combat dearth and famine, but rather out of the sheer amount of free time hunter-gatherers (see also Gowdy 1998) have at their disposal. Succinctly put, economy (and in extension management) can anthropologically be understood less as a necessary function, and more as a symptom of idleness in early communities, as the continued scratching of a social itch brought on not by pressing need but by a desire to pass the time.

3. THE MORALITY OF EXCHANGE

> Hunters and gatherers have by force of circumstance an objectively low standard of living. But taken as their *objective*, and given their adequate means of production, all the people's material wants usually can be easily satisfied. The evolution of economy has known, then, two contradictory movements: enriching but at the same time impoverishing, appropriating in relation to nature but expropriating in relation to man. (Sahlins 1972, pp. 36–7)

Such a view suggests two things. One, exchanges contain a fundamental element of grooming behaviors, of creating interpersonal comfort by engaging in social intercourse mediated through mechanisms we have later come to call economic. Two, in assessing the makeup of economic orders, we need to be wary of teleological explanations, insofar as they do not necessarily function as adequate descriptions of the assumed foundation of the order itself. Put somewhat differently, if we assume exchange is at the heart of economy, and that economy is a necessary precondition of talking about management, we cannot through this immediately assume that there is any specific functional form which we can go back to in order to debate ethics and morality. The notion of a moral foundation may in fact be misleading, in that it assumes that there is a specific rationality that this morality is keeping in check. What Sahlins and Gustafsson so brilliantly showed was that there might never have been a definitional moment of calculative rationality that kick-started economic thinking, no reckoning of transaction-costs or stakeholder analysis, but rather something much more like a game, a set of exchanges played out in order to instill into the community a sense of a shared ritual. In other words, what if economy started out as a form of comforting?

In fact, if we look to the existing anthropological data regarding exchange, and compare the patterns between intra- and inter-community exchange, a very clear pattern emerges. In most societies where exchange has been analysed, exploitation of a partner that exists within the group that engages in the most intensive exchange – i.e. the partners within a community – is frowned upon, even punished. However, cheating somebody who comes from very far away is seen as less problematic, and in some cases even laudable. In traditional economic analysis (as well as in most cases of business ethics) this would be explained by reference to cost–benefit analyses. Since a trader from far away will not come by often, and might never come by again, it is 'economic' to cheat him, since the gains outweigh the risks. The same would then be inverted within the community. This is, however, a very odd way of looking at it. If one wants to look at the pecuniary or material value-benefits, intra-community exchanges have little to none. Rather, these exchanges often represent institutions that in time and work expended cost more than they bring in – situations an economic agent who coordinates behaviors through cost–benefit analyses would not engage in. Instead, our assumed rational agent would (if we believe those arguing for an economics-based understanding of man) be more likely to cheat a person the greater a chance this represents a case where cost-efficient exchange can be engaged in. In cases with low to no profits, and thus low to no economic losses to be had through exclusion – be moral. In cases with high profits, and thus high losses to be had – cheat away. This, seemingly, would be how an economist would explain early trading behaviors.

The error in this argument is identical to the fallacy that besets much of the thinking on business ethics, namely that exchange (as the basic form of economic behavior) must be understood as driven by the strive for benefit for either of the parties. Important to note here is that in Sahlins now often forgotten treatment of early economies, his argument was that not only could a person enter into exchange relations without expecting a profit, the other party might as well. This is exceptionally important, for it establishes that when querying the logic of exchange we need not try to find a specific form of analysis of outcome, but can instead study the exchange *as it is*.

This, which we could call a phenomenological analysis of exchange (cf. Bibard 2007), would thus look at what takes place when, for example, early man started exchanging material goods within a tight-nit community dominated by kinship ties. Looking to how, for example, gifting behaviors, for instance the exchange of ceremonial tokens or icons, is conducted shows us how early exchange built not so much on the creation of wealth or material value (in fact, the process is in many cases highly wasteful (cf. Bataille 1967/1991)) but the establishment and upkeep of identities and social relations – as we can see in the case of the *kula*.

4.   THE RETURN OF THE *KULA*

Based on extensive fieldwork among the people of the Trobriand Islands in Melanesia, Bronislaw Malinowski published a series of books and articles on the different aspects of their culture. Of these, two books are particularly well known, *Argonauts of the Western Pacific* (1922) and *Sex and Repression in Savage Society* (1927). It is in the earlier of the two in which the particular institution of the *kula* is expounded upon, and the description of this circulation of valuables in the Trobriand Islands still holds a central place in the history of economic anthropology.

The analysis begins with an observation that stands at odds with the then generally held belief that 'primitive' societies lacked economies, a fallacy that still exists, albeit in a somewhat modulated and subconscious form, in modern thought concerning economic organizing. Although such societies may exhibit some barter, even some trade, they were not seen as developed enough to have mastered the art of economic exchange. As they lacked financial institutions, their economic behavior was assumed to be of a non-developed kind, which (assumedly) in time could grow into a real system of exchanges, that is, a market economy. But what Malinowski observed on, for example, the island of Kiriwina, was that there was a continuous and omnipresent exchange of goods, and that these exchanges were extensive both in their geographical dispersal and with regards to the amount of time and resources the islanders put into them. Within the islands there existed advanced and deeply embedded forms of interaction, where exchange and kinship relations were intertwined so as to make them indivisible, but it was the far more dramatic exchanges between the islands that became the focus of Malinowski's early study. He noticed that there existed a traditional system of exchanges that covered the islands as a whole, one where valuables circulated in a '*kula* ring' spanning several hundred miles. In this, two specific articles circulate in opposite directions, creating both a trade route and a distinct cultural pattern, one that encompasses all the members of the societies that take part. The first object, which circulated clockwise (assuming you could observe the islands from above, a vantage point from where they form a kind of circular pattern), was the *soulava*. These were shell necklaces, considered to be male and worn by women, which were constructed by stringing together disks of shells with red mother-of-pearl. The opposite object, the *mwali*, were armbands constructed through breaking off and polishing rings from large shells. Mwali were seen as female, worn by men and circulated counterclockwise. Together they are referred to as the *vaygu'a* and the exchange of these within the *kula* ring constituted an economy unto itself where an intricate structure of rules and conventions ordered their movement.

In the *kula*, the possession of one of the *vaygu'a*-objects is a matter of great pride and satisfaction. The present custodian of an object will often gather people around him and tell the tale of the object, complete with lists of previous custodians. Still, these objects must continuously be kept in motion and given away to the next member in the *kula* ring. As the objects travel in opposite directions, a participant will have a partner or partners to whom all *mwali* are subsequently given and from whom *soulava* will be received. Likewise he will have an opposite partner or partners, to whom *soulava* goes and *mwali* is received. These relations are often enduring and life-long, although new participants can enter from time to time. In some areas, the *kula* is reserved for tribal chiefs, but this exclusivity isn't total. And although it is true that *mwali* are continuously exchanged for *soulava*, this exchange is not conducted in a way that would enable us to liken it with trade.

Superficially viewed, the *vaygu'a*-objects are mere trinkets of extremely limited economic value. But the *kula* system in which these circulate can be seen as the most important institution on the islands, and to a great extent a person's social standing is determined by his position in this system. The travels entailed in these exchanges marked a significant exertion and usage of tribal resources, and to a great degree this exertion was only compounded upon, with participants working hard to create, for example, special ceremonial boats with which to travel. The travels that were undertaken in order to give the objects away could furthermore be very perilous, but were undertaken with diligence and a pronounced enthusiasm. And what is more, all this activity was in order to get and give objects that participants very well could have manufactured themselves, at a fraction of the cost in time and resources (the shells are not particularly rare, and the objects are not hard to create). Despite the 'uneconomic' nature of this, the institution is seen by both Malinowski and Mauss (and later scholars) as both central and functional to the inter- and intra-tribal economies. Mauss, who devotes much of the beginning of his *The Gift* (1924/1950) to a description of the *kula*, sees in this a pure example of the 'total social phenomenon' of the gift as it exists in archaic societies. But what Malinowski tries to do, something that gives his analysis a particularly political bent, is to show that far from being a childish and irrational custom of childish and irrational natives, the *kula* is in fact an inherently functional institution, even an efficient one. The perspective of classical economics is for him ethnocentric and arrogant as it trivializes all such economic behavior that doesn't fit into the market system of exchange. He writes in the conclusion of *Argonauts of the Western Pacific*:

> At one or two places in the previous chapters, a somewhat detailed digression was made in order to criticise . . . the conception of a rational being who wants nothing but to satisfy his simplest needs and does it according to the economic principle of least effort . . . Now I hope that . . . the meaning of the Kula will consist in being instrumental to dispel such crude, rationalistic conceptions of primitive mankind, and to induce both the speculator and the observer to deepen the analysis of economic facts. (Malinowski 1922, p. 516)

When a participant in the *kula* has possession of one of the objects, he will for a time hold on to it and his status will be higher due to this. As tales about the objects are in continuous motion, and he has received the object from one of his trading-partners, his possession of the object in question will be well known to those that interact with him. After a while these will, within the boundaries for propriety both with regards to the time it has been in his possession and to the rules of *kula* exchange, engage with him in order to keep the gift circulating. They may give smaller gifts to make him bound by reciprocity, or otherwise attempt to influence him. As there may be several partners to whom he can give the *vaygu'a*-object, he will choose between these and after a while prepare his boats and voyage to a trade-partner. Here, he will give the object to him, as is befitting the ritual. This is done in a fashion that intentionally downplays the value of what is given:

> The act of giving itself assumes very solemn forms: the thing received is disclaimed and mistrusted; it is only taken up for a moment, after it has been

cast at one's feet. The giver affects an exaggerated modesty: having solemnly brought on his present, to the sound of a seashell, he excuses himself for giving only the last of what remains to him, and throws down the object to be given at the feet of his rival and partner. (Mauss 1924/1990, pp. 22–3)

To conduct oneself honorably, you cannot show any greediness or trading behavior in the *kula*. Although there is continuous talk about what one wishes to gain [*sic*] or what someone else has received in the *kula*, to do this in an open manner would be inappropriate. As the objects are never traded directly, which is further exemplified in the custom of not even giving them hand-to-hand but by throwing them to the ground instead, there is none of the direct and explicit comput-ability we are accustomed to present in trade. Trading, which exists in parallel but which is strictly distinct, is called *gimwali* and is markedly 'economic'. Here, you haggle over prices and try to negotiate maximiz-ing outcomes. To engage in this is fully normal, and not associated with any moral stigma; it is merely a normal trading situation. But if the boundaries between these two institutions are breeched, condemnation will ensue. If a *kula* is conducted in a sloppy way, too quickly or without proper keeping with etiquette – or if a participant tries too overtly to negotiate better terms for himself in the exchange – it is said that it is conducted 'as if it were *gimwali*' (Malinowski 1922, p. 97), something that is unfitting honorable men. One of the most important aspects of the *kula* is that it must portray and represent the generosity, freedom and unselfishness of the participants, as well as their power in being able to forgo valuables. This power can be viewed in many ways, but what such a ritual shows is that the participants can communicate their inde-pendence of material restraints, i.e. their affluence. And at the same time show us that exchange need not be founded on efficiencies in the tra-ditional, 'economic' sense, but instead on processes of building friend-ships, displaying friendships, proving oneself to be a man of honor, and so on – all processes of social feelings. All of this is old news to the field of economic anthropology, but it contains a puzzle when talking about morality in the field of business.

What social feelings – by which I mean the set of emotional and sense-making processes that constitute embodied knowledge of interaction behaviors in the social animal – represent here is something quite different from the assumed calculative rationality of *Homo œconomicus*, and my contention is that this set of feelings can be referred to as the actual moral foundation of management. This as the capacity for empathic response and emergent social grooming functions (Gustafsson 1994) for me stands as both by necessity more primal than the equally cultural capacity for calculative rationality – as the need for the latter should only emerge in more complex settings whereas the former will be necessary in all social interactions – and having greater explanatory force than models reducing human interaction to algorithms and cost–benefit analyses.

5.   MANAGEMENT AS MONKEY BUSINESS

In the context of this chapter this points to social feelings being something more complex than merely veneer applied to a state of *Homo homini lupus*, and instead something much more fundamental, a natural state from which the economic grows rather than vice versa. It also points to exchange as something which finds its base in an indelible and quite possibly biologically given preference to keep up social contacts. The latter point demands an explanation. Within the social sciences, the change in thinking that has been described by and through terms such as 'the linguistic turn', 'social construction', 'post-structuralism', 'cultural studies' and a plethora of others, has made calls to biology and genetics anathema. For many, particularly in the field of critical management studies or critical business ethics, there is no greater sin than invoking explanations from biology, as this is often mistakenly assumed to be a call to social Darwinism. This, however, is a tragic mistake.

One common origin-myth of organizing refers to the necessity of co-operation for sheer survival, in effect arguing that Neolithic man (or whichever early ancestor one wants to use as origin-point) started the first organization for necessary, rational and calculable reasons – something akin to a Neanderthal *Homo œconomicus*. Some, like Paul Seabright, even refer to economic life as having a biological basis, and talk about the 'natural history of economic life' (the subtitle of Seabright 2004).

> Task-sharing takes place to a limited degree in all species that reproduce sexually . . . but human beings' capacity – unique in nature, as we have seen – to share tasks regularly and elaborately with others to whom they are unrelated has enabled them to exploit the presence of large numbers in a way unavailable to higher mammals. (Seabright 2004, p. 36)

Here unique capacities lead, in full accordance with the precepts of strategic management, seamlessly to exploitation of an advantage. Simple as that. However, very little in these socio-biological explanations show why simple task-sharing (such as the all-time favorite example, sexual reproduction) would lead to advanced organizations. And although the Darwinian solve-all of 'survival' is regularly brandished, this actually solves very little. The existence of an advantage may seem like enough of a reason to utilize it, but obviously this is not a logical necessity.

Let us ponder this in the context of our earlier discussion for a moment. According to Sahlins (cf. Gowdy 1998), Neolithic man led a fairly nice and uncomplicated life. Four hours of daily work (or less) sustained his/her needs, and the rest was spent chatting, playing, having sex and napping. Now, obviously, some would see this as a utopian existence. Still, it is conceivable that some of these antediluvian layabouts got bored, and made up alternative amusement – like organizing! As Richard Wrangham and Dale Peterson (1996) show in their study of chimpanzees, organizing among these normally takes place not due to any specific stimulus, but as a reaction to boredom. All of a sudden, a chimpanzee may start beating on the ground with some branches, screeching and jumping around. After a while, others will join in, until a critical mass is reached. This can then lead to a war-party, which will attack neighboring flocks of apes, killing and raping with some abandon. In such a manner, even our animal cousins can create at the very least a temporary organization, but not out of any rational reason or distinct necessity. Chimpanzees may enjoy these little forays into organized mayhem, but they do not form these bands out of any pressing need – unless breaking up the monotony of a peaceful and unproblematic existence is seen as a need. Obviously, this kind of diversion takes on many forms. Chimpanzees play, engage in frivolous sexual activity, fling dung at each other for fun, and so on. None of these have clear-cut evolutionary advantages, and as socio-biologists invent ever-more fanciful explanations regarding such behavior, the great apes seem to find new ways to simply amuse themselves. Even hunting, which many reference as an origin-point of sorts for organized behavior, seems to be less than rational when observed among the chimpanzees:

> My work at Gombe has shown that the energetic balance involved in hunting rarely tips in favor of a nutritional motive. Most members of the hunting party receive very little meat for their effort, and the number of chimp-hours expended on the hunt plus the long begging and sharing session that follows it can be enormously costly relative to the quantity of meat that is usually available. The most typical catch is a one-kilogram baby monkey, divided among up to twenty hunters. So chimpanzees engage in an energy-expensive behavior, and most fail to recoup their caloric investment. (Stanford 1999, pp. 97–8)

The difference between my position (drawn from the work of prima-tologists such as de Waal and Stanford) and that of socio-biologists in the social sciences (see for example, Nicholson 1997, Seabright 2004) should be obvious. I contend that we can trace complex social behaviors back through the biological veil of our separation from the other great apes, but not in order to claim that our social feelings are strictly biological or genetic, but rather that culture and social feelings exist on a much more fundamental level than socio-biologists are normally prepared to admit. Where this debate has often hinged on finding 'rational genetic' explanations for human behavior, even a passing interest in primatology shows that the kind of rationality that one seeks is not necessarily present in 'nature' either. Chimpanzees hunt for fun, capture small monkeys and use them as dolls (Stanford 1999), engage in war parties and so on, behaviors that are closer to the argument for the development of human economies as presented by Sahlins and Gustafsson than anything remotely like the actions of a purely efficient self-interested optimizer.

Returning to our Neolithic ancestors, we can now ask whether the adoption of increasingly intricate task-sharing so praised by Seabright (2004) is a result of a necessity a priori, or in fact born out of the luxury of abundant leisure time? If we accept the works of Sahlins (1972) and Gowdy (1998) as at least possible conjectures, then the development of organizations would not have been started due to a need for such, unless we account for their importance as social activities. The hunting behaviors of chimpanzees and the organizing activities of early man might in fact best be seen as precisely the kind of grooming activity postulated earlier, activities engaged in because animals with social feelings (i.e. capacity for empathic response) have something akin to a biological propensity (cf. Popper 1990) to engage in social activities. We should of course not see this need as a need in a limited sense, but rather as the likely realization of a biological possibility, much as the development of language in *Homo sapiens*, which in part was dependent on the complex genetic contingency of how our mouth cavities, tongue and vocal cords happen to match and make complex sounds possible. Nor should we see it as a given, except after the fact. But with this fact, with these activities, and seeing to the problems in presenting calculative rationality as an explanation, it becomes evermore clear that we need to revisit the notion of a moral foundation.

6. AGAINST ANTHROPOCENTRISM: EMPATHIC RESPONSE AND THE MORAL FOUNDATIONS OF MANAGEMENT

Regardless if we look to the economic life of early man or the organizing behavior of our close ancestors, we will find a much more complex set of behaviors than is normally assumed. In the former case, economic and organizational development appears as something much more complicated than just a response to the stimulus of dearth and famine. In the latter, we cannot discount the existence of complex organized behavior engaged in for reasons going beyond simple survival. In both cases we

need to go beyond the simple surface, the veneer referred to by Frans de
Waal (2006; cf. Cheney and Seyfarth 2007).

> In fact, things may be exactly the other way around. Instead of language and
> culture appearing with a Big Bang in our species and then transforming the way
> we relate to each other, Greenspan and Shanker (2004) propose that it is from
> early emotional connections and 'proto conversations' between mother and
> child (cf. Trevarthen 1993) that language and culture sprang. Instead of empathy
> being an endpoint, it may have been the starting point. (de Waal 2006, p. 23)

The critical part of de Waal's argument is that he wants to move the
debate regarding morality and ethics away from the assumption that these
are behaviors that have endowed upon the human animal, and upon the
human animal alone, as a kind of veneer given by the advance of civilization. By studying ongoing social behaviors among monkey and apes,
he has been able to show in them complex and ongoing interactions that
seem to fit very well with social emotions such as generosity, gratitude,
fairness and even community concern. All these build on the capacity
for empathic response, i.e. the capacity of 'putting oneself in the place
of another', realizing that one is interacting with a being that is also an
individual, and being able to translate between one's own emotional states
and those of the other. For instance, de Waal (2006, p. 29) references a
study by Masserman et al., which showed that rhesus monkeys would not
interact with a food delivery system when they realized that doing so sent a
painful shock to another monkey. Rather than continuing to hurt another,
the monkeys would simply refuse food, even starve. In other words, on a
basic level of ethics, monkeys were shown to be quite capable of making
a long-term ethical decision that went against its own self-interest, simply
in order not to hurt another being. This kind of empathy is at the base of
social feelings, and de Waal carefully lays out the wide variety of moral
behaviors that apes and monkeys are in fact capable of.

By doing so, de Waal delivers a stinging criticism against those who
would see ethics and morality as something that is merely applied on top
of an assumedly brutish nature, and claims that morality is as much part
of our 'natural makeup' as the capacity for complex calculations is. We
are moral *to begin with*, and have been so for a very, very long time, much
longer than we have engaged in anything like more complex economic
behaviors. Insights from primatology could thus be used to critique those
forms of ethical argumentation that would postulate self-interest as a
natural state – the popularity of dressing up reductionism as 'methodo-
logical individualism' would be a good candidate – by showing that this
is not only sociologically problematic and philosophically weak, it builds
on a mistake regarding nature as well. In a move that will surely be seen

as downright perverse by some, the natural sciences might actually be a friend of critical management studies (by any other name).

Similarly, the arguments that can be drawn from economic anthropology attack the notion that economy started out of a 'natural state' where dearth and the war of all upon all reigned. Rather than seeing the cultural aspect of the economy as a veneer applied to a necessity of profit and a relentless fight against lack, we can from people like Sahlins infer a quite different history, one where dearth, lack and radical competition are in fact *effects* of the cultural move towards collecting things, setting up permanent homesteads, establishing trade. The natural foundation we normally if implicitly assume simply isn't there. This is why it is necessary to inquire more deeply into the moral foundations of management – they may be quite different from the ones we are used to.

Both insights, that primates may be more fundamentally moral than we give them credit for and that the early stages of economy might have been a case of serious play bring us back to social feelings as a shared foundation. There exists a moral foundation for management simply because there exists a moral foundation for our very being as social animals, and this can be traced back far beyond the usual borders of how business ethics is thought about. By challenging the usual assumptions about self-interest (or not) in novel ways, the field could be extended, and old argumentations broken up. But there also exists a moral foundation to the birth of economy, namely that in the development of exchange behaviors, by necessity, there existed a dimension of social feelings, and in order to have a fully developed theory of economy we need to revisit this anthropological core. This dual query regarding the standing of social feelings in the possibility to establish an original economy to actually manage might seem to touch upon a rather abstract, even irrelevant issue, but I contend that in order to have a theoretical foundation one needs to free the discussion of overly anthropocentric ideas. This would include at least entertaining the notion that we are at heart creatures of comfort, and that the grooming we still engage in is in fact something basic and necessary rather than a marginal and contingent phenomenon.

7. MANAGEMENT AS COMFORT, MANAGEMENT STUDIES AS COMFORTABLE

In other words, to me management is impossible without social feelings, and the category of comfort is critical if we want to fully understand the origin and the trajectory of economy as a human endeavor. From early on, we comfort each other and engage in activities that represent grooming behaviors – chatting, agreeing, puttering about. And this is in fact what we have been doing throughout the ages. Grooming is a social activity that builds on social feelings, and existence of this even in animals such as chimpanzees gives us the possibility of re-imagining the trajectories and connections of social development. If we accept the challenge from economic anthropology that exchange need not be a case of profit-seeking but might instead have originated out of empathic relationships and their continuation, we get a situation where comfort and economy in fact are irrevocably intertwined, giving us a very clear moral foundation of management.

However, the term 'comfort' also contains another side, one that might be analytically much more problematic. As I have argued elsewhere (Rehn 2008b), management studies is to a great extent defined through the ways it has chosen to remain affixed to a set of unchallenged assumption, i.e. defined by a kind of epistemological comfort. By sticking to the same ideas and the same assumptions, the field itself has become something akin to a gang of baboons picking each other's nits – lovely but far removed from an active intellectual debate. The field of business ethics can likewise be criticized for being too nice for its own good, with the same references and the same calls to theorists repeated *ad infinitum* out of an unconscious desire to keep the debate comfortable. So where comfort might be exceptionally important to establish and keep up an economy, the same comfort might very well stifle an intellectual debate.

Therefore, this text has quite consciously been written in order to be uncomfortable. I make no claims to have fully shown how economic anthropology and primatology can be used to query business ethics, I have merely tried to show that there are questions about the foundations of our field that are rarely asked, because we are not comfortable with seeing apes as moral agents or questioning the origins of economy. However, *exactly* because this is uncomfortable, these are questions and issues that should be raised. If we are to discount things because they do not fit in elegantly with our prevailing ideas about things, we are not researchers but ideologues. And if we are to understand morals, we cannot let our moralizations about the world guide us. In other words, if we truly want to inquire into the moral foundations of management, we can never let ourselves be creatures of comfort.

REFERENCES

Argandona, A. (2007), 'Economics, ethics and anthropology', in M. Djelic and R. Vranceanu (eds), *Moral Foundations of Management Knowledge*, Cheltenham, UK and Northampton, MA, USA: Edward Elgar.

Bataille, G. ([1967] 1991), *The Accursed Share, Vol. 1: Consumption*, New York: Zone Books.

Bibard, L. (2007), 'Towards a phenomenology of management: from modelling to day-to-day moral sensemaking cognition', in M. Djelic and R. Vranceanu (eds), *Moral Foundations of Management Knowledge*, Cheltenham, UK and Northampton, MA, USA: Edward Elgar, pp. 3–30.

Cheney, D. and R. Seyfarth (2007), *Baboon Metaphysics: The Evolution of a Social Mind*, Chicago, IL: University of Chicago Press.

Davis, J. (1992), *Exchange*, Buckingham: Open University Press.

de Waal, F. (2006), *Primates and Philosophers: How Morality Evolved*, Princeton, NJ: Princeton University Press.

Godelier, M. (1972), *Rationality and Irrationality in Economics*, New York: Monthly Review Press.

Gordon, K. and R. Thietart (2007), 'From hunter-gatherer to organizational man: a morality tale', in M. Djelic and R. Vranceanu (eds), *Moral Foundations of Management Knowledge*, Cheltenham, UK and Northampton, MA, USA: Edward Elgar, pp. 47–63.

Gowdy, J. (eds) (1998), *Limited Wants, Unlimited Means: A Hunter-Gatherer Reader on Economics and the Environment*, Washington, DC: Island Press.

Greenspan, S., S. Shanker (2004), *The First Idea: How Symbols, Language and Intelligence Evolved From Our Primate Ancestors To Modern Humans*, Boston, MA: Da Capo Press.

Gustafsson, C. (1994), *Produktion av Allvar: om det Ekonomiska Förnuftets Metafysik*, Stockholm: Nerenius and Santérus.

Koslowski, P. (ed) (2000), *Contemporary Economic Ethics and Business Ethics*, Berlin: Springer.

Malinowski, B. (1922), *Argonauts of the Western Pacific: An Account of Native Enterprise and Adventure in the Archipelagos of Melanesian New Guinea*, London: Routledge.

Malinowski, B. (1927), *Sex and Repression in Savage Society*, London: Kegan Paul.

Mauss, M. ([1924] 1950), *The Gift: Forms and Functions of Exchange in Archaic Societies*, London: Cohen and West.

Newton, T. (2001) 'Organization: the relevance and the limitations of Elias', *Organization*, **8** (3), 467–95.

Nicholson, N. (1997), 'Evolutionary psychology: toward a new view of human nature and organizational society', *Human Relations*, **50** (9), 1053–78.

Popper, K. (1990), *A World of Propensities*, Bristol: Thoemmes Press.

Rehn, A. (2001), *Electronic Potlatch – A Study on New Technologies and Primitive Economic Behaviors*, Stockholm: Royal Institute of Technology.

Rehn, A. (2008a), 'Wittgenstein's iPod, or, the familiar among us', in D. Wittkower (ed.), *iPod and Philosophy*, Chicago, IL: Open Court.

Rehn, A. (2008b), 'On meta-ideology and moralization – prolegomena to a critique of management studies', *Organization*, **15** (4), 598–609.

Sahlins, M. (1972), *Stone Age Economics*, New York: Aldine de Gruyter.

Seabright, P. (2004), *The Company of Strangers: A Natural History of Economic Life*, Princeton, NJ: Princeton University Press.

Slater, D. and F. Tonkiss (2001), *Market Society: Markets and Modern Social Theory*, Cambridge: Polity Press.

Stanford, C. (1999), *The Hunting Apes: Meat-Eating and the Origins of Human Behavior*, Princeton, NJ: Princeton University Press.

Trevarthen, C. (1993), 'The function of emotions in early communication and development', in J. Nadel and L. Camaioni (eds), *New Perspectives in Early Communicative Development*, London: Routledge.

Wilk, R. (1996), *Economies and Cultures: Foundations of Economic Anthropology*, Boulder, CO: Westview Press.

Wittgenstein, L. ([1953] 2001), *Philosophical Investigations*, Oxford: Blackwell Publishing.

Wrangham, R. and D. Peterson (1996), *Demonic Males: Apes and the Origins of Human Violence*, Boston, MA: Houghton Mifflin.

10. 'Is your manager a psychopath? . . . Are you?' The human–animal divide at work

Rasmus Johnsen

1. INTRODUCTION

He is good at making friends and alliances, but these relations never seem to last. He is extremely confident, maybe even self-important. He is very ambitious, but seldom finishes what he started. He is innovative, charming and good at convincing other people that his ideas are ingenious, but following them most likely will have catastrophic consequences for everyone involved. He has a personality disorder from which he seems to be the only one who doesn't suffer, while people around him, his colleagues, his employees and even the organizations he works for, come apart. He is a *psychopath*. But instead of being in prison like Hannibal 'The Cannibal' Lector he works around the corner and is probably a middle manager on his way up the corporate ladder.

Over the last decade the debate concerning clinical psychopathy among employees and managers in contemporary business organizations has found its way to international news stories (for example, Desai 2004; Deutschman 2005). When the white-collar crime and Machiavellian behavior behind the bankruptcies of some of the world's largest companies is exposed or the investments of rogue traders lead to severe economic loss, this psychiatric diagnosis comes up and the media starts questioning the sanity of those responsible.

But if these examples refer to the sense-making process after huge corporate scandals and to the exposure of unbelievable immorality and ruthlessness following them, then the use of the diagnosis in organizations also leads a more precarious life. It does so when it refers, not to the extraordinary rogues, but to the assumption of the potential threat that a co-worker or a manager in the organization may be a psychopath in hiding; an individual who works and lives among us, looks like everyone else, but is cunningly camouflaging anti-social behavior under a veneer of friendliness and slick charm. The psychopath lurking in the world of work is successful because his ruthlessness and desire for power is mistaken for ambition and good leadership skills – while he is really scheming, manipulating, lying and using people around him for his own benefit. In times where human resource management has become a key factor in the management of subjectivity at work, incorporating most of the managerial tropes concerned with the productive appropriation of generic human qualities, the image of the psychopath reflects the fear of abuse of this vocabulary.

The seriousness of this fear is reflected for example on the web pages of Danish unions that try to warn their members and give advice on how to recognize a psychopath. A union for lawyers and economists (Santesson 2006) call them 'Masters of Lying' and warn that even though you might have been in contact with one and think you know the characteristics, you can easily be fooled again. A league for IT-workers organized under the Danish Metal Workers Union claim that the 'charismatic psychopath' manipulates, terrorizes and intimidates, and that he leaves a trail of people behind that might never return to work (IT2U 2009). A large Danish union for commercial and clerical employees has put a test on their homepage to assist their members in determining if the manager is a psychopath (HK 2007). The test is framed by yellow and black stripes (like hazard warning tape at a building site) and asks the question: 'Is your manager a PSYCHOPATH?' A text in smaller letters below states that the test is not intended to be used for 'labeling others psychopaths' and curiously also states that to do this you need a professional background. There are eight questions to be answered on the test formulated along the line of: 'Does it sound hollow to you, when your manager tries to express repentance?' Or: 'Is your manager arrogant? Haughty? . . . Does he act like the centre of everything?' Answering the questions with either No, Maybe/Somewhat or Yes, will eventually reflect on a meter, also in black and yellow, that shows where the individual in question lands on a scale from 0–12. While scoring a zero on the scale gets the commentary: 'Be happy', a score of just one means: 'Be frustrated' and a score of 12: 'Be very scared'. The web page also asks the members of the union to share their experiences with others, offers the opportunity to read some already published stories, and contains a number of interviews with political parties about possible legislation in the area.

The research into the field of non-forensic psychopathy, however, stands against these serious efforts to warn about psychopaths lurking in organizations. This research suggests that the assumption of the disorder among successful workers in organizations is very doubtful. As Harris et al. (2001) in a study of the construct of psychopathy conclude, it is unlikely that there are more than a few, if any, adult psychopaths who have not engaged in substantial criminal behavior and who would meet socioeconomic definitions of success. Apart from the problem that there is very little evidence to support the fact that clinical psychopaths hide in contemporary business organizations, other researchers who have tried to recruit psychopaths from the community (Widom and Newman 1985; Widom 1977) have failed to make it clear that these participants would meet diagnostic criteria. Additionally most of the subjects in these studies had been arrested, and as many as half, incarcerated. Contrary to what the assumption of a kind of organizational psychopath seems to suggest, Widom (1977) reports that the socioeconomic status of allegedly non-forensic psychopaths is not substantially higher than that of those who have landed in prison. A later replication study (Widom and Newman 1985) shows that the community-recruited psychopaths had serious financial problems and had almost all been arrested. They held short-term jobs and were frequently on welfare and unemployed. In other similar studies (Belmore and Quinsey 1994) the subjects who met the criteria for psychopathy appear to have been between prison sentences when assessed. Lykken (1995) adds that psychopaths are more likely than others to have been raised by single mothers with the higher risk of poverty this entails. The most influential classical study of psychopathy, Cleckley's *The Mask of Sanity* (1976), takes notice of the history of failure in the lives of psychopaths, because of their recklessness and their dishonest, exploitative behavior.

The striking difference between the findings in clinical research and the assumptions made in the considerable amount of popular literature published on the subject of organizational psychopathy over the last decade, with titles like *Snakes in Suits – When Psychopaths Go to Work* (Babiak and Hare 2006), *The Sociopath Next Door* (Stout 2005), *Working with Monsters: How to Identify and Protect Yourself from the Workplace Psychopath* (Clarke 2005), suggest that entirely different subjects are being treated here. The aggressive and self-destructive character presented in psychiatric research is not the same as the slick, charming and unscrupulous character presented in the popular discourse. From a critical standpoint this discrepancy could surely be taken to reflect the problematic issues in understanding socially unacceptable behavior as mental illness and the dangerous implications in using pathology instrumentally in power struggles on the labor market. But the discrepancy can also be taken to mean something else and more.

In the following, I will argue that the organizational psychopath, characterized as a corrupt and immoral success with a good conscience, plays a marginalized, yet important role in the identity formation of the subject in human resource management. Rather than representing an individual who is in constant contact with the mental health or the criminal justice systems, but is found impossible to rehabilitate, the organizational psychopath represents a boundary phenomenon of monstrous hybridization, in which the human and the inhuman in the contemporary management of subjectivity at work – as 'human resource' – become enmeshed in an inclusive, heterogeneous, and dangerously unstable zone. In this, I will argue, the organizational psychopath comes to represent a modern version of the *lycanthrope* – the werewolf – as a creature that through several centuries of our cultural history possessed a fundamental role in the mechanisms of how the 'human' came to be understood through the human–animal divide. Like the lycanthrope, the precarious character representing the lack of self-knowledge that enabled man to be more than an animal and thus came to define the human being, the organizational psychopath represents the collapse of the distinction between the spontaneous judgments and moral acts of authentic human behavior and the managerial codification and instrumentalization of the human as a resource. The psychopath, I will argue, emerges in the organizational setting as a grotesque hybridization of the 'human' as an authentic quality and the 'human' transformed into a resource by managerial intervention and practice. In this sense the psychopath constitutes a flip side to management in contemporary organizations – the dark side of Human Resource Management.

In order to examine this monstrous hybrid I will introduce the French psychoanalyst Julia Kristeva's theory of *abjection*. The theory of the abject – the 'something' that the subject must separate itself from in order to be human, but that uncannily remains in the separation – is useful to understanding the role of the psychopath in the identity formation of the working subjectivity, because it illustrates the instability of the distinction between the authentically 'human' and the instrumentalized 'human' in HRM of which the organizational psychopath is a problematization. When Kristeva defines the abject as 'above all a revolt against an external menace from which one wants to distance oneself, but of which one has the impression that it may menace us from the inside' (Kristeva 1996, p. 118), she is touching upon a profound insight that the image of the organizational psychopath may provide us with: that the assumption of something authentically human, which becomes instrumentalized in HRM, is itself the result of a separation and not a generic factor. In this perspective the 'organizational psychopath' emerges with the uncanny indistinctiveness of a separation that has not been made, as a hybrid between the human and the inhuman. Through a discussion of the human–animal divide in the 16th century's prosecution of alleged werewolves, I will argue that Kristeva's theory of abjection can illustrate how the organizational psychopath – as a modern version of the lycanthrope – emerges as a problematization of the assumption of the authentically 'human' and its position on organization. As a reflection of the managerial injunction to 'be yourself', the assumption of psychopathy in organizations represents the precarious problem of knowing exactly what that means.

The chapter has a philosophical perspective. Performing an inquiry into the role of the psychopath in organizations is meant to be a constructive examination of what 'the human' in HRM means, of how it works and what it relates to when it does so. In this respect it neither aims to synthesize different paradigmatic positions within the field in order to affirm it, nor does it seek to criticize in order to undermine the praxis and clear the way for a radical alternative. Rather, what the following aims for is an illumination of that which is often left out in the debate about contemporary managerial strategies. As Steyaert and Janssens have argued, the field of HRM studies suffers from a too one-sided orientation towards normative models and lacks a more reflexive approach that aims to develop the theorizing of the field itself (Steyaert and Janssens 1999; Janssens and Steyaert 2008). The philosophical approach in this chapter seeks to respond to this lack by maintaining a constructive attitude that develops and contributes something. In this sense the approach complies with the plea for a *reconstructive reflexivity* (Janssens and Steyaert 2008; Alvesson et al. 2008) in the studies of human subjectivity at work. In a broader sense this is also what lends the chapter its *ethical* perspective. As Jones et al. have argued, ethics in business is often reduced to a *technology* that works to reduce undecidability – almost as if just knowing the right rules would immediately enable us to do the right thing (Jones et al. 2005). In a philosophical perspective, ethical thinking is not reducible to a mechanical normative perspective like this (see also Jeanes and Muhr, and Rehn in this volume). In fact, in a more radical sense, ethical thinking is not at all concerned with the stability of some solution. Instead, it works hard to keep and retain openness, difficulty and a problematizing horizon, seeing that the 'ontological conditions' of ethics is freedom (to choose an alternative), which is why ethics is the reflective form given to this freedom (for example, Foucault and Rabinow 1984; Foucault 1988, 1990, Raffnsøe et al. 2008). Giorgio Agamben even maintains that such an experience addresses the fundamentally unfinished character of being. Ethics becomes effective only when things do not necessarily speak for themselves (Agamben 2004). Engaging in an examination of the organizational psychopath and its relation to the 'human' in HRM amounts to a constructive complication of things in this sense of 'the ethical'.

2.   ABJECTION AND THE IMAGE OF THE WEREWOLF

It makes perfect intuitive sense to understand both the psychopath and the werewolf along the lines of Julia Kristeva's theory of abjection, when she defines the abject as 'immoral, sinister, scheming, and shady: . . . a hatred that smiles' (Kristeva 1982, p. 4). Yet to understand the relevance and meaning of the abject to the present perspective may be more challenging when Kristeva points to the pivotal aspect of the abject as its status of being 'something rejected from which one does not part'. The paradoxical designation of the abject as an ambiguous in-between, which incessantly emerges on the inside in spite of its expulsion, is not straightforward. A scene from Jules Verne's classic *From the Earth to the Moon* provides us with a powerful illustration that may be helpful here. The novel's narrators Ardan and Barbicane, travelling with two dogs as companions, are hurled into space in an oversized projectile arranged much like a Victorian closet. By accident, when the travel companions are shot out of the huge underground cannon, one of the dogs – Satellite – suffers a fatal wound and dies. Worried that the body will contaminate the air in the narrow space, the two men decide to quickly open the scuttle and throw out poor Satellite, but soon find that the dead dog that they sought to get rid off does not disappear. Instead, the corpse seems to hang outside the window of the projectile that holds the little community from which it was expulsed. Mounting and ever mounting 'this deformed, unrecognizable object, reduced to nothing . . . flattened like a bagpipe without wind' (Verne 1874, p. 201) follows the spaceship through empty space on its way towards the moon.

Like the corpse of the dead dog Satellite that used to be a family pet, the abject represents the massive emergence of uncanniness in something radically separate and loathsome that is no longer exactly subject or object, but is haunting because it is not reducible to any of them – but is not nothing, either. To Kristeva the abject refers to the human reaction to the threat of a breakdown in coherence or meaning brought about by the loss of a distinction between self and other (Felluga 2003). The corpse provides an especially good example of this, because it represents something beyond the mere knowledge or meaning of death. The corpse, like the materiality of other refuse, *shows* what is thrust aside in order to live (Kristeva 1982, p. 3). The deformed body of the dead pet Satellite forms a continuous relation with the little community aboard the Victorian projectile by showing both the death that is ejected into empty space and the death that eerily remains among the living. In this sense we can speak of the abject as *a distinction that has not been made*; it is the sickening, disgusting, unhealthy, appalling and paradoxical 'thing' that is marked by a fundamental indistinctness. When Kristeva argues that a 'wound with blood and pus, or the sickly, acrid smell of sweat, of decay, does not *signify* death', it is not because somatic extrication has no symbolic function, but rather because it has much more than just that.

Nowhere, perhaps, is the rejection of something from which one does not part as lucidly illustrated as in the trials against alleged werewolves in 16th century Europe, a period in which the notion of the 'human' was extremely vulnerable and unstable, and was secured, as the historian Erica Fudge (2003) argues, largely by forms of self-mastery over the passions which reasserted the domination of reason over the body. The concept itself – *werewolf* – suggests a fundamental indistinctness. Originating most probably from the Anglo-Saxon *wer*, meaning simply man, and *wulf* meaning wolf, the term *werewolf* means *man-wolf* (Otten 1986; Lawrence 1996). Another suggestion by Baring-Gould that holds the Norse *vargr*, signifying either a wolf or a godless man, to equal the English *were* leads to the same conclusion. The Anglo-Saxons called the evil man a *wearg*, *vargs* in Gothic is a fiend, and old Norman laws said of criminals condemned for certain offences to outlawry: *Wargus esto!* (Baring-Gould 1995). As a monstrous hybrid between incongruities: human and animal, man and beast, lawful and outlawed, the werewolf represented a zone of indetermination, in which the elements were dangerously indiscernible and a distinction had to be made. The trial records of cases against werewolves testify that this distinction was much more than a metaphorical matter. Including detailed accounts of raving madness, horrible crimes, rape, incest, cannibalism and savage murder (Otten 1986, p. 51; see also: Baring-Gould 1995), the verdicts in such cases were based on realistic attempts to determine the physical shape of the defendant during the crime, often through demonic theory drawing on historical authorities like Aristotle, Augustine and Thomas Aquinas. This dilemma is very well exemplified in the following excerpt from the interrogation of the lycanthrope Jacques Roulet convicted in 1598 of murder and cannibalism:

> When rubbed with this ointment do you become a wolf?
>
> No; but for all that, I killed and ate the child Cornier: I was a wolf.
>
> . . .
>
> Do your hands and feet become paws of a wolf?
>
> Yes, they do.
>
> Does your head become like that of a wolf – your mouth become larger?
>
> I do not know how my head was at the time; I used my teeth; my head was as it is to-day.
>
> (Baring-Gould 1995, p. 65)

Constituting a complete – and painstakingly real – indiscernibility between man and animal this excerpt illustrates eminently how the cases against werewolves had to deal with much more than merely the question of guilt in order to determine the nature of the defendant.

One example is the case of Jean Grenier, which began as terror spread during the year of 1603 among the villagers in the St. Sever districts of Gascony in the south-west of France. Several young children had begun to mysteriously disappear off the fields and roads without a trace, discoveries had been made of partially eaten children, and a man-wolf was reported attacking little girls tending sheep. In one instance even an infant was stolen from its cradle in a cottage where the mother had left it to sleep. In late May a boy about the age of 14 was arrested. On 2 June, Jean Grenier confessed to the higher court to lycanthropy. He told the court that after he had run away from home, he had been taken to meet the Lord of the Forest. This lord was a tall dark man, dressed all in black, who provided Jean Grenier with a wolf-skin and a salve he would smear himself with, when he was hunting for children at the command of his master. From that time on, he said, he had 'run about the country as a wolf' (Baring-Gould 1995, p. 72). When questioned about the children, whom he said he had killed and eaten as a wolf, he told the court that he had on one occasion entered an empty house and dragged a sleeping child out of its cradle. He had eaten as much of it as he could and given the remains to a wolf. He had then developed an uncontrollable appetite for the flesh of young girls. Through confrontations it was established that Grenier had killed and eaten several children and wounded others.

The problem that the court faced in the case of Jean Grenier was the nature of the defendant: can a human being change or be changed physically and in this shape commit abominable crimes for which he cannot be held morally responsible, because of the metamorphosis? Is the physical transformation real or is it a delusion? Although Jean Grenier did not plead insanity, the judge determined that he was incapable of rational thought, 'so dull and idiotic that children of seven or eight years old have usually a larger amount of reason than he' (Baring-Gould 1995, p. 74), and hence could not be held morally responsible for what he had done. Instead of execution he was sentenced to life imprisonment in a monastery. Here he ended his days seven years later, shortly after a visitor had described him as running frantically around on all fours, unable to comprehend the smallest things: 'His eyes were deep set and restless, his teeth long and protruding, his nails black, and in places worn away' (Baring-Gould 1995, p. 74). As to his claims about being turned into a wolf, the statement of the president was that 'the change of shape existed only in the disorganized brain of the insane; consequently it was not a crime and could not be punished' (Otten 1986, p. 51).

The relevance of Kristeva's theory of abjection to the human–animal divide, exemplified in the case against Jean Grenier, is indicated not only by the disgust and abomination that the indistinctness between man and beast provokes, but also by the precarious instability of the distinction resulting from it, because this distinction presupposes and passes through the human. Rather than constituting something generically *inhuman*, the werewolf reflects a fundamental indiscernibility between the human and the inhuman *in man himself*. This indiscernibility threatens the identity and the natural quality of the 'human' as such and must incessantly be taken care of. When Kristeva paradoxically speaks of the abject as that which remains, even in the attempt to expulse it, the terror that it provokes consists in the realization that it is the expulsion itself that articulates the elements in the distinction. What remains is the nagging suspicion that before the act of separation, there was nothing but a formless and primordial chaos out of which the distinction emerged. The abject of the werewolf is terrifying, because it is the material manifestation of a distinction that has not been made. Attesting to the precarious instability of the human–animal divide, it constitutes an uncanny reminder that the subject of this divide is inscribed in a fundamental *lack* of distinction, out of which it emerges, not with a qualitative and natural difference, but as man *defined as the result of a separation*. In other words, the terrible abomination of the lycanthrope consist not in the fact that it is different from me, but in the anxiety-provoking possibility that I might resemble it more than I like. It is this precarious dilemma, as we shall see, that makes the organizational psychopath a contemporary cousin of the werewolf.

3. THE ORGANIZATIONAL PSYCHOPATH

If lycanthropy reflected a fear that beasts might be lurking in the gloomy shadows just beyond the thresholds of civilization, the clinical construct of psychopathy grew out of the fear of the animal that evolutionary theory had given shelter in darker regions of the human soul. It was the general obsession in the 19th century with the brutish origins of the species, reflected for example in Baring Gould's assumption in *The Book of Werewolves* ([1865] 1995) that a child is naturally inclined to strike at a butterfly 'because it has *life* in it and he has an instinct within him impelling him to destroy life wherever he finds it' (Baring-Gould 1995, p. 133), which saw psychopathy emerge as a theory about degeneracy. Generally the concept itself is credited to the French physician Philippe Pinel, by many recognized as one of the founding fathers of psychiatry, who advocated moral treatment for the disorder instead of the more traditional cruel, physical interventions like bloodletting or ice-cold baths (Arrigo and Shipley 2001, p. 327). In the early 19th century Pinel had observed that some of his patients engaged in impulsive and often extremely violent acts. They caused self-harm, but were perfectly capable of comprehending the irrationality of what they were doing and their reasoning abilities appeared unimpaired. Pinel described the disorder that these men were suffering from as *manie sans délière* (insanity without delirium) and expressed surprise to find 'many maniacs who at no period gave evidence of any lesion of understanding' (Pinel 1962, p. 9). But it was in the work of Benjamin Rush, an American psychiatrist who maintained that the moral derangement he found in his patients was congenital and that it was caused by 'an original defective organization in those parts of the body which are preoccupied by the moral faculties of the mind' (Rush 1812, p. 112), that psychopathy emerged as a problematization of the 'human'. Some years later the British physician J.C. Prichard defined the 'morbid perversion of the natural feelings, affections, inclinations, temper, habits, moral dispositions, and natural impulses, without any remarkable disorder or defect of the intellect or knowing and reasoning faculties' (Prichard 1835, p. 16) that he found in some patients, as *moral insanity*. This classification of moral alienation saw insanity in some individuals separate them from the natural human qualities that they were supposed to possess. To Prichard the disorder was characterized by involving a deranged state, where:

> moral or active principles of the mind are strangely perverted or depraved; the power of self-government is lost or greatly impaired and the individual is found to be incapable, not of talking or reasoning upon any subject proposed to him, but of conducting himself with decency and propriety in the business of life. (Prichard 1835, p. 85)

Although the understanding of psychopathy in psychiatry has undergone considerable changes and is still embossed by the diagnostic confusion that has always surrounded the disorder, Prichard's description of the morally insane to a large extent meets the contemporary definitions of the disorder. As Arrigo and Shipley (2001) argue, many of the items that make up the PCL-R (Psychopathy Check List – Revised) proposed by Robert D. Hare (Hare 1970), the Canadian psychiatrist who refined and empirically validated the modern construct of psychopathy, can be identified in Prichard's description of the morally insane (Arrigo and Shipley 2001, p. 340). The understanding of psychopathy as a corruption or degeneration of a natural moral ability to conduct oneself with decency and respectability is reflected in Hare's description of the psychopath as a 'self-centered, callous, and remorseless person profoundly lacking in empathy and the ability to form warm emotional relationships with others, a person who functions without the restraints of conscience' (Hare 1993, p. 9). It is as the 'morally insane', who scrupulously takes advantage of others in the 'business of life', without a sense of wrong and right that the organizational psychopath emerges.

A quick overview of the literature published over the last decade on the subject of individuals in organizations with characters 'rooted in lying, manipulation, deceit, egocentricity, callousness and other potentially destructive traits' (Babiak and Hare 2006, p. x) will confirm this. Some of the bestsellers include dramatic and evocative titles like Hare's *Without Conscience – The Disturbing World of the Psychopaths Among Us* (1993), *Snakes in Suits – When Psychopaths Go to Work* (2006) published with industrial psychologist Paul Babiak and psychologist Martha Stout's *The Sociopath Next Door* (2005). Law scholar Joel Bakan's *The Corporation* (2004), also a popular documentary movie, discusses psychopathy as a diagnosis for business corporations as such. In Scandinavia, titles like psychiatrist Dahl and journalist Dalsegg's *Charmør og tyran* [*Charmer and Tyrant*] (1999), Sanne Udsen *Psykopater i jakkesæt* ([*Psychopaths in Suits*] (2006) and Lars-Olof Tunbrå's *Psykopatiske Chefer – lige så farlige som charmerende* ([*Psychopathic Managers – as Dangerous as Charming*] (2004) have added to the list of titles that popularize the idea of a group of non-forensic psychopaths lurking among us.

The literature generally assumes that 1–2 percent of the population are clinical psychopaths, with a higher prevalence among men than among women, but also that this number is much higher – up to 4–5 percent and growing – in contemporary business organizations. Hare, whose Psychopathy Check List is used worldwide to screen for psychopathic personalities, holds that psychopaths 'make up a significant proportion of the people the media describe – serial killers, rapists, thieves, swindlers, con men, wife beaters'. He adds to this list 'white-collar criminals, hype-prone stock promoters . . . disbarred lawyers . . . and unscrupulous businesspeople' (Hare 1993, p. 104). He also speculates that such people are well represented in the business and corporate world, where 'they ply their trade with few formal or serious contacts with the law'. His co-author of *Snakes in Suits*, Paul Babiak, elsewhere has presented a study of an employee in an industrial organization, who received a high score on the psychopathy checklist. This 'industrial psychopath', Babiak suggests, is someone without the progression of increasing antisocial behavior and deviant lifestyle typically found in forensic psychopathy (Babiak 1995). Babiak insists that it is one of the dominant abilities of this type 'to *mask his/her antisocial traits*' (Babiak and Hare 2006, p. 172, emphasis added). The assumption that antisocial behaviors 'are almost always never apparent to the casual observer, being covered by a convincing veneer of charm', and that 'it is only after prolonged exposure that the psychopath's manipulative nature becomes apparent' (Babiak 1995, p. 173) is reflected broadly in the literature in chapters instructing readers how to recognize a psychopath. These chapters include practical suggestions about what to do and suggest precautions to take when it happens (for example, Babiak 1995; Tunbrå 2004; Babiak and Hare 2006; Udsen 2006).

Hence what sets the character of the organizational psychopath apart from the violent and self-destructive character of the classical psychopath is the ability to manage his disorder in a way that makes it imperceptible to others and useful to him. This dominant trait is reflected in the precarious assumption that the managerial culture of many contemporary organizations may in fact promote and invite psychopathic behavior. Before beginning his study of what he refers to as an 'industrial psychopath', Babiak considers some initial questions concerned with the relation between contemporary organizations and what he understands as 'individuals with psychopathic tendencies' (Babiak 1995, p. 175). According to his study the psychopath is likely to enter into contemporary organizations because 'exceptional charm and appearance of higher intelligence may, in fact, make him/her appear to be an ideal candidate'. The kind of organization likely to suit him will be one looking to attract entrepreneurial, business start-up types to new ventures that will not frustrate the psychopaths' excessive need for stimulation. This 'chaotic business world' could grant the psychopath an ideal environment for success, because it offers 'variety and stimulus without the controls found in more stable organizations, and may offer an environment conducive to psychopathic manipulation' (Babiak 1995, p. 175 f.). Elsewhere Hare and Babiak suggest that 'some hiring managers may mistakenly attribute "leadership" labels to what are, in actuality, psychopathic behaviors' (Babiak and Hare 2006, p. xiii). They also suggest that psychopathic individuals 'known for ignoring rules and regulations, coupled with a talent for conning and manipulation' will find the structure of the new 'transitional' organizations style that came out of the 1990s inviting. Udsen (2006) maintains something similar, when she argues that contemporary corporate culture in the Western world creates environments, where psychopathic personality traits among the employees are not being subdued, but are rather encouraged and produced. To understand how this is possible we will have to look closer at the dilemma of the 'human' in Human Resource Management.

4.   THE DILEMMA OF THE 'HUMAN' IN HUMAN RESOURCE MANAGEMENT

Profoundly contradicting the contemporary narrative of HRM as a champion of the human and humanity in organizations, early HR-theory found its sources in a philosophical tradition from Hobbes to Freud that was generally deeply suspicious of 'the human factor'. Reflecting also the popular theories of degeneracy of its time, it viewed the spontaneity of sentiments and drives as something that needed to be manipulated or even eradicated. Although Townley's critical perspective on HRM as 'the black box of production, where organizational inputs – employees – are selected, appraised, trained, developed, and remunerated to deliver the required output of labour' (Townley 1993, p. 518) may be problematic to a contemporary perspective, to the theories of Elton Mayo the definition is quite precise. As O'Connor (1999) has effectively illustrated in a study of theory and practice in Mayo's work, Mayo specifically located the human being in the context of the workplace and referred 'the human' to the worker's subjective and maladjusted state, which had to be corrected. This correction, Mayo believed, was not only an asset to the productivity of the organization, it was also necessary in order to save the impending collapse of Western civilization: 'There is nothing so dangerous, individually and socially, as a mind which has escaped conscious control; it is such minds which are cause of crime, war, and social revolution' (Mayo 1922, p. 16). Mayo shared with his contemporaries the broad modernist critique of the disenchantment of the world, according to which industrialism had destroyed previously tight social bonds. But in contrast to many of his contemporaries, his solution was not revolution (or democracy, for that matter, which he viewed as a 'decivilizing force') but the development of a strong managerial elite, who would have the skills to drive out of the working class the irrational sentiments, which possessed them. Mental delusion, he believed, was attributable to maladjustment and could be treated through psychotherapy. One example, provided by O'Conner, tells of an artisan, who was helped to realize that he had suffered child abuse from an alcoholic father. Through this care, Mayo asserts, the man was led to understand his maladjustment, and when he left the hospital, he 'had completely lost interest in ideas of political revolution. He . . . took a clerical job and kept it' (Mayo 1972, p. 15). Mayo's idea of a social system aimed to create a nesting situation comparable to the properties of a Russian doll, where the individual would be captured by an informal group and the informal group in its turn would be captured by the firm. The successful continuity of the system would then eventually shape the perceptions of the employee the way the firm needed (Johnson 1993). As O'Conner (1999, p. 242) concludes, 'the human' in Elton Mayo's work refers to the 'worker's subjective and maladjusted state, manifested through discontent with, disputes with, and resistance to authority.' The practice of 'human relations' ultimately means to 'facilitate adjustment to industrial life'.

Mayo's designation of 'the human' in the worker as a dysfunctional resource represents the dilemma of Human Resource Management in a very pure form. Implying the continuous task of resolving the moral dilemma of the distinction between 'human' and 'resource', the managerial practice of Mayo's theories constitutes an *exclusion* that is simultaneously representable as an *inclusion*. Excluded are the unproductive and mal-adjusted states, isolated within the human being as irrational sentiments and drives, which resemble the animal forces that the early modern period believed had the power to transform man into beast. Included, however, in this process of exclusion is the 'outside' that these forces represent. Taking Mayo's dilemma seriously will mean accepting that the functional subject of his theory is man *plus* the separation that passes through man himself. The abject character of this exclusion, in other words, is not radical enough to allow for a secure differentiation in the subject, but must continuously be rearticulated, reappropriated, dislocated and displaced anew.

Interestingly, although the work of the so-called school of neo-human relations saw itself, if not in opposition, then surely as an alternative to Mayo's human relations (Johnson 1993), this dilemma was only further intensified by the introduction of the aspect of self-actualization into the development of the individual at the workplace, although here it has largely become a question of self-management. If Mayo's work insisted that the human side of the worker was a dysfunctional state that had to be corrected by managerial control, the theories of Douglas McGregor in *The Human Side of Enterprise* (1960) placed the task of continuously resolving the dilemma *within* the individual subjectivity by introducing the workplace as the space for the realization of a whole human being. Inspired especially by Abraham Maslow, who developed his influential theory about the 'needs hierarchy' through empirical studies of dominance in monkeys (Cullen 1997), McGregor's work represented an alternative theory of the human being that held the re-establishment of the moral worth, freedom and dignity of the individual at work to be the only way to the redemption and resolution of societal problems. In the words of Heelas (2002, p. 80), the *self-work ethics* that has developed out of McGregor's introduction of the self as a resource into the workplace, invites the working subjectivity to resolve the dilemma in HRM by seeking to make the distinction between the authentically 'human' and the instrumentalized and codified 'human' *within* itself: 'the self as a self which considers itself to be something more, something much deeper, more natural and authentic'.

5.   THE ORGANIZATIONAL PSYCHOPATH AS AN *ABJECT*

As Costea et al. (2008) have shown, Human Resource Management, understood as a loose, complex phenomenon, today has become the most important exemplar in the managerial agenda of the trend to make subjectivity, and notions of the self, productive and profitable in business settings. On this background the development of management techniques, designed to expand and intensify the productivity of these resources through different forms of normative control, have proliferated (see, for example, Barley and Kunda 1992; Kunda 1992; Alvesson 2002; Fleming and Spicer 2003). Also the related aspect of de-emphasizing organizational control and letting employees 'be themselves' at work in order to achieve superior production and maximization of value is becoming increasingly popular. Many progressive organizations are encouraging employees to express personality authentically in all its uniqueness and difference (Fleming and Sturdy 2008). The emphasis here, like in some of the recent popular management literature (for example, Peters 2003; Bains 2007), is on the control-free organization that allows authentic displays of sexual identity, life-style and 'fun' instead of insisting on the organization as a place for work. One example is the celebration of differences and idealization of individuality at Google's headquarters in California, where the physical and emotional well-being of the employees is characterized as an object for management and sports and food are integrated parts of the organizational culture (Cederström and Grassman 2008). In place of controls founded on regimentation (technical control), standardization (bureaucratic control) and normalization (normative control), thought to undermine individual notions of, for instance, lifestyle, sexuality, consumption or leisure, the advocates of this paradigm argue that they are setting the employee free (Fleming and Sturdy 2008).

The popular image of the organizational psychopath that through the last decades has come to be a dominant trope in the designation of dysfunctional organizational behavior, I will argue, is a problematization of exactly this precarious freedom. If the practice of contemporary HRM internalizes the precarious separation – of the real from the merely appearing, of the creative from the shameless, of the committed from the manic, of the intimate from the superficial – out of which the 'human' in HRM emerges as a resource, then the psychopath represents the dysfunctional management of this injunction. But rather than representing a distinct pathology, the motif of the organizational psychopath marks a fundamental and precarious *indistinctness* between authentic human qualities and the managerial demand for a humanity that can be identified, isolated, manipulated, mobilized and recombined in organizational practice. The sleek, charming hatred of the psychopath, his 'moral insanity' does not consist merely in the instrumentalization and codification of human behavior, but rather in the immoral *privation* of this instrumentalization. It is in this sense that we can understand the psychopath at work as an abject. Representing a distinction that has not been made, the psychopathic privation of the organizational demand collapses the difference between the self at work that considers itself to be more than just that and the superficial self of the 'human resource'. Like its relative the werewolf, the psychopath represents the material manifestation of a distinction that must be made in order to separate the human from the inhuman. As a disturbing and grotesque hybrid between authentic humanity and the humanity that I assume to appear human, the terrible abomination of the organizational psychopath is not primarily constituted by the fact that his scrupulous attempts to take advantage of others in the business of HRM makes him different from me. Rather it is constituted by the eerie fact that the expulsion of the inauthentic from my innermost, authentic being disturbingly remains in the expulsion. As the ghost of a werewolf the organizational psychopath reminds me of the uncanny fact, constituted by the distinction that passes through me, that I might be like him.

REFERENCES

Agamben, G. (2004), *The Open – Man and Animal*, Stanford, CA: Stanford University Press.

Alvesson, M. (2002), 'Identity regulation as organizational control: producing the appropriate individual', *Journal of Management Studies*, **39** (5), 619–44.

Alvesson, M. and H. Willmott (2002), 'Identity regulation as organizational control: producing the appropriate individual', *Journal of Management Studies*, **39** (5), 619–44.

Alvesson, M., C. Hardy and B. Harley (2008), 'Reflecting on reflexivity: reflexive textual practices in organizations and management theory', *Journal of Management Studies*, **45** (3), 480–501.

Arrigo, B.A. and S. Shipley (2001), 'The confusion over psychopathy (I): historical considerations', *International Journal of Offender Therapy and Comparative Criminology*, **45** (3), 325–44.

Babiak, P. (1995), 'When psychopaths go to work: a case study of an industrial psychopath', *Applied Psychology: An International Review*, **44**, 171–8.

Babiak, P. and R.D Hare (2006), *Snakes in Suits – When Psychopaths Go to Work*, Regan Books: New York.

Bains, G. (2007), *Meaning Inc. – The Blueprint for Business Success in the 21st Century*, London: Profile Books.

Bakan, J. (2004), *The Corporation – The Pathological Persuit of Profit and Power*, London: Constable.

Baring-Gould, S. (1995), *The Book of Werewolves*, London: Senate.

Barley, S.R. and G. Kunda (1992), 'Design and devotion: surges of rational and normative ideologies of control in managerial discourse', *Administrative Science Quarterly*, **37** (3), 363–99.

Belmore, M.F. and V.L Quinsey (1994), 'Correlates of psychopathy in a non-institutional sample', *Journal of Interpersonal Violence*, **9**, 339–49.

Cederström, C. and R. Grassman (2008), 'The masochistic reflexive turn', *Ephemera*, **8** (1), 41–57.

Clarke, J. (2005), *Working with Monsters*, New York: Random House Publishers.

Cleckley, H. (1976), *The Mask of Sanity*, St. Louis, MO: Mosby.

Costea, B., N. Crump and K. Amiridis (2008), 'Managerialism, the therapeutic habitus and the self in contemporary organizing', *Human Relations*, **61** (5), 661–85.

Cullen, D. (1997), 'Maslow, monkeys and motivation theory', *Organization*, **4** (3), 355–73.

Dahl, A. and A. Dalsegg (1999), *Charmer og tyran*, Copenhagen: Munksgaard.

Desai, L. (2004), 'Corporate Psychopaths at Large', accessed 26 December 2008 at www.cnn.com/2004/BUSINESS/08/26/corporate.psychopaths/index.html.

Deutschman, A. (2007), 'Is your boss a psychopath?', accessed 26 December 2008 at www.fastcompany.com/magazine/96/open_boss.html.

Felluga, D. (2003), 'Modules on Kristeva: on the abject', accessed 4 November 2008 at www.cla.purdue.edu/academic/engl/theory/psychoanalysis/kristevaabject.html.

Fleming, P. and A. Spicer (2003), 'Working at a cynical distance: implications for power, subjectivity and resistance', *Organization*, **10** (1), 157–79.

Fleming, P. and A. Sturdy (2008), '"Just be yourself!" – towards neo-normative control in organizations', Cambridge University working paper.

Foucault, M. (1988), *Politics, Philosophy, Culture: Interviews and other Writing 1977–1984*, New York and London: Routledge.

Foucault, M. (1990), *The History of Sexuality*, reprint edn, Harmondsworth: Penguin Books.

Foucault, M. and P. Rabinow (1984), *The Foucault Reader*, New York: Pantheon Books.

Fudge, E. (2003), 'How a man differs from a dog', *History Today*, (June), 38–44.

Hare, R.D. (1970), *Psychopathy Theory and Research*, New York: Wiley and Sons.

Hare, R.D. (1993), *Without Conscience – the Disturbing World of the Psychopaths Among Us*, New York: Pocket Books.

Harris, G.T., T.A. Skilling and M.E. Rice (2001), 'The construct of psychopathy', *Crime and Justice*, **28**, 197–264.

Heelas, P. (2002), 'Work ethics, soft capitalism, and the "turn to life"', in P. Du Gay and M. Pryke (eds), *Cultural Economy*, London: Sage Publications, pp. 78–86.

HK (2007), homepage of HK website, accessed on 3 November 2008 at www. hk.dk/www/job_og_loen/arbejdsmiljoe/psykopat_testen.

Honneth, A. (2004), 'Organized self-realization: some paradoxes of individualization', *European Journal of Social Theory*, **7** (4), 463–78.

IT2U (2009) homepage of IT2U website, accessed 3 November 2008 at www.it2u. dk/sw11178.asp.

Janssens, M. and C. Steyaert, 'HRM and performance: a plea for reflexivity in HRM studies', *Journal of Management Studies*, **46** (1) 143–55.

Johnson, P. (1993), *Management Control and Organizational Behaviour*, London: Paul Chapman.

Jones, C., M. Parker and R. ten Bos (2005), *For Business Ethics: A Critical Text*, London: Taylor & Francis.

Kafka, F. (1979), *Report to an Academy*, Pretoria: M and M Productions.

Kristeva, J. (1982), *Powers of Horror: An Essay on Abjection*, New York: Columbia University Press.

Kristeva, J. (1996), *Julia Kristeva Interviews*, New York: Columbia University Press.
Kunda, G. (1992), *Engineering Culture: Control and Commitment in a High-tech Corporation*, Philadelphia, PA: Temple University Press.
Lawrence, E.A. (1996), 'Werewolves in psyche and cinema: man–beast transformation and paradox', *Journal of American Culture*, **19** (3), 103–12.
Loehr, J.E. and M. McCormack (1997), *Stress for Success*, New York: Three Rivers Press.
Lykken, D.T. (1995), *The Antisocial Personalities*, Hillsdale, NJ: Erlbaum.
Mayo, E. (1922), 'Industrial peace and psychological research. I – civilization and morale', *Industrial Australian and Mining Standard*, **67**, 16.
Mayo, E. (1972), *The Psychology of Pierre Janet*, 2nd edn, Westport, CT: Greenwood Press.
McGregor, D. (2006), *The Human Side of Enterprise*, New York and London: McGraw Hill.
O'Connor, E. (1999), 'Minding the workers: the meaning of "human" and "human relations" in Elton Mayo', *Organization*, **6** (2), 223–46.
Otten, C.F. (1986), *A Lycanthropy Reader: Werewolves in Western Culture*, Syracuse, NY: Syracuse University Press.
Peters, T. (2003), *Re-imagine!*, Harmondsworth: Penguin Books.
Pinel, P. (1962), *A Treatise on Insanity*, translated from French by D.D. Davis, facsimile of London 1806 edition, New York: Hafner Publishing Co.
Prichard, J.C. (1835), *A Treatise on Insanity, and Other Disorders Affecting the Mind*, London: Sherwood, Gilbert, and Piper.
Raffnsøe, S., M. Gudmand-Høyer and M.S. Thaning (2008), *Foucault*, Frederiksberg, Denmark: Samfundslitteratur.
Rush, B. (1812), *Medical Inquiries and Observations, Upon the Diseases of the Mind*, Philadelphia, PA: Kimber & Richardson.
Santesson, T. (2006), *Er din chef psykopat?*, last updated, 14 November 2006 accessed 28 January 2008 at www.djoef.dk/blog/print_tekst?ID=10755&type=a rtikel&navn=Er+din+chef+psykopat%3F.
Stallybrass, P. and A. White (1986), *The Politics and Poetics of Transgression*, London: Methuen.
Steyaert, C. and M. Janssens (1999), 'Human and inhuman resource management: saving the subject of HRM', *Organization*, **6** (2), 181–98.
Stout, M. (2005), *The Sociopath Next Door*, New York: Random House.
Townley, B. (1993), 'Foucault, power/knowledge, and its relevance for human resource management', *Academy of Management Review*, **18** (3), 518–45.
Tunbrå, L. (2004), *Psykopatiske Chefer – Lige så Farlige som Charmerende*, Kolding, Denmark: Birmar.
Udsen, S. (2006), *Psykopater i Jakkesæt – når Chefen er Psykopat*, Copenhagen: Aschehoug.
Verne, J. (1874), *From the Earth to the Moon Direct in 97 hours 20 minutes*, translated by L. Mercier, New York: Scribner, Armstrong and Co.
Widom, C.S. (1977), 'A methodology for studying non-institutionalized psychopaths', *Journal of Consulting and Clinical Psychology*, **45**, 674–83.
Widom, C.S. and J.S. Newman (1985), 'Characteristics of noninstitutionalized psychopaths', in D.P. Farrington and J. Gunn (eds), *Aggression and Dangerousness*, New York: Wiley, pp. 57–80.

11. The sublime object of corruption – exploring the relevance of a psychoanalytical two-bodies doctrine for understanding corruption

Thomas Taro Lennerfors

> For the King has in him two Bodies, viz. a Body natural, and a Body politic.
> (Kantorowicz 1997, p. 7)

1. INTRODUCTION

Nowadays, corruption is receiving great attention in various types of media, in research and in everyday discussions. To draw on a discursive strategy often used by business ethicists, there have lately been a large number of scandals related to corruption (Parker 2003). The international NGO Transparency International publishes a daily corruption newsletter, producing a steady stream of scandals. Research on corruption is proliferating as well. While it is difficult to demonstrate that corruption talk is more present in society than ever before, research on corruption has certainly taken a particular path. It is the aim of this chapter to show that this path might do more to limit our understanding of corruption than to guide it forward.

To do this we cannot, of course, avoid the question 'what is corruption?' Drawing on psychoanalysis and a mystical theory called 'the two bodies doctrine', I want to develop an alternative or complementary theory to use for understanding corruption. The main conflict or antagonism of this chapter is that between economics and psychoanalysis. Framed in the broadest possible way, it is about structure vs. subject, matter vs. mind, or desire-free vs. desire-based understanding. I want to argue that one cannot understand corruption if one ignores desire. However, research on corruption has taken exactly this desire-free path; corruption is mostly framed as a principal–agent issue. Against this, I argue that corruption is something that we attribute to those who already are in the wrong (symbolic) place. This leads to the provocative claim that *corruption is a place*. Corruption is therefore not totally relativistic as might be argued from those claiming that corruption is a discursive construction. It cannot occur anywhere.

We must therefore move away from both principal–agent based understanding and those relativistic understandings that corruption is just socially constructed. The psychoanalytical understanding helps us to understand how corruption is constructed. And, an important step towards the psychoanalytical understanding of corruption is to understand the two bodies doctrine – the idea that the King has in him two bodies.

The chapter is rather theoretical. In order to make it easier to follow and to show the potential relevance of the alternative theory, I will use examples of corruption talk from Transparency International and Sweden, but my main sources of inspiration are Ernst Kantorowicz, who wrote an extensive thesis on the two bodies doctrine, and Slavoj Žižek who did a psychoanalytical reading of the same doctrine. Probably the most central source of inspiration, however, is the work of Peter Bratsis (2003a, 2003b, 2006), who has indicated the connection between corruption and the two bodies doctrine. This chapter is an attempt to elaborate on this connection, relating it to previous research on corruption.

The first part of the chapter offers a critique of the traditional way of theorizing corruption. By framing corruption as a principal–agent problem it is construed as structurally similar in public and private sectors, and in all different countries and continents. Corruption, on this view, is an agent breaching the trust of his or her principal. This is the usual conceptualization in economics and business studies, including business ethics. According to this theory, the agent must completely separate his or her private interests from the interests of the principal. At work, the agent must solely act according to the will of the principal. This strict separation between the interests at work and the interests off work is sometimes described as a misunderstood interpretation of the two bodies doctrine. This is the split between the symbolic office and the person. By separating your body at work, from your body off work, you can stay clear of corruption – because if you keep your private body outside the workplace, you cannot be anything but an agent of the will of the principal at the workplace. This is what the principal–agent model of understanding corruption leads to. And this is also a connection to the two bodies doctrine. As I will show, however, it is too simplified an interpretation of the two bodies doctrine.

In the second part, I will show that a more accurate understanding of the two bodies doctrine really *can* lead us to a more rewarding understanding of corruption. This reading is based not only on Kantorowicz, who is the scholar that one traditionally associates with the two bodies doctrine, but also on Slavoj Žižek who bases his reading of the two bodies doctrine on Lacanian psychoanalytical concepts, especially the sublime desirable object *a*. This reading suggests that the principal–agent version of corruption is not enough to understand what corruption is. This is the psychoanalytical turn in corruption research that I want to suggest. Drawing on a variety of examples, I will then, in the third part, discuss how the two bodies doctrine has spread from kings to public officials. The claims of the received view notwithstanding, we do not really use the principal–agent model when discussing cases of corruption. I will therefore conclude with a discussion of how psychoanalysis can help researchers bring the repressed themes of research on corruption to light.

2. CORRUPTION, PRINCIPALS, AND AGENTS

There are many fascinating issues or mysteries related to how corruption is discussed world-wide. One such mystery lies in the conflation of the idea of corruption in the public and the private sector. Peter Bratsis has very poignantly remarked that there is no anti-corruption law in the world, only laws against different corrupt practices, such as embezzlement, bribery, etc. (Bratsis 2003a). To take just one example, the Swedish law on bribery has encompassed both public and private sectors since 1974. One can be bribed (and thus corrupted), both in the private and the public sector. Yet many people I have discussed corruption with state that corruption is essentially related to the public sector. This conflation of public and private sectors regarding the issue of corruption is also clearly visible when we take Transparency International's (TI) definition of corruption into account. Let us pose a frequently asked question to the TI. How do you define corruption?

> Transparency International (TI) has chosen a clear and focused definition of the term: Corruption is operationally defined as the misuse of entrusted power for private gain. TI further differentiates between 'according to rule' corruption and 'against the rule' corruption. Facilitation payments, where a bribe is paid to receive preferential treatment for something that the bribe receiver is required to do by law, constitute the former. The latter, on the other hand, is a bribe paid to obtain services the bribe receiver is prohibited from providing. (www.transparency.org. FAQ)

It is interesting that transparency has chosen to define corruption as the misuse of *entrusted power* for private gain, instead of what has been the mainstream definition of corruption in the last, at least, 40 years, i.e. the misuse of *public office* for private gain (Nye 1967; Friedrich 1990; cf. Della Porta and Vannucci 1999; Rose-Ackerman 1999). The earlier definition, which was used by the World Bank, inevitably led to limiting corruption to the public sector, and I have argued elsewhere that this limit is arbitrary and misleading; corruption is theoretically indistinguishable in the public and private sectors (Lennerfors 2008). One can misuse one's office whether one is a government bureaucrat or a purchasing manager in a private sector business. Still, many believe that corruption in the private sector must be a completely different issue. For example, the Anti-Corruption Institute of the Swedish Chamber of Commerce has recently submitted a petition to change the law on bribery in Sweden (Institutet mot mutor 2006). According to the Anti-Corruption Institute, the public and the private sectors are different and the anti-bribery law should consequently differ between the public and the private sectors. I would suggest, in any case, that there is mismatch between the TI definition of corruption and what people generally consider to be corruption. I will argue that this is the result of a deficient theoretical understanding of what corruption is.

The mainstream theoretical understanding of corruption is constructed upon the principal–agent model (Leiken 1997; Jain 1998; Lennerfors 2008). Let us take bribery as an example. The principal embodies the 'public' interest and when the agent takes a bribe and does not act in the interest of the principal, he or she has committed an act of corruption. He or she has used his or her position for private gain. It may not surprise the reader that this principal–agent model of bribery is the predominant one, even though some argue that this conceptualization is a rather new way of understanding bribery and that the mainstream notion of the bribe before the 1980s was 'a payment or inducement for someone to do something illegal or unethical' (D'Andrade 1984; Carson 1985, p. 70).

If we believe that this is an accurate characterization of the theoretical debate on corruption, then it is not remarkable that TI has a definition that is sector-neutral. The principal–agent model does not distinguish the public from the private sector. The principal might be the totality of shareholders in a private corporation or the residents in a nation-state. The important factor is not whether the act of bribery took place in the private or the public sector, but rather whether the agent acted according to the will of the principal, or in other words, whether a trust was breached (Gustafsson 1988, pp. 38–41). This model also applies to other kinds of corruption; embezzlement consists of extracting resources from the principal in violation of their trust. In either case, it does not matter whether the principal is a company or the state.

The principal–agent model is structurally similar to the naive version of the two bodies doctrine. The principal–agent model seems to imply that agents must leave all their personal life outside the office. The agent should be an angel as ten Bos and Kaulingfreks put it – a pure messenger who only delivers the message of the principal (Kaulingfreks and ten Bos 2005). Du Gay has argued that bureaucrats are not robots nor angels but that they are working for the public ethos of impersonality and equal treatment (du Gay 2000). Still, du Gay holds that there are different ethics and values in different spheres of life. There is a tendency to talk about a body at work and a body off work, i.e., one self at the workplace and another outside.

In my thesis on the discourse of corruption at the Swedish Road Administration (SRA), I saw some examples of this split into a body at work and a body off work (Lennerfors 2008). The SRA, an organization responsible for constructing and operating state roads, buys construction work and consulting services from the private sector and they have to act impersonally and professionally since they are administering taxpayers' money. Corruption is unthinkable at the SRA. Many agree that it can sometimes be difficult to clearly distinguish between bribes (a form of corruption) and gifts (legitimate contributions). Instead of distinguishing these concepts, a respondent that I talked to said that he clearly separated his job from his private life. He could play golf with a friend of his, even though this friend happened to be working in an organization that was a supplier to the SRA. This respondent clearly separated the two parts of his existence from each other. Even though he received gifts as a private person, he could act according to the will of the principal. Another person could be friends with a supplier off work, and scold him at work. This way of separating the two bodies is an effective strategy against corruption.

There is another case of this bodily separation, which has been appearing now and then in Swedish media. In 2006, Ilmar Reepalu, the head of the municipal executive committee in the Swedish city Malmö, was arraigned for taking bribes in the form of a trip to South Africa. Ilmar Reepalu says that:

> I have never been offered anything by any company. The short trip to South Africa was a private gift from a private friend. (DN 2006b)

Reepalu claimed that what he received was between friends. Since they were good friends, a trip need not be corrupt, was the verdict of the District Court in Malmö. Reepalu seems to subscribe to the logic that the public body, the body at work, is and should be unrelated to the personal body. The public body, or the body 'at work', had nothing to do with the gift, according to Reepalu. This is how one can try to separate the natural body (Ilmar Reepalu) from the public body, or the body at work (the head of the municipal executive committee).

Reading Bratsis and observing these empirical examples of separation was what drew my attention to the two bodies doctrine. It has been discussed by both Slavoj Žižek and Giorgio Agamben and was therefore somewhat known to me (Agamben 1998; Žižek 2002). When reading the main treatise of the two bodies doctrine, namely the one of Ernst Kantorowicz, I realized that there are some similarities between the two bodies doctrine and the cases of corruption that I studied. Many respondents have expressed the view that the case of Ilmar Reepalu is rather strange. Does he really believe that he has two existences? One of those who were surprised was Christer van der Kwast, the director of the Swedish public prosecution authority. He disagreed with the outcome of the legal process and appealed to a higher instance (DN 2006a). Van der Kwast was probably thinking that Reepalu is Reepalu, both at work and at home.

However, to try to think corruption with the help of the two bodies doctrine did not help me in the way I thought. Instead of relating corruption to the separation of the two bodies and thus being aligned with the principal–agent understanding of corruption, the two bodies doctrine gives us another understanding of corruption, an understanding which help us to take a step towards the psychoanalytical understanding of corruption. The issue at hand is not the separation between the symbolic office and the natural person, which Reepalu intends to do. Slavoj Žižek explains:

> What is at stake is thus not simply the split between the empirical person . . . and his symbolic function. The point is rather that this symbolic function *redoubles his very body*, introducing a split between the visible, material, transient body and another, sublime body, a body made of a special, immaterial stuff. (Žižek 2002, p. 255, emphasis in original)

So the two bodies doctrine is not simply the separation between one's symbolic office and ones empirical person, they are a separation of something like *substances*. This metaphysical separation underwrites the practical separation of the body that is at work from the body that is off work. These two bodies must be kept apart in order to avoid corruption. This leads to interesting situations where people try to create the fiction of separating bodies, suggesting that the two bodies doctrine is a way of understanding this fiction. The question now is: If the two bodies doctrine is not a question of separation of the two bodies, as the principal–agent model of corruption indicates, what is it? And how does it help us to understand corruption?

3.   THE TWO BODIES DOCTRINE – KANTOROWICZ AND ŽIŽEK

The two bodies doctrine can be traced back to metaphysical descriptions of the king in seventeenth-century England. 'The King has in him two Bodies, viz. a Body natural, and a Body politic' (Kantorowicz 1997, p. 7). An excerpt from the writing of one of the crown jurists under Queen Elizabeth reveals, on a more detailed level, that the king:

> has a Body natural, adorned and invested with the Estate and Dignity royal; and he has not a Body natural distinct and divided by itself from the Office and Dignity royal, but a Body natural and a Body politic together indivisible; and these two Bodies are incorporated in one's Person, and make one Body and not divers, that is the Body corporate in the Body natural, et e contra the Body natural in the Body corporate. So that the Body natural, by this conjunction of the Body politic to it, (which body politic contains the Office, Government, and Majesty royal) is magnified, and by the said Consolidation hath in it the Body politic. (Kantorowicz 1997, pp. 7–9)

This mystic two bodies doctrine was ridiculed before Kantorowicz wrote his treatise. One of those ridiculing the doctrine was a scholar named Maitland of whom Kantorowicz speaks. Maitland tells us about King George III who had to go to Parliament for permission to hold some land since rights denied to any of His Majesty's subjects were denied to him (Kantorowicz 1997, p. 3). Was the king a king or a man? Maitland concluded his discussion by stating that the two bodies doctrine was a marvelous display of metaphysical – or we might say metaphysiological – nonsense (Kantorowicz 1997, p. 3). But the metaphysiological nonsense does not concern two separable bodies of the King, but rather two bodies that intermingle. The Body politic, in the above excerpt from the crown lawyer of Queen Elizabeth, seems to enhance the Body natural inter-mingling with it. In the body politic dwell 'truly mysterious forces which reduce, or even remove, the imperfections of the fragile human nature' (Kantorowicz 1997, p. 9). It is this two bodies doctrine that Kantorowicz writes the history of.

What Kantorowicz intends to do in his treatise is to trace the genealogy of the two bodies doctrine throughout history, making visible the intri-cate relationships between religion and politics. Kantorowicz claims that the two bodies doctrine ultimately stems from the two natures of Christ (Kantorowicz 1997, p. 49). Throughout his treatise, he distinguishes between different important periods in the development of the two bodies doctrine, moving from a religious version to a more secular one. The most religious version is what he calls Christ-centered kingship. The idea of the king is based on the idea of Christ. In very simple terms: Christ was God and man. Analogously, the king was God and man. As said, the two bodies doctrine gradually evolved to become one where the second body of the king was not based on God, but on Law, on the Fisc, on the Polity, and the State. Kantorowicz's work is thus echoed by the claim of Carl Schmitt that all significant concepts of the modern theory of the state are secularized theological concepts (Schmitt 1985).

The king's second body is thus in early medieval times stemming from God, but later on more secular concepts. An interesting aspect is that more people started to get an extra body in later medieval ages (see also Johnsen's chapter in this volume). For example, in those times jurists were often depicted as angels. Jurists are certainly thought of as embodying the Law. So even though the two bodies doctrine might have evolved from a way of understanding the king, it did spread to other groups of people, like jurists:

> In this respect, then, it may be said that the political and legal world of thought of the later Middle Ages began to be populated by immaterial angelic bodies, large and small: they were invisible, ageless, sempiternal, immortal, and sometimes even ubiquitous; and they were endowed with a corpus intellectuale or mysticum which could stand any comparison with the 'spiritual bodies' of the celestial beings. (Kantorowicz 1997, pp. 282–3)

Kantorowicz thus manages to argue that there are religious foundations of the problem of the King's two bodies. The doctrine ultimately stems from the twinned nature of Christ. We might remember that Kantorowicz's fascination with this doctrine was probably caused by some excerpts from crown lawyers under the Elizabethan rule. One might wonder what the two bodies doctrine consisted of in that period. Kantorowicz, and even Maitland – the scholar who ridiculed the two bodies doctrine – knew that the two bodies doctrine provided an important heuristic fiction to bring into agreement the personal with the more impersonal concepts of government and to harmonize modern and ancient law (Kantorowicz 1997, p. 5). This leads us to conclude that the doctrine very likely had a religious origin, but then evolved more and more to become a certain mystical stain amongst rather secularized political concepts. The two bodies doctrine would in this reading be equal to a remnant from past times. To revitalize the two bodies doctrine, and to eventually see how it can help us to understand corruption, I would like to draw attention to the recent re-reading of it done by Slavoj Žižek. Instead of religion, he used Lacanian psychoanalysis.

Žižek, when reading Kantorowicz, ties the mystical body, which is intertwined with the natural body of the King, to the Lacanian concept of the *objet petit a.* Žižek clarifies that it is a particular position in the symbolic order that creates this sublime body. We do not discuss the separation between the symbolic office and the empirical person. Rather, it is the symbolic office that creates this *objet petit a.*

That Žižek argues that the *objet petit a* is the second body of the king might not seem very helpful. One religious concept seems to be exchanged in favor of an equally problematic psychoanalytic concept. What then is this *objet petit a*? One explanation is that the *objet petit a* is a thing of nothing. Furthermore, Žižek explains it as that which is in a person more than himself. This is some unfathomable and untouchable matter serving to draw the attention and desire of others. The *objet petit a* is that 'something in me more than myself' on account of which I perceive myself as 'worthy of the Other's desire' (Žižek 1997, p. 8). Or put in another way, it is the object which is 'in the subject more than the subject itself', that which I fantasize that the Other (fascinated by me) sees in me' (Žižek 1997, pp. 9–10). The *objet petit a* is a 'chimerical object of fantasy', an object 'causing our desire and at the same time . . . posed retroactively by this desire' (Žižek 1989, p. 65).

The *objet petit a* is a main component in Lacanian psychoanalysis since this is the object that we chase, the object that we want, or the object we want to destroy. It is not a material object, but it is sublime. It can be that 'something' that causes us to desire another person, that 'something' that we are trying to get when buying the latest gadget, or that 'something' that we are repelled by in adherents of a different religion. This object is unreachable, since if we would get it, our desires would be extinguished. The *objet petit a* is that limit which ultimately stops us from enjoying fully.

Is this the limit for our understanding of the *objet petit a*? No, Žižek holds that the *objet petit a* is always situated within an ideological edifice. Therefore, the *objet petit a* has no positive ontological status. Rather, it is the void, which according to Lacanian psychoanalysis, characterizes all structure, which means that in the very core of any ideological edifice there is a void.

So Žižek's account of the two bodies doctrine is that the symbolic office, a position of power, creates this special stuff in the king, redoubling his very body. The point is thus that when a person occupies an office, his body gets supplemented with an inseparable, sublime substance. But why is Žižek really interested in the two bodies doctrine? It is probably because he sees similarities between the kings and the leaders of political parties. One of Žižek's favorite examples is the speech that Stalin delivered at Lenin's funeral. Stalin allegedly said: '"We, the Communists, are people of a special mould. We are made of special stuff" . . . It is quite easy to recognize the Lacanian name for this special stuff: *objet petit a*' (Žižek 1989, p. 145).

As has been mentioned above, the *objet petit a* does not have only a positive aspect, namely, that it is what arouses the desire of the Other. From another perspective, the *objet petit a* becomes the fundamental blockage to enjoyment, the *objet petit a* becomes what has to be removed in order to create a complete society. Above, I stated that the *objet petit a* is the void around which any symbolic or societal order is constructed. With this void, the order is incomplete. Without it, then, would it be complete? Sometimes the *objet petit a* is vacillating between different material objects, for example, in a capitalist system of consumption. Sometimes, the *objet petit a* is embodied by some particular group of people that is seen as an obstacle to reaching a perfect society. For example, in Fascist societies, Žižek claims that this internal psychological impediment to enjoyment was embodied in the Jew. Žižek often discusses the idea that the Jew was seen as the only obstacle to reaching a complete, harmonious society. A function of ideology is to project this fundamental blockage to some positive entity, such as the Jew. 'If these Jews were not there, our society would be complete' was the message of the Fascist ideology. The Jew occupied this place of the *objet petit a*.

What Žižek adds to Kantorowicz's account is the relation between the second sublime body and desire. I stated in the beginning of the chapter that any desire-free theory of corruption is bound to be fictional. Corruption has some relation to principals and agents, but also to the *objet petit a*. What I am arguing is that it is this *objet petit a* that works as the founding principle for corruption. Without *objet petit a* there would be no corruption because, if the people engaging in 'corrupt practices' do not arouse our desire, they will not appear corrupt to us. The *objet petit a* is therefore the base of any understanding of corruption.

4.   WHERE IS CORRUPTION POSSIBLE?

Kantorowicz's two bodies doctrine has been studied and re-read by Žižek as a psychoanalytical thesis, the second body being a sublime body – the *objet petit a*. I hold that this is the phantasmatic foundation that creates the perception of corruption. Instead of focusing on whether there has been any breach of trust or contracts between principal and agent, I turn the focus towards the very possibility of corruption, which I hold is created by the sublime body. I want to argue that it is the existence of this sublime body that make us hold those working in the public sector to a higher standard than those in the private sector.

Let us start by turning to how the two bodies doctrine has spread to the entire public sector. Already in the reading of Kantorowicz, we saw that not only kings have a second body. Also the jurists were depicted as angels, being a pure instrument of Law. Here, we can be informed by Peter Bratsis' reading of Norbert Elias. In this reading, it is held that the structural position of the King has been transformed into a public bureaucracy. The king has become transformed into public functionaries (Bratsis 2003b, p. 32). The power of the King has gradually become transformed into a more distributed power exercised by public functionaries. One of the possible explanations for the symbolic position that redoubles the body of the public functionaries, making them susceptible to corruption, is that they occupy a position of power. Žižek claims that the position of power in democratic societies should be empty, since it is the abstract concept of 'people' that should be in power. In Žižek's own words:

> [T]he radical break in the very mode of the performing of Power introduced by the emergence of democratic political discourse. Lefort's fundamental thesis – which has today already acquired the status of a commonplace – is that with the advent the 'democratic intervention', the locus of Power becomes *an empty place*; what was before the anguish of interregnum, a period of transition to be surmounted as soon as possible – the fact that 'the Throne is empty' – is now the only 'normal' state. In pre-democratic societies, there is always a legitimate pretender to the place of Power, somebody who is fully entitled to occupy it, and the one who violently overthrows him has simply the status of an usurper, whereas within the democratic horizon, *everyone* who occupies the locus of Power is by definition a usurper. (Žižek 2002, p. 267)

The locus of power should be empty, it seems. This might also be the reason why bureaucrats are held to be pure agents, empty bodies to be filled by the will of the principal, exactly as in the principal–agent model of understanding corruption. However, could it not be the case that occupying a position of power is what creates the *objet petit a*, and thus, the possibility of corruption? This particular construction of the place of corruption is most probably possible to relate to a liberal-capitalist ideology, with a belief in the functioning of markets and a mistrust against the state. The people working for the state are, from this point of view, usurpers who illegitimately occupy a place of power, which should be empty. It is state employees that can be susceptible to corruption – and this is only because they are in the wrong place. The *objet petit a* is embodied by public officials and this is why we fantasize about them inter alia as being corrupt.

The *objet petit a* representing a void creates different contradictory representations of that, which embodies it. If we go back to Žižek's account of the Jew embodying *objet petit a*, we can see that there is a 'phantasmic richness of the traits supposed to characterize Jews (avidity, the spirit of intrigue, and so on)' (Žižek 1989, p. 99). But none of these positive traits could really capture the unfathomable *objet petit a*. They had that inexplicable 'something'. Žižek explains:

> Already at the level of a simple phenomenological description, the crucial characteristic of this cause is that it cannot be pinpointed to some clearly defined observable property: although we can usually enumerate a series of features that annoy us about 'them' (the way they laugh too loudly, the bad smell of their food, etc.), these features function as indicators of a more radical strangeness. [. . .The name of this] paradoxical uncanny object that stands for what in the perceived positive, empirical object necessarily eludes my gaze and as such serves as the driving force of my desiring it, *objet petit a*. (Žižek 2005, p. 246)

An example of this 'something' existing in the public sector bureaucrats can be found in Paul du Gay's work, whose work clearly indicates that there is something special in the bureaucrats, something unfathomable that is created by their position as being bureaucrats. A passage that I would like to draw attention to is where du Gay, drawing on Robert Parker, describes two contradictory popular representations of the bureaucrats.

> [P]opular anti-bureaucratic sentiment trades on two dramatic, but rather contradictory representations of the 'typical bureaucrat'. One has this creature endlessly drafting diabolical regulations, 'cunningly contriving new controls over the private citizen' while extending its own, malign influence. The other has bureaucrats positioned as idle loafers, spending their days – as two enthusiastic and influential advocates of contemporary public sector reform have it – 'reading magazines, planning sailing trips, or buying or selling stocks', all at the taxpayers' expense. (du Gay 2000)

As can be noticed, the bureaucrats are both cunning and incompetent, zealous and lazy, partial or not enough understanding.

David Levine has also studied corruption from a psychoanalytical perspective. He holds that corruption is an attack on norms concordantly with individuals developing 'certain of the key qualities associated with corruption: greed, arrogance, a sense of personal entitlement, the idea of virtue as personal loyalty, and the inability to distinguish between organizational and personal ends' (Levine 2005, p. 724). He finds corruption is based on a type of greed called 'ultimate narcissistic fulfillment' – the experience of the self as uniquely good and uniquely worthy. This is also part of the fantasies of the enjoyment that corrupt people derive from their actions, and how special and 'unlike us' the corrupt people are.

The most important message here is that the *objet petit a*, which makes us desire, and which creates the possibility of corruption is probably only occurring in the public sector. If we understand the two bodies doctrine in its psychoanalytical version, we can also understand that corruption cannot occur in the private sector, i.e. we do not label such practices 'corruption'. What this perspective gives us is a psychoanalytical perspective on corruption, a perspective which makes much more empirical sense than the principal–agent model. The principal–agent model is sector neutral, while the psychoanalytical model does indeed consider social structure and pinpointing where the *objet petit a* is today. The position of the *objet petit a* can certainly change, but, even though the definitions of Transparency International and the Swedish law against bribery are sector neutral, we still think that corruption really only exists in the public sector.

What this theory leads us to suggest is that when we label somebody as 'corrupt', we probably do not mean that he or she is corrupt, but that he or she is situated in the wrong symbolic position, whether it be in a public bureaucracy or in a monopoly organization (Lennerfors 2008, Chapter 10). We do not mean 'corrupt' but we mean 'monopoly' or 'state bureaucracy'. This is in line with some interesting papers about corruption in ancient Greece – accusations of corruption were often only added as a complement to other accusations (Taylor 2001a, 2001b). Such accusations might today amount to being a public functionary, or working in a monopoly. The main crime is thus not the actions of the agent, such as breaching trust against a principal, but the main crime is the place, a place that is vested ideologically with desire, a place which creates the *objet petit a*.

5. DISCUSSION

There are signs that we are moving towards a definition of corruption that is sector-neutral. Corruption is no longer explained as the misuse of public office (implicitly understood as public sector office) for private gain. However, many still cannot accept this expansion of the corruption concept from just public sector to both private and public sectors. I have argued that this expansion of the corruption concept is probably related to how the corruption concept is defined theoretically, namely as a principal–agent issue. In the principal–agent model of corruption, there is no reason to expect that there should be any difference between public and private sectors, since there are principals and agents in both sectors.

Therefore I suggest that corruption, despite appearances, is probably not really derived from the principal–agent model. The main contribution of this psychoanalytical perspective on corruption, in any case, is to theorize corruption beyond the principal–agent model through the two bodies doctrine. The psychoanalytical perspective on corruption thus brings another possible theoretical framework to understanding corruption.

Corruption is also, of course, socially constructed in different discourses. Even though this chapter does not explicitly deal with this idea of discursive construction, the psychoanalytical perspective advanced in the chapter tries to point to the *objet petit a* that guides and is guided by any discursive constructions. We all know that everything is socially constructed, but we might not know how. The psychoanalytical perspective might give us an understanding of why corruption is constructed as in particular ways.

Lacanian psychoanalysis might both help us to escape desire-free theoretical models, such as the principal–agent model, and purely semiotic, language-based, understandings such as corruption as discursively constructed. To understand corruption, there is a need to move beyond the principal–agent model and understand psychoanalysis in order to grasp the psychic structure of corruption. If we generalize from corruption, there might be a possibility that psychoanalytic theory can provide alternative understandings of perceptions of other forms of wrongdoing than corruption. In that case, psychoanalytical theory can indeed guide the field of business ethics and organization theory forward. However, all this work remains to be done. This chapter has only tried to indicate a possible way of introducing psychoanalysis into our attempts to understand a particular evil.

REFERENCES

Agamben, G. (1998), *Homo Sacer: Sovereign Power and Bare Life*, Stanford, CA: Stanford University Press.
Bratsis, P. (2003a), *Corrupt Compared to What? Greece, Capitalist Interests, and the Specular Purity of the State*, London: Hellenic Observatory, European Institute, London School of Economics and Political Science.
Bratsis, P. (2003b), 'The construction of corruption, or rules of separation and illusions of purity in bourgeois societies', *Social Text*, **21** (4), 9–33.
Bratsis, P. (2006), *Everyday Life and the State*, Boulder, CO: Paradigm Publishers.
Carson, T. (1985), 'Bribery, extortion, and 'the foreign corrupt practices act', *Philosophy and Public Affairs*, **14** (1), 66–90.
D'Andrade, K. (1984), 'Bribery', *Journal of Business Ethics*, **4** (4), 239–48.
Della Porta, D. and A. Vannucci (1999), *Corrupt Exchanges: Actors, Resources, and Mechanisms of Political Corruption*, New York: Aldine de Gruyter.
DN. (2006a), 'Friande dom mot Reepalu överklagas', *Dagens Nyheter*, 15 September.
DN. (2006b), 'Reepalu till motattack efter friande dom', *Dagens Nyheter*, 29 August.
du Gay, P. (2000), *In Praise of Bureaucracy: Weber, Organization and Ethics*, London: Sage.
Friedrich, C.J. (1990), 'Corruption concepts in historical perspective', in A.J.

Heidenheimer, M. Johnston and V.T. LeVine (eds), *Political Corruption: A Handbook*, New Brunswick, NJ: Transaction Publishers, pp. 15–24.
Gustafsson, C. (1988), *Om Företag, Moral och Handling*, Lund, Sweden: Studentlitteratur.
Institutet mot mutor (2006), *En Kritisk Analys av den Svenska Mutlagstiftningen*, Stockholm: IMM.
Jain, A. (1998), 'Models of corruption', in A. Jain (ed.), *Economics of Corruption*, Boston and London: Kluwer Academic Publishers, pp. 13–34.
Kantorowicz, E.H. (1997), *The King's two Bodies: A Study in Mediaeval Political Theology*, first published 1957 copyright renewed 1985, seventh paperback printing, with an introduction by William Chester Jordan, Princeton, NJ: Princeton University Press.
Kaulingfreks, R. and R. ten Bos (2005), 'Are organizations bicycles? On hosophobia in neo-gnosticism in organizational thought', *Culture and Organization*, **11** (2), 83–96.
Leiken, R.S. (1997), 'Controlling the global corruption epidemic', *Foreign Policy*, **105**, 55–76.
Lennerfors, T. (2008), *The Vicissitudes of Corruption – Degeneration – Transgression – Jouissance*, Stockholm: Arvinius.
Levine, D.P. (2005), 'The corrupt organization', *Human Relations*, **58** (6), 723–40.
Nye, J.S. (1967), 'Corruption and political development: a cost–benefit analysis'. *American Political Science Review*, **61** (2), 417–27.
Parker, M. (2003), 'Business, ethics and business ethics: critical theory and negative dialectics', in M. Alvesson and H. Willmott (eds), *Studying Management Critically*, London: Sage, pp. 197–219.
Rose-Ackerman, S. (1999), *Corruption and Government: Causes, Consequences, and Reform*, Cambridge: Cambridge University Press.
Schmitt, C. (1985), *Political Theology: Four Chapters on the Concept of Sovereignty*, Cambridge, MA: MIT Press.
Taylor, C. (2001a), 'Bribery in Athenian politics part I: accusations, allegations and slander', *Greece and Rome*, **48** (1), 53–66.
Taylor, C. (2001b), 'Bribery in Athenian politics part II: ancient reaction and perceptions', *Greece and Rome*, **48** (2), 154–72.
Žižek, S. (1989), *The Sublime Object of Ideology*, London: Verso.
Žižek, S. (1997), *The Plague of Fantasies*, London: Verso.
Žižek, S. (2002), *For They Know Not What They Do: Enjoyment as a Political Factor*, 2nd edn, London: Verso.
Žižek, S. (2005), *Interrogating the Real*, London and New York: Continuum.

Index